MW00956118

Impossible is Nothing
My Fight to Live a Softball Dream

BY BETH NORTHWAY AS TOLD TO BOB NORTHWAY

Love you always!

Beth

Copyright © 2011 Beth Northway and Bob Northway
All rights reserved.

ISBN: 1-4679-5173-0
ISBN-13: 9781467951739

This story is dedicated to my family, friends, and coaches. You taught me how to dream big and then encouraged me to reach for everything I could imagine. Go Irish!

"Impossible is just a big word thrown around by small men who find it easier to live in the world they've been given than to explore the power they have to change it. Impossible is not a fact. It's an opinion. Impossible is not a declaration. It's a dare. Impossible is potential. Impossible is temporary. Impossible is nothing."

—Muhammad Ali

Leading Off

It was the sixth inning of the last Big East game of my Irish career. We were deadlocked 0-0 in the championship game of the league tournament, and Becca Heteniak, DePaul's all-conference pitcher, had a stranglehold on our hitters. I would be the leadoff batter in the inning. No sweat, though. I had been the Irish leadoff hitter most of the season. And with only three Irish batters reaching base so far, this would be my third leadoff appearance of the day.

The way the game was going, I knew there was a good chance this would be my last at bat. As I left the on-deck circle for the batter's box, I heard Coach Gumpf call out, "Come on Beth, we need you on base!" I knew that was my job, but I also knew it would take a good at bat to get the inning started right. Both pitchers had feasted all day on the home plate ump's wide strike zone. Hitting a 65 to 70 mph rise ball or drop thrown from 43 feet away is hard enough without having to cover a corner eight inches off plate. But that's what we train for. Hitting pitchers' mistakes in the middle of the plate is nice if you can get it. But pitchers like the DePaul ace don't slip up like that very often.

As I dug my right foot into the batter's box, I took a couple of practice cuts and looked down the third base line to see what Coach wanted me to do. I'm not the typical leadoff hitter. Slapping or bunting for a hit isn't my game. I'm a line drive hitter with decent power, but I bat leadoff because I do my job. I get on base.

As expected, Coach signaled me to swing away, punctuating her sign with an emphatic clap of her hands. She had confidence in me, although I had popped up and struck out in my two previous trips to the plate. I was hitting over .350 for the season...that's about one hit for every three at bats...and my on base percentage was over .500, so I was due.

I knew I had my work cut out for me and Heteniak didn't give in. She was working that outside corner like it was her job and, based on her success all day, I'm sure she felt it was. It took all of my focus to work the count to three balls, two strikes. The next pitch was a rise ball heading for that outside corner again. I triggered and began my swing but held up as I saw the pitch was going to be too wide for even this ump to call a strike. I was on my way to first with a leadoff walk...as good as a hit for a leadoff batter. Now it was up to my Fighting Irish teammates to turn Heteniak's mistake into a rally.

In keeping with Notre Dame's Fighting Irish tradition, our next batter came out battling, but she couldn't get on top of a rise ball on a first pitch bunt attempt. It was a pop-out to first base. Not a problem, I thought. We have a lineup full of hitters and two more outs to work with.

I watched Heather Johnson, our number three hitter, settle into the batter's box. She had checked in with Coach, and received the swing away sign followed by that clap of the hands. There'd be no bunting or slapping for Heather either. She was one of our most disciplined and powerful hitters. Heather wouldn't be playing "small ball" with one out and the game on the line. She was going to swing away and see how far she could hit it.

Heteniak was careful with Heather, playing around the outside edge of the strike zone until she fell behind two and one. That's a hitter's count, and Heather took full advantage of it on the next pitch. She got on top of a rise ball that strayed over the outside corner of the plate. The ball was drilled hard and long toward right field.

As Heather made contact, I was already in motion. In an instant I had to decide if the ball would be caught. If so, I needed to wait for the catch, tag the bag and decide if I could beat a throw to second. If the ball is going to drop in, I needed to recognize it right away if I was going to make it to third or even score. The rules say I can leave the bag as soon as the pitcher releases the ball. I timed it perfectly and was on my way to second as the ball left Heteniak's hand. When Heather made contact, a quick glance as the ball took off told me she'd hit it a ton and that there was no chance it would be caught.

As I approached second base I had to make another quick decision: should I play it safe and stop at third or gamble that the ball would elude the outfielders long enough to give me a chance to make it all the way home? By the time I had rounded second I'd made my decision, this was no time to be timid. In a close game against a tough pitcher, we needed a run, now!

Rounding second, my first responsibility is to look for Coach. The play is behind me, so she's my eyes. If Coach has her hands up, it means the outfielder has intercepted Heather's hit before it reached the gap and the ball is on its way to the cut off or maybe even on a line to the plate. If she's wind-milling like crazy, she agrees with my decision to go for broke. I'm really rolling now, so whatever Coach is doing is a blur, but I sense her urgency and see the wind-milling left arm as the right hand points toward home. I round third and from the corner of my eye can see the ball is on its way in from right field. "No way," the thought flashes through my brain. "There is no *way* that throw is going to beat me home!"

Softball Angel

I started playing softball when I was three or four. Actually, that's when I started playing catch with a ball and glove. My Dad was my first target, and I started out throwing a baseball, not a softball. Not only was the smaller ball easier to grip, it was the only ball we had around the house. My older brother, Andy, was just starting out in the local Kentwood Baseball League (everyone just called it KBL) and he and my Dad would play catch in the back yard to get ready for practice and the games. Most days, I would stand on the sidelines and watch. I would wait for Andy to say he'd had enough. Then, before my Dad could follow him to the house, I'd pick up the glove and ball and make it clear that it was my turn next.

Once I started throwing, I didn't want to quit. If this was something my brother was doing, I wasn't going to sit on the sidelines. Of course, I probably wouldn't have been as eager to continue if my first experience with a ball and glove had been discouraging or, worse yet, painful. Fortunately, Dad knew that nothing would discourage me quicker than getting hit in the face or chest. I think he also knew my Mom would put an end to our throwing sessions pretty quickly if I ended up with bloody nose or lip. So, he perfected a short overhand lob that arced softly into my glove while not endangering what he called my "pretty little face".

Over time, the arc became less obvious and the throws a bit harder as I learned to turn the fingers of the glove down on a low ball and up on a higher throw. Pretty soon I was moving my feet to get to balls thrown to my left and right. I learned to react quickly and snag balls thrown wider to my left or glove side. And I learned how to make a backhand catch across my body with fingers pointed down on throws to my right.

My throw developed right along with my ability to catch. I'm a right hander, so learned to lead with my left foot toward my target, and bring the ball over the top on a line to my Dad's glove, clearing my left side out of the way so I could follow through. Dad saw to it there'd be no flatfooted, wide-open "throwing like a girl" in our backyard.

Pretty soon, I had a glove of my own (one of my brother's old mitts, I think) and I would bug my Dad to throw with me when Andy had better things to do. But I would also get in on the action when we were supposed to be watching my brother play. On game nights, if Andy wasn't actually hitting or playing in the field, I'd goad my Dad into playing catch on the sidelines. Looking back, I could have been more supportive of my brother's baseball career, but throwing and catching was almost an obsession with me. It was as if I had to constantly answer the unspoken question: How many times can Dad and I throw and catch this thing without a miss? Sorry Andy. My only excuse is, I was mentally and physically addicted to throwing that ball back and forth, over and over again.

Fortunately for my brother, when I was seven, my own KBL career began and I could let him play his games in peace. By then I'd reluctantly accepted that, while boys played baseball, girls were supposed to play softball. As much as I enjoyed playing catch with my Dad, I was really pumped up to be on a team, wearing a real uniform, with a coach, teammates, and an actual diamond to play on. I'd watched enough of Andy's games and the Detroit Tigers on TV to know that this was the real deal. I just knew this was going to be fun!

Sometimes in sports, you get lucky. In my career, I've discovered that you often don't know how lucky you are until you look back several years later. I know now that being selected in the random preseason player selection lottery to play for Greg Youtzy's KBL team was the best possible way to begin the first chapter of my organized softball career.

Coach Youtzy's sports philosophy was simple: Play your best, be aggressive, and, most important of all, HAVE FUN! Greg would always tell us not to take losing too hard, but to remember, "Winning is more fun." As his *Youtzy's Angels* teams racked up several championships in our progression from T-ball, to pitching machine ball, and then to live pitching, Greg's coaching philosophy probably ruffled the feathers of opposing coaches who didn't take the games as seriously as we did. But Greg really was right...doing our best and winning was a lot of fun.

Greg taught me there is only one way to play the game, and that is "all out, without holding anything back." It doesn't matter if you are at bat, running the bases, playing in the field, or pitching. Anything less than total effort isn't doing your best. I also learned another lesson both on and off the field: you can't have better friends than the ones you form with teammates. I have been lucky to share close friendships with the girls (and, in high school and college, young women) on each of my teams. I have to mention my Angels teammates, Deanna, Melissa, Brooke, and later on, Kristi, who were my first softball buddies. They made it easy to follow Coach Greg's most important rule: have fun!

Say Hey!

I played a lot of different positions growing up in KBL. The rules for the younger age groups said everyone had to play a minimum number of innings in the field and everyone on the team was in the batting order, even if they were not playing in the field at the time. Oh, and you couldn't play the same position the entire game. My first position was shortstop – because I had range and I could throw – but I played all over the infield and in the outfield. I also caught. And, when we went to live pitching, I pitched.

Between games in the evening and on weekends, and in the off season, my Dad and I worked on infield and outfield drills. We'd find a ball field with reasonably smooth dirt for infield practice and he'd hit a lot of groundballs to me at shortstop. If we were lucky enough to have Andy, my Mom or a buddy along, we'd also work on that long throw to first. We had a big back yard, so we'd often do our fly ball drills there. Dad would spend hours hitting or throwing pop ups and fly balls and I'd learn to take the best angles to track the ball down. To get a quick jump and catch everything within range, you had to visually pick up the ball off the bat and make the all-important first step in the right direction. It was an instinct we worked on relentlessly.

We also worked on dive drills to the left and right and on short balls in front of me. I learned that, even on hard ground, diving for the ball and catching it was very satisfying and any pain from the impact of flesh on turf was forgotten as I scrambled to my feet to chuck the ball back in to Dad. On those occasions during KBL practices or games where one of us hit the ground a bit harder than normal and were slow to get up, Coach Greg would jokingly ask, "Is the bone sticking out?" Once we realized that there were, indeed, no bones protruding from our flesh, we'd get up, brush ourselves off, and get ready for the next play.

My favorite backyard drill from the early days, and the one that probably really tried Dad's patience, was our 'Say Hey' drill, named after Willie Mays, the all-time major league baseball great of the 1950's and 60's. Mays was famously known as the 'Say Hey Kid' and many still say he is the greatest and most complete player who ever played major league baseball. He was well known for his skill as a hitter and a fielder and for his exuberant playing style. His running, over the shoulder catch of Vic Wertz' long drive in the 1954 World Series is legendary and symbolic of the talent and desire that set Mays apart from other baseball greats.

My Dad told me about his great catch and I wanted to be just like the great Willie Mays, which is why we took to calling my over-the-head catching practice the Say Hey drill. I would make my Dad hit fly ball after fly ball over my head so I could sprint back and make the catch. One catch wasn't enough. I had to catch a dozen or more at full extension like a wide receiver going deep in football. The last one had to be the best one of all...or we'd keep going until it was.

Over time, my Dad became a pretty good fly ball hitter but no one could hit it just right every time. That made for a lot of long afternoons in the backyard and, later, on the softball diamond when I graduated from the backyard to larger practice fields. The Say Hey drill was so much a part of my early days as a softball player that I had Dad take my picture next to Willie Mays' plaque when we visited the Baseball Hall of Fame in Cooperstown on one of our summer vacations. At the age of seven or eight, I couldn't match Willie's skill as a ballplayer, but I was right there with him when it came to my enthusiasm for practicing and playing the game.

My poor Dad. He told me later I was so enthusiastic and devoted to improving my skills that he made a personal resolution to never be the one who called an end to our practices. I'm sure there were times when, after already working all day long, he was ready to call an end to the evening's Say Hey drill long before I was.

Game Time!

As much as I liked practicing, I was really excited to play the games. Greg always had us arrive early so he could count heads and make sure we were all there, then get us warmed up. We'd start with some light throwing, then throw harder, hit some wiffle balls to get our swings loosened up, and line up to make a few running catches.

Then it was game time! From the start, Greg used me a lot in the infield. I threw the ball hard and accurately and I could field it if it was hit anywhere near me. Plus, I wasn't afraid to be aggressive and I think Greg liked that in me. Melissa, Brooke, Deanna and the other girls on my earliest teams were also good fielders...so if one of us fielded the ball, we knew our teammates would catch our throw and we'd record the out.

In tee ball, almost everyone could hit the ball, but those of us with strong level swings tended to hit it hard enough to get it past the opposing fielders almost every time. Even with the league's five runs per inning limit, we scored a ton of runs in most games.

We also didn't forget Greg's most important rule. We really worked hard at having fun. We'd be all decked out in our red and white uniforms, singing our songs from the bench while our team was at bat, and chirping back and forth to encourage each other when we were in the field. We were aggressive base runners, so even little hits often turned into doubles and triples. And we always slid into the base in a cloud of dust or a splatter of mud to be sure we'd be safe. Our Moms must have loved washing our white uniform pants. I'm pretty sure, no matter how much they were washed, those pants were never very white after the first few games of the season.

At the end of each game, Greg would ask us to share our thoughts on why we won (most of the time) or, on those rare occasions when we got beat, why we lost. This was his chance to re-inforce the lessons we could take from each game. If one of us had struggled, he'd find something positive in the way we had played.

Greg always named a player of the game, mentioning the little things we did that made a difference in the outcome. Everyone was player of the game at least once each season. Greg gave us each a treat ticket to wrap up our postgame talk, and the player of the game was awarded a second ticket. After a quick reminder about the date and time of our next game, Greg would lead us in one last cheer before we'd sprint off to the refreshment stand to spend our tickets.

Although winning and losing wasn't supposed to be important for the younger age groups, my teammates and I kept track. I don't think we lost a game until our fourth year together. All the way up to our last year, we were consistently the team to beat in KBL.

One year, just after I started playing ball, I got a taste of the big time. Greg had pulled some strings and the *Angels* were invited to join the West Michigan Whitecaps, our local Class A minor league baseball team, on the field for the national anthem before their game. It was KBL night at the ballpark, so there were hundreds of Kentwood kids in the stands screaming and yelling. We ran out on the field and each took a position next to one of the players. Some of my teammates had to double-up, because there were twelve of us. But Greg had me stand on the pitcher's mound all alone with "Crash", West Michigan's team mascot. I sang as loud as I could with a big grin on my face. No stage fright for me! My parents still have that picture on display at home. It was my first time on a really big stage, and it was big stuff for me at the time.

The Importance of Finishing

As much as I loved playing ball with Coach Greg, as I grew older, I learned that there was another level of ball available for really serious softball players...travel ball. I wouldn't quit Coach Greg's team, having fun and supporting my coach were still important to me. But by the time I was 11, I wanted to take on the challenge of higher level competition. This decision was the first step on the path that would lead to my college recruitment and my career at the University of Notre Dame.

I probably could have left Greg and my teammates as soon as I started playing travel ball and they would have understood. My passion for playing the game was obvious to everyone, and I was clearly driven to get better. But quitting my KBL team wasn't an option. My parents had always talked to me about loyalty and quitting, or rather, NOT quitting. I learned at an early age that it's important to be loyal to friends and teammates and coaches who have supported you, and it's never OK to quit.

When I began asking to sign up for one activity or another, one of the first rules my parents had was, live up to your commitments; if you start something, finish it. That wasn't a problem when it came to sports. Whether it was basketball, soccer, ice hockey, or any of the other sports I tried, I never wanted to quit. I just wanted to play and practice more.

When it came to non-sports school activities, I was also motivated. I was a good student, mostly because I studied hard, tried to stay ahead in my assignments, and did all of the extra credit assignments my teachers offered. I wanted to be the best at everything.

If I struggled in a class, I would just study harder. Giving up wasn't an option.

I also wasn't one to give up easily when it came to making friends. At one point a boy from Korea transferred to my elementary school and was assigned to my third grade class. We quickly became friends, but there was a communication problem. John spoke little English. I solved that problem by having my parents get me a book of Korean vocabulary words and I carried it to school with me so I could learn enough Korean to keep up my end of the conversation. John was doing his part by improving his command of English, learning a little Korean was the least I could do. John wasn't my only friend. I had a really good buddy named Jeff, and I especially liked hanging out with all the boys at recess. We'd play basketball and football together and they respected my ability to keep up with them in both sports.

I wasn't excited about every activity I tried. One year, my Mom wanted me to become a dancer. We signed up for a beginning ballet and tap dance class that lasted several weeks and culminated with a big dance recital in a high school auditorium. I hated it. But I sucked it up and finished the class, even dressing up in a sequined costume and taking the stage for a brief dance number in front of Dad, Mom, Andy, my Grandma and Grandpa and an audience of other parents and relatives. Whew! I was glad when that was over with. I think my Dad sensed my relief. He met me in the hallway and rewarded me with a trophy and a rose for a job well done. They even convinced me to smile for the camera before I ditched the sequins for a tee shirt and jeans.

My belief in finishing what you start has become even stronger as I have grown older and it still drives me forward today...even when things aren't going well. Sure, I've been burned a few times when being loyal or not quitting has resulted in some personal disappointment or pain, but the good that has come from my perseverance far outweighs the bad.

Taking My Game
on the Road

As I mentioned, by age 11 I became aware that I needed to move up to a more competitive level of ball if I was really serious about the game. Travel softball was where the best players competed. In our area the first level of travel ball was for girls 12-and-under. It seems unbelievable today, but I didn't sign up to play as an 11 year old (the age most players enter 12-and-under ball). I was having a lot of fun playing in KBL with Coach Greg, and I had another passion even stronger than softball...I was really into basketball.

But the next year, my best friend Deanna was asked to play catcher for a local travel ball team, the *Blaze*. After, her first couple of practices, Deanna was really excited about her new team and I was a little envious. Meanwhile, Deanna's Dad took my Dad aside and tried to talk him into going to the next practice for a tryout. We were both pretty pumped up and ready to go, but first we had to convince Mom.

Mom loved watching me play ball a lot, but I was playing basketball and soccer at the time, plus KBL softball, and, of course, going to school. Oh, and did I mention that both of my parents were working full time? And that my brother also had activities and interests that involved the rest of us? Looking back, we had a lot on our plates already. How would we find the time for travel ball, too?

Lucky for me, Mom couldn't resist my pleading. It helped that my soccer career was winding down, so we wouldn't really be adding a sport, we'd just be replacing one (at least, that was my argument).

With Mom's hard-won support, I was ready for the tryout. Now I just had to make the team.

I was full of confidence. Still, walking into that high school gym on Sunday morning and having a team full of unfamiliar, but obviously very confident, softball players give me the once over was a little intimidating. It was late fall and the core of the team had been selected weeks earlier. Most had played the previous year; they were travel ball veterans. Deanna had joined late, but by now had a couple of practices under her belt and was an accepted member of the team. I felt a little like an intruder in a private club.

Fortunately my Dad was all business. He grabbed our gloves and said I should warm up my arm before the tryout. I soon forgot about being nervous. We started tossing the ball lightly back and forth, gradually lengthening the distance between us until my arm was loose. Then we began to throw harder and before long I was making Dad's glove "pop", just like at home. The team manager, Coach Furlong, approached my Dad as we finished our warm up and after some introductions said the head coach wanted me in the batting cage to see what I could do. I grabbed my bat and a batting helmet and stepped into the cage.

I was greeted by a compact bundle of energy in a baggy sweat-shirt and baseball cap who introduced himself as Coach Green-man. He motioned me toward the plate and retired to his position behind the batting machine to begin feeding balls to me. I came out swinging aggressively and before long, I was hitting them pretty good. I was still an undisciplined hitter. In KBL, the pitching was slow enough you could get away with a long, looping cut and still make contact and drive the ball hard into the outfield. Despite my raw technique, Coach Greenman seemed impressed. "You're an aggressive hitter," he called out a couple of times during our session.

Then, the coach turned the pitching machine off and said, "Nice job, Kiddo" in a raspy voice. (Later on Coach Greenman gave me my own official team nickname, but on that first day he used the all-purpose nickname we all answered to.) The coach motioned for me to leave the cage as he turned back to the pitching machine and I walked back across the gym to where my Dad was waiting. Coach Furlong joined us a couple of minutes later and said, "Coach wants to know if you want to do this."

I waited anxiously, expecting to hear my Dad immediately answer, "Of course we do!" But instead, Dad followed my Mom's coaching and calmly asked, "How much will this cost?" I couldn't believe it. Put a price tag on my sports career? You have _got_ to be kidding!

Coach Furlong showed my Dad the schedule of payments and explained the fundraising opportunities. He also described the uniforms and equipment I'd receive, and what equipment we'd have to buy. Bottom line, the cost to play would be $650 plus the cost of the family's travel and my personal equipment (glove, spikes, batting glove and bat). I looked expectantly at Dad. Fortunately, he didn't leave me hanging for too long. "Let's do it," he said, and I headed straight for the team huddle across the gym before he could change his mind.

Only Perfect Practice Makes Perfect

My first experience in travel ball was a real eye opener. In KBL, we had four or five players whose softball skills were better than those of the other members of our team and who were more interested in doing what it takes to get better. On my first *Blaze* team, every player was good, and they were all willing to put in the practice time to keep getting better. Coach Greenman was a stickler for doing things the right way, from warming up our arms before practices to how long we should show up before practice, and later on, for our games. During the long Michigan winters, we practiced in a high school gym. Since there were teams practicing before and after us, we couldn't exceed our allotted two hours. Coach Greenman made sure we didn't waste a second. We moved quickly and efficiently from one drill to another as an entire team and then split up to run through a series of individual hitting stations. We rotated from one station to the next around the gym working on various fundamentals, then putting it all together with a visit to the cage to hit off the machine.

Although we worked quickly and efficiently with no standing around, Coach made sure we didn't hurry through the drills. "Practice makes perfect isn't really true," he'd tell us. "Only *perfect* practice makes perfect." He would watch us closely whether we were tossing the ball to warm up, hitting off the tee, or flailing at golf ball-sized wiffle balls with a broom handle. Even when he seemed focused on another player, he'd call out over his shoulder to correct a bad habit, or improve the way we executed a drill. He seemed to have 360 degree vision, Although Coach Furlong and two or three Dads helped as assistant coaches, it was clear that there was only one real coach…and that was Coach Greenman. He was the teacher that we believed could and would make us better.

The biggest difference between travel ball and KBL was the pitching. Even in the 12-and-under age group, many girls in travel ball were throwing the ball in the 50's from a pitching rubber 35 feet from home plate. They were also throwing with movement and at different speeds. Many had good command of their drop balls and a well-disguised changeup, in addition to a fastball. A few girls could even throw a rise ball, a pitch that looked like "meat" to the batter until it arrived at such speed and at enough elevation, the hitter couldn't come close to making contact.

Learning to hit good pitching was an essential if you were going to last in travel ball and I struggled to incorporate the tips that Coach Greenman gave us to shorten our swings up, meet the ball out in front of the plate, and keep the bat in the hitting zone as long as possible on the follow through. Hitting had always been the most natural part of my game. Now it was something I had to work at, contorting my arms and hips into seemingly unnatural positions to start my swing early enough, make contact and drive the ball hard to the grass in the outfield. I worked hard at it and I improved.

Coach believed strongly in playing "small ball"; using the slap and bunt to surprise opposing fielders, make them rush their fielding and throws, get on base, move runners, and score runs. Especially in the younger age groups, a travel ball team that could execute small ball could win a lot of games at the expense of teams that couldn't field the ball cleanly and make plays at every base. I had decent speed and good eye-hand coordination, so I quickly became a good bunter and could even slap for an occasional in-field hit.

There are a variety of bunting strategies in small ball and Coach Greenman used them all. Each of us had to be able to sacrifice bunt, drag bunt, drop-step (or sneaky) bunt, plus slap from the right side and the left side. Some of our girls were too big or didn't have the speed necessary to get on base as bunters, but we all had to learn to do it and do it well.

If our leadoff batter got on base, the most valuable bunt in our arsenal was the sacrifice bunt. When you were facing a really good pitcher in 12-and-under ball, it was important to be able to move the runner closer to home with a sacrifice bunt. The object of the sacrifice bunt isn't to get on base yourself, it is to advance the base runner who is already on base. The batter gives herself up (or sacrifices herself) to get the runner into scoring position. Getting the bunt down in fair territory was "job one" with Coach Greenman.

He made it very clear that there was no excuse for hurrying a sacrifice bunt in order to get a head start running to first base. "Admire it," he'd yell when one of us would bunt foul or miss it entirely because we were leaving the batter's box too soon to run to first. Coach wanted us to square and show that you are going to bunt early so the fielders would all charge in and commit to fielding it. He said to "catch" the ball with the bat to absorb the impact of the pitch and deaden the ball. By squaring early, you improved the chances of placing the bunt on the ground in fair territory. Once the ball rolls far enough to be out from under foot, you sprint for first. The worst thing you can do is run into the ball. If you do, you're automatically out and the runner stays at first. No one wanted to trot back to the dugout with head down after running into the ball and ruining a great sacrifice bunt.

I could lay down a sacrifice as well as anyone on the team, but my favorite bunt was the drop-step or sneaky bunt and I was really good at it. With the drop step, you don't let the fielders know you are going to bunt until the last moment after the pitch is already on its way to the plate. The idea is to use the element of surprise to turn a bunt into a hit.

As a right handed batter, I would wait for the pitch with my bat cocked behind my right ear like I was going to hit away. As the pitcher released the ball, I'd step back away from the plate with my right (back) foot, which lowered my body. At the same time, I'd quickly slide my top hand up the barrel of the bat as I brought the bat into the bunting position. I'd stay still long enough to place the bunt down in fair territory (along the third base line if at all possible) and take off immediately for first.

Neither the pitcher nor the third baseman would be expecting a bunt, so they wouldn't be charging to field it in time to get me at first. The catcher might have a chance, but if the bunt was far enough up the line, there's no way she could get to it, then turn and plant her feet to make the throw before I was safe. I turned these "sneaky" bunts into a lot of singles in my early travel ball career and continued to use the element of surprise more than a few times to successfully convert bunt singles in high school and college.

As a right hander, I didn't use the slap very often. Conventional wisdom says left hand batters will have more success slapping. When slapping, the batter strides toward the pitcher as the pitch arrives, swinging the bat sharply or "slapping" it hard to generate a hard ground ball through a hole between the infielders or a short fly ball over their heads for a "Texas League" hit. If the hitter is really fast, it is sometimes possible to beat out a slap even if it is fielded cleanly in the infield. A lefty is a step closer to first base as she makes her running start, so she has a better chance to beat the throw to first.

Coach Greenman was more likely to have me hit away than slap, but I was fast enough and coordinated enough that he had me slap occasionally from both sides of the plate and I took pride in my ability to do it successfully. I even recall surprising my varsity high school softball coach in a game during my freshman year with a perfect slap through shortstop. The coach had unintentionally tapped the right side of her face while I was watching for the hitting sign before an at-bat. I recognized the motion as the team's designated "slap" sign, and dutifully slapped the first pitch into left field for a single.

I was batting fourth, or cleanup, at the time and the coach wasn't real pleased with my ability to execute the slap. Line drives in the gaps were what she expected. In four years of varsity high school ball, it was the only time she gave me the slap sign, either intentionally or by mistake. After our early misunderstanding, and the scolding I received afterwards, I think she could have slapped herself silly in the coaching box and I still would have swung away!

First Season

As soon as the weather broke in the spring of my first travel ball campaign, we moved outside and, hard as it was to believe at the time, the intensity of Coach Greenman's practices went up a couple of notches. Now we could field real ground balls off of a dirt infield, track fly balls against the gray Michigan sky and take our turn in the batter's box against live pitching from Coach as well as the pitching machine.

By this time I was playing third base most of the time. As a latecomer to the team, I was filling one of the few remaining positions still open for competition. Coach's daughter, Katie, was set at second base, Ashley, an intense competitor with a rocket for an arm, was firmly in charge of shortstop, our pitchers—Ali, Jen, Mouse and Molly—rotated in at first base when they weren't on the pitcher's rubber. Deanna and Amanda were our catchers. And in the outfield we had Coach Furlong's daughter Lauren, plus Kayla, and Amanda or Deanna when they weren't catching.

With Coach Greenman, you had to earn your spot every day. There were no guarantees of playing time except for our best pitchers. I had worked out all over the infield and outfield and was even one of several girls Coach tried at catcher. I was a good catcher in practice—I could "drop and block", get rid of the mask to catch a pop up, and I put my throwing arm to good use trying to gun down runners at second or third base. But my catching career came to a close before the season got started. I had grown quickly over the winter and had become one of the taller girls on the team. Not only did that make catching a bit more awkward for me, but I was also suffering from what my doctor described as growing pains in my legs. Crouching behind the plate was making them even more painful.

That's when Coach began using me primarily at third base. I thrived at the "hot corner". I had good range to get to pop flies behind me, I could get to hard ground balls to my left and right, and I fielded the bunt well in front of me. I had a strong, accurate throw to gun runners down at first or second on a force play, and to throw home. And I could get my glove up in time to snag the line shots that are why third base is considered the hot corner of the infield.

My travel ball game career began strangely. In my first at bat, I hit a hard groundball to short stop and ran as fast as I could to first base. I lunged to cross the bag just after the throw arrived and tripped over the first baseman's foot, flying head over heels onto the hard stone dust of the infield. Not only was I out on the play, my back was a bloody mess. After some quick first aid, though, I was back on the field.

Fortunately, the rest of my inaugural travel ball season wasn't as painful. Even though it was the first time I had practiced softball all winter and spring, then played six straight weeks of tournaments capped by a week-long trip to a national tournament, my first year playing for Coach Greenman flew by almost before I knew it.

The team played well enough to finish as tournament runner up several times. We never did take home the first place hardware, but we got close enough to feel that, if we kept working hard to get better, we'd be a force to be reckoned with in the future. Best of all, we qualified to play in the National Softball Association 12-and-under national tournament in Columbus, Ohio. There must have been 150 teams in all age groups at the tournament. The field complex was huge, and we savored every minute of what seemed like nonstop games against strong opponents, practices on local recreational fields, and lots of team chill-out time in the hotel lobby at night.

At the end of the season, I couldn't wait for the fall tryouts so I could re-earn my spot on Coach Greenman's team and start the whole cycle again. Looking back, I knew I hadn't burned it up at the plate but I had hit respectably for a rookie. I also raised some eyebrows with my solid play at third base. Most important of all, I was getting better in all aspects of the game and I really enjoyed playing this more challenging level of ball.

Becoming a Hitter

A few weeks after my first travel ball season ended, it was time for tryouts to earn a spot on next season's team. Several of my teammates would be joining me and moving up an age group to try out for the *Blaze* 14-and-under team. A few decided to go their own way and try out for other clubs. And a couple decided that playing softball year round was not their cup of tea. Fortunately, Coach Greenman and Katie would be moving up to the next age level with me, so I'd have a chance to play for the man I now referred to simply as "My Coach", or just "Coach".

Blaze tryouts were "open", which meant you were not guaranteed a spot on the team, even if you had played the previous year. But it didn't hurt that Coach knew what we could do. While we didn't have a lock on a spot, Coach made it clear he wanted to build his team around players who worked hard and wanted to get better. He already knew that those of us who had played for him last year were hard workers, driven to get better, and that we would soak up everything he could teach us.

Still, there were dozens of new girls at the tryouts, including some really good players—girls that would make our team better. Only seven of the girls from the previous year's team were returning. So if all of us made the team, Coach would need to add five new players to build our 12-girl roster. After the first of two tryouts, Coach made it official. He offered all seven returning players a spot on the team. None of us hesitated to accept. As I said earlier, we were committed and would have been heartbroken if Coach had turned us away.

By the end of the second tryout the following week, he had also made offers to five new girls. Within a couple of days, he had firm commitments from all of the new players and we had a team. Now it was time to start practicing again. Joining me as teammates were Katie, Deanna, Ashley, Jen, Amanda, and Ali from 12-and-under ball. The new players were Ally, Shannon, Kaprice, Jenna and Amber. Amber and Allie were pitchers and would join Ali, Katie and Jen in a deep rotation. Jenna had blazing speed and, like Deanna, was an accomplished slapper, Shannon was a great athlete who could play just about any position on the diamond, and Kaprice was a really a special player. She was tall and powerful, capable of dominating just about any pitcher/hitter matchup. She was also a great fielder.

With a lineup like ours, competition for playing time would be fierce. I felt pretty good about my ability to play in the field. I had a strong throw and I covered a lot of ground...so much so that Coach began using me at shortstop as well as third base. This was due, in part, to the makeup of our new team. We had an abundance of larger, physically imposing players who were well-suited to playing the corner infield positions. My range, good glove and decent but not awe-inspiring size made the switch to shortstop a natural for me. I also worked out in centerfield where my speed, range and arm were also assets.

But as well as things were going in the field, I was struggling at the plate. I'd made some improvement in my first year of travel ball, but I was still having trouble absorbing all of the tips I was getting from Coach, my Dad, high school coaches, and others. It was hard to turn all that advice into a consistent, powerful swing that worked for me.

After one particularly bad hitting session I was so frustrated, I broke into tears in my Dad's car as we drove home from the fields. After I calmed down a little, my Dad and I began to talk about what we could do to improve my hitting. We had heard about a hitting coach in town who worked with both baseball and softball players and, although we didn't know a lot about picking a hitting coach, we knew we needed expert help. It turned out that Curtis Morgan was exactly the expert I needed.

Curtis was a former minor league ballplayer with a reputation as a strong hitter. In addition to running Morgan's Hitting Club out of an old warehouse near downtown Grand Rapids, Curtis coached club baseball teams and was well known in local baseball circles as a consultant to college teams and some of the better high school baseball and softball programs in our area.

My first visit to Morgan's Hitting Club was a bit intimidating. Curtis' headquarters was a creaky brick warehouse located between the railroad tracks and the Grand River in an area of town my parents had never thought to bring me to before. We entered through a heavy steel door beneath a dingy sign that read, Morgan's Hitting Club. Up a flight of wooden stairs lit by a couple of bare light bulbs, another gray door opened into the second floor of the building. Passing through that door was like entering another world. It was a world where Curtis ruled and where, if you didn't take hitting as seriously as he did, he'd send you on your way. It didn't matter if you were a paying customer that helped support his business, as far as Curtis was concerned the business of hitting was a lot more important than any profit you might represent to him or his club.

I had never seen another place like it. Beneath banks of fluorescent lights was a row of net batting cages, each framed by thick wooden beams that supported the ceiling. The sound of batted balls echoed off of those beams and the hard rubber tiles that covered the wooden floor. Players ranging from about eight-years-old to college age worked on their swings off of tees, pitching machines and live tosses from instructors.

Here and there, individual hitters received instruction, and in one cage, a baseball pitching coach watched closely as a young pitcher worked on his windup and delivery. Amid all of the activity and noise, a loud voice directed traffic from cage to cage, yelled instructions to hitters and his assistants, and showed that, without a doubt, he was the headmaster in charge of this loud, sprawling school of batsmanship.

My Dad and I stood in the aisle outside of the cages and took in the action while we waited for Curtis to turn his attention to us. My Dad had called ahead to arrange our first visit, so Curtis was expecting us, or at least we thought he was. But he was so absorbed in teaching, criticizing and occasionally roaring his approval, that we weren't sure if he remembered we were supposed to meet with him or even knew we were there.

Finally Curtis noticed us. He stood up from the bucket he'd been sitting on and walked over and said, "You must be Beth." That was probably the quietest greeting I would get from Curtis in all of the years I worked with him. As we met almost weekly to improve, refresh, fine tune and otherwise keep my swing working at its peak, Curtis was more likely to greet me with a loud shout, either asking how my last practice or game had gone, or if I'd worked on the drills he'd assigned me.

Curtis was all ears as I described my frustration with all the conflicting advice I was getting on how to hit better, and my inability to make any of it work for me. I showed him some of the things I was working on as he threw "soft toss" to me. In soft toss, the coach sits on a bucket just across the plate and out in front of the hitter. He tosses the ball lightly over the plate so the hitter can practice making solid contact on a moving ball. After a few cuts, Curtis stopped me and began to make some adjustments.

The first thing he did was put the bat on my right shoulder, set my elbows close to my chest, and we began to work on a simple repeatable swing that allowed me to get the bat from the shoulder to the hitting zone on a short, direct path. I began to make consistent, solid contact hitting off the pitching machine at a moderately high speed.

Curtis also changed the position of my feet. He favored a wider stance, although not so wide I couldn't turn my hips. We started with them about shoulder wide and then widened them out a few inches more. He said we'd probably incorporate a stride next, but for now, we'd keep my feet on the ground.

Then Curtis introduced me to the "trigger", which, next to the stride, was one of the most controversial elements of Curtis' hitting philosophy. The trigger is the movement of the hands back, and away from the pitcher as the batter gets ready for the pitch. It is a timing device—sometimes accompanied by a shift and plant of the front foot as the hitter "loads" weight behind the head. It seems crazy today, but at the time, most coaches in our area taught a short swing that was almost all forearms, with no trigger and never a stride of any kind.

Curtis was accused by many old school softball coaches of teaching girls a "baseball" swing, a cut his critics said was too long to ever catch up with pitches traveling 55 to 60 miles per hour from a pitcher whose release point was just 40 to 43 feet away.

While most coaches said that an effective swing had to be short and quick, Curtis believed with the right swing, a hitter didn't need to worry about being fast enough. To Curtis, trying to be quick just ruined timing and swing mechanics as the batter became over anxious and jumped at the ball. Curtis taught a swing that used the trigger to ensure that the hitter was *ready* for the pitch to arrive...ready to hit the ball with coordination and power. "You don't need to worry about being quick to hit well," he told me over and over again. "Just be ready."

I had noticed that the best college softball players triggered and swung the bat powerfully, involving their legs as well as their upper bodies. The swing Curtis was teaching me not only looked like the swings I saw elite softball players using, it also felt natural to me. It was far more athletic than the swings others had tried to teach me. It allowed me to keep my hands back and attack explosively as the ball reached the hitting zone. And, it fit my approach to the game, arming me with a powerful swing I could use to aggressively compete against power pitchers.

Later, as I attended hitting clinics at colleges and universities, I found that the swing Curtis helped me build wasn't considered a baseball swing, the coaches at those camps said it was a college softball swing. One afternoon during a clinic at the University of Michigan, Coach Carol Hutchins walked by the cage where I was hitting and paused for a minute to say, "Look at that...high school girls are now swinging like college players."

In the first few weeks I worked with him, Curtis stripped my swing down to the basics and built it back up, piece by piece. Although we started with the bat on my right shoulder, before long we had moved past that very basic trigger position to one where the bat was held upright behind my right ear. Soon thereafter, he added a short stride to my swing. Working over and over without ever releasing the ball, Curtis would fake the toss and train me to trigger back with the hands, simultaneously stepping forward and planting the left foot.

Through the years, we would experiment with adjustments to stride and hand position, but the basic swing I learned that first winter with Curtis would become the foundation for the hitting that would propel me to a spot in an elite softball program at one of the nation's most highly regarded universities.

While he was focused on improving my swing, over the years Curtis and his assistant, Sean, also worked on teaching me the finer points of hitting. For example, they taught me how to adjust to hit a changeup at 45 miles per hour when facing a pitcher with a fastball in the mid 60's. If you are lucky, that off speed pitch is not a strike, so even if you are out on your front foot and overcommitted as it arrives at the plate, you can just watch it sail by for a ball. But if it's in the strike zone and you already have a couple of strikes, you have to be able to hit it. Curtis would say, if it's a good pitcher who disguises the change of speed well, there is no question you are "going to be fooled" by the pitch. But even though your weight will already be forward when the ball arrives, you aren't completely beaten. Curtis instructed me to keep my hands back as my weight shifted forward and then throw them out when the ball finally arrived. By keeping my hands back, I could still drive, or at least dump, the ball into right field. Even if the best I could do was a foul ball down the first base line, that was better than a strike out.

His approach for dealing with a pitcher who throws hard inside was equally useful. Don't flinch or jump out of the way, he'd say. Hold your ground and show her you are not afraid. If there was a chance the inside pitch would be called a strike, he'd say to swing early and pull the ball hard and foul past third base to send the pitcher a loud message: "Don't bring that stuff in here!" Curtis would bellow the words loudly to emphasize the attitude my bat expressed each time I drove an inside pitch hard off of the posts lining the left side of his batting cages. When it came to hitting, Curtis was all about showing the pitcher who was boss.

As I moved up in travel ball, it became apparent that good pitchers could throw the ball four or five inches off the outside corner of the plate and many umpires would call it a strike. If you couldn't hit the outside pitch—or at the very least, foul it off to avoid striking out—you weren't going to have much success at the plate.

Curtis spent a lot of time training me to hit the outside pitch effectively without conceding the inside half of the plate to the pitcher. Some will tell you that you need to stride toward the plate in order to hit to the opposite field. But if you stride in, it can prevent you from making solid contact with anything inside and sometimes even balls over the middle of the plate. Crowding the plate can help, but there's a catcher right behind you watching your batting position. If she sees you move in, the next thing you know the pitcher is going to bust you inside. You'll have a hard time making contact with a strike on the inner edge of the plate, and if you do, it will likely be off the handle of the bat, or your hands. Ouch!

To successfully hit balls on the "black" or a few inches off the outside corner of the plate, Curtis taught me to move in a little bit but otherwise set up and stride normally. As the pitch arrived, he said to wait a fraction of a second longer and meet the ball slightly back in the hitting zone. Because the bat is late and not yet squared to the pitch, the impact sends the ball hard "the other way" to right field. If you are a little too late, you try to put a foul ball into the seats along the first base line. With two strikes, swinging for a foul ball is far better than watching a borderline outside pitch go by for a looking "K". On any count, "going with" the outside pitch instead of trying to pull it to left field can mean the difference between a solid drive to the outfield and a weak groundout. Even if I couldn't connect solidly, I'd be glad to frustrate the pitcher by wasting her pitches with foul balls in the stands along the right field line.

In the cage, Curtis would toss balls from behind a screen or use the pitching machine to zero in on a spot off the outside corner. The goal was to hit the target he placed on one of the massive wooden posts that supported the ceiling along the right side of the cage. Hit that post hard, Curtis would say, and it is a solid drive to right field. To spice things up, Curtis told me and my hitting partners he would reward us with a big ham for the holidays if we could hit that post. Curtis was big on hams. When we were working on the more basic skill of driving the ball hard on a line, he would offer the same reward if we could smash the ball on a line and hit the screen at the back of his very long, tunnel-like batting cages without hitting the net on the sides or top of the cage.

Once Curtis figured out that I had a thick skin and could take just about any razzing he could dish out, he would spice up most of my sessions with some good natured trash talk. Taunting us about the ham was part of the loud, stinging, non-stop banter we expected from Curtis. It wasn't too long before I was driving the ball hard all around that post until I finally smacked it dead center. Curtis was tickled that I'd earned the ham and immediately turned his taunts to everyone else in the place including my hitting partner and good friend, Christina. Luckily she hit the post soon after I did and he stopped razzing her. Curtis still owes us those hams!

Ham or no ham, my ability to hit the outside pitch was a key to my success as a hitter in every level of ball I played after that. During critical at-bats in tight games, I took a lot of satisfaction in my ability to "waste" several otherwise unhittable outside pitches until the pitcher either gave in and walked me or piped one down the middle that I could drive right back up the middle.

Almost Over Before It Began

My second season of travel ball couldn't have begun at a better time. After a second winter of training with Coach Greenman, plus about eight months of working with Curtis Morgan, my game was peaking. I was still playing AAU basketball and a schedule conflict with the state AAU tournament caused me to miss the first game of the travel ball season in nearby Lansing. But I arrived in time for the second game and Coach immediately installed me at shortstop.

I wasn't really expecting to get the start at short, but I guess I had convinced Coach in practice that I had earned the job. He had moved last year's shortstop, Ashley, to right field where she could use her gun to turn sharply hit balls that looked like sure singles into outs at first base. He had decided that Kaprice's size would be an asset at third base. So I started the season at short, my favorite spot on the diamond and a position that usually saw a lot of action.

Despite hurrying the first ball hit to me and tossing the throw over the first baseman's head, I settled down and played solid defense the rest of the game. Meanwhile, in my first at bat, I waited on an outside pitch the way Curtis had taught me and lashed it on a line past first base and into the corner in right. The fences on the field were set up deep for adult slow pitch softball, which meant there was nothing to stop my hard hit once it got past the right fielder. I rounded the bases for a home run well ahead of the throw from the hustling but otherwise helpless outfielder.

Coach moved me around between short and third the rest of the tournament and I continued to hit as we closed out the weekend with a solid team performance. We left the fields filled with confidence that our combination of power hitting, good pitching, and strong defense could make this a special season.

Our next tournament was the following weekend in Merrill-ville, Indiana, about two hours from home and an hour from Chicago. It was Memorial Day weekend and there would be a lot of strong teams from Michigan, Ohio, Indiana and Illinois competing for the first place hardware.

As we began our drive from Grand Rapids on Thursday evening, the sky didn't look promising. But we didn't let the dark clouds and occasional lightning dampen our enthusiasm. We had my Mom's van painted with the team colors and drew honks from other cars as we headed south and west on Interstate 196. What's a little rain to girls who practice indoors all winter while harsh winds blow and snowdrifts accumulate outside? In our part of the world, people say if you don't like the current weather, just wait five minutes, because it is sure to change!

Sure enough, the sky was clear when we arrived at the fields later that evening and a full slate of games was underway under the lights. We weren't scheduled to play until early the next morning. After watching a few innings, Coach made it clear we should all head back to the hotel and get to bed so we'd be rested for our early wakeup calls. He got no argument from us.

The next morning, we met in the hotel lobby for breakfast and then it was time to head to the fields. Coach always wanted us ready to warm-up at least an hour and a half before game time. This morning was no exception. It was light out when we reached the fields, but there was no sun. The fields were damp and there were a few puddles on the paved driveways, the residue from an overnight rain. A low dark sky made it look like there was more rain to come.

We started our warm-up routine with our synchronized throwing drill, facing each other in pairs arranged in two rows about ten feet apart. We started with wrist snap throws to our partner in the opposing line and then came soft tosses from about 30 feet. We moved back some more to begin stretching our arms out with longer throws. Then the two rows would move closer again to within about 15 yards with all the balls in the hands of the players on one side. The assigned captains would call out "throw" and all of us would simultaneously throw a strike directly at the target presented by our partners' chest high gloves. The captains would call out, "throw" again and the return throws would fly in the opposite direction.

The idea was to have all of the throws arrive in our partners' gloves with one loud "smack". A "popcorn" effect caused by unsynchronized throwing was unacceptable to Coach. We practiced the drill all the time and were good at it. The precision of our pregame throwing drills frequently attracted spectators who were impressed with the difference between our disciplined warm up compared to the lackadaisical drills of many other teams.

The final step in our throwing warm-up was a rapid-fire game of catch with our partner, designed to combine proper footwork, a quick release, and accuracy. The object was to complete 21 exchanges in a row before any of our teammates. If you missed, you had to chase the ball down and start over, often while getting an earful from Coach.

After completing our throwing drill in the damp morning air, we set up our hitting stations and began working from tees, hitting soft toss and facing Coach's wiffle ball pitches. By now our opponents, the Indiana *Magic*, had also arrived and were warming up. The *Magic* were always one of the best travel clubs in the Midwest and this would be our first real competitive test of the year. We'd soon find out if we were ready to compete against the best. All around us, other teams were warming up on adjacent fields and fans were arriving and filling the bleachers behind the backstops. Our *Blaze* fans were loud and in great spirits. They were mostly family members, but there were a few friends and coaches from other teams as well. Then the umpire crew arrived and it was game time.

After the coin flip, we took the field and the home plate ump called out, "Play ball!" The *Magic* proved to be every bit as tough as we thought they would be. Their pitching and defense held our hitters at bay through the first few innings. Meanwhile, our pitcher and fielders were hanging tough as well. The *Magic* managed some solid hits, though, and took the lead. It was now the fourth inning and the skies had grown darker and a light rain was falling. We hoped we'd be able to finish the game, but we desperately needed to record *Magic* outs and get our bats going.

Then the game score and threat of rain suddenly became a lot less important to me. With a runner on second and no outs, Kaprice was playing in front of third base to defend against a bunt. With the next pitch, the runner suddenly bolted for third in a steal attempt. I raced from my shortstop position to cover third, arriving at the same instant as the catcher's throw and the runner. I heard the sickening 'thwak' of bone on flesh and the next think I knew I was on the ground and in excruciating pain. The *Magic* runner had not slid into the bag on the close play. Instead she came in standing up and the full momentum of her body was concentrated in the impact of her knee as it speared my left thigh.

Afterward, my Dad said he could hear the sickening sound of the impact from the stands and he was sure the collision had torn every ligament in my knee. Both Dad and Mom started to the field as I lay on the ground. But they could see that the coaches from both teams and the umpires were doing everything they could to help me. I was on the ground for quite a while, but was relieved to find that, after the initial pain, the damage wasn't in my knee. I had an ugly bruise above the knee, but no pain in the knee joint and I had full mobility. It looked like I would be alright.

Back on my feet, I walked around under Coach's watchful eye and he was convinced—with some lobbying from me—that I could continue playing. The game resumed as I grew accustomed to the ache in my leg. I was relieved that the "bone wasn't sticking out", which had always been Coach Youtzy's measure of serious injury in KBL. We played another inning before the sky opened up and rain began to fall in buckets. Both teams retreated to the dugouts, but it wasn't long before the game was called. We had lost to the *Magic* in a rain-shortened contest.

The tournament organizers told the coaches they would monitor weather updates and field conditions and would let them know by telephone when play would resume. Wet and unhappy with our performance in the loss, we headed back to our hotel to shed our soggy uniforms and wait for word on our next game time. As the day progressed the weather didn't improve and we soon learned that all of the day's action would be cancelled. As the fields grew wetter, the welt on my leg grew larger. The ugly bruise had turned into a swollen mass about the size of the ham Curtis had promised me. We began applying heat and ice alternately to try to reduce the swelling and loosen up the leg, which was growing stiff as the swelling increased. Nothing seemed to work, and I could tell Coach was worried.

The next day, the rain continued and we amused ourselves with movies, shopping trips, a euchre tournament, and by just hanging out with teammates at the hotel. I also spent a lot of time icing my leg and trying to stretch and loosen it up. It was growing a lot stiffer. Finally on Sunday the tournament was cancelled entirely and we loaded up our cars and headed for home. Despite our best efforts, we had not been able to stop the swelling in my leg. Even if the games had continued, it was doubtful I could have played.

By the time we arrived home, I could barely walk. We kept icing, but finally called the family doctor and made an appointment to see him. It was clear something was seriously wrong. Upon seeing my leg, the doctor referred us to an orthopedic clinic for x-rays and further evaluation. When the clinic doctor came in to examine me she immediately called out to others on the staff, "Take a look at this hematoma!" X-rays confirmed that, while nothing was torn or broken, I had sustained a severe bruise all the way to the bone. The injury had a serious impact on my mobility. I could only bend my leg 40 percent of its normal range.

Then came the real blow. The doctor said there was a real danger of causing further, more serious injury. I could not practice or play softball, or engage in any other athletic activity involving my legs until the swelling could be reduced and my range of motion could be restored. I would need to apply ice repeatedly every day, perform careful stretching exercises and undergo physical therapy to get my leg to bend normally again. Until I regained normal use of my leg, I was on the sidelines. I couldn't even practice hitting. My season might be over almost before it began.

Sidelined

I was devastated to learn I could not play and that my season might be over. When I looked at my leg, I was baffled at how a big bruise could put me on the sidelines. It didn't hurt all that much anymore except for the lingering stiffness. And the bones weren't sticking out. I should be able to stretch it out and then get back on the field. But I couldn't. I faced a long, slow recovery process that could not be rushed, even with weekly physical therapy and total dedication to my rehab exercises at home in between the supervised sessions at the medical clinic. Sitting on the bench for the first time in my short career hurt me a lot more than the injury itself.

Looking back, my injury brought me to the first serious crossroads in my softball career. There was no question about doing physical therapy. I needed to do that to ever see the field again. The question was: What else would I do during my enforced absence from the field? I suppose I could have sulked and felt sorry for myself. And don't get me wrong, there were plenty of times when I thought "Why me?" during my time away from the game I loved. I also could have used my time off to find other interests. I had a lot of friends outside of softball, and enjoyed spending time just hanging out, going to the movies, and all of the other things any normal thirteen-year-old wants to do. It wasn't like I didn't have options.

But instead of those paths, I told my Dad and Mom I wanted to participate as much as I could in my team's practices and games, even if it meant serving as chief cheerleader from the dugout during the games and taking part in only limited practice drills. We called Coach and broke the news to him. I wouldn't be able to play or participate in practice fully until I regained mobility in my leg. But I wanted to come to practice and listen to his coaching, do what I could to help my teammates, and participate in all of the drills that did not require a left leg.

Coach gave his tentative O.K. He explained later that he had some reservations because as he put it, "A girl who can't play can distract the team and become a negative influence in practice and during games." Coach didn't have anything to worry about on that score. I was still all about softball, frustrated by my inability to play, and committed to working my hardest to maintain my skills and stay in peak softball condition. The problem was, the limits the doctor had placed on me included no full swings of the bat and no full throws, both of which required a strong and supple left leg.

Physical therapy began right away. I was referred to a clinic across town because I was told one of the therapists specialized in sports injuries and even worked part time with the Grand Rapids *Rampage*, our local Arena Football League team. That was my introduction to Jolene Bennett, a no-nonsense professional with a quick wit and a contagious upbeat and positive attitude. If I had had any thoughts of feeling sorry for myself, Jolene quickly dispelled them. There would be no sulking on her watch.

In our first session, she sketched out our therapy plan and set our goal. I had to regain 80 percent of normal mobility to get back on the field. Based on her previous experience with professional football players who had similar injuries, she said recovery could take six to eight weeks. Unfortunately, in six weeks the relatively brief travel ball season would be over and my season would be washed out as surely as our last game in Indiana had been. But I had to take Jolene's advice to heart: "Do everything you can to get better, you can't do any more than that."

What followed was the first of many painful stretching and deep muscle massage sessions. I'd lie on my stomach as Jolene would try to bend my leg back as far as it would go. She would relax the tension before trying it again, and again. The most painful technique Jolene used was stem stimulation treatment to try to break up the knotted mass beneath my skin. Electrodes were attached to my thigh and electrical impulses were applied to stimulate the muscles. At the same time, Jolene would bend my leg back as far as it would go toward my backside. If my leg wasn't hurting much when I walked into the therapy session, it sure was when I walked out! After a few weeks of therapy with Jolene, my Mom and I affectionately nicknamed her "Mean Jolene" because of the pain she administered while healing my leg.

I came away from the first session with a set of daily stretching and exercise drills to do at home and some large rubber bands to create resistance. I also came away with the recipe for Jolene's secret icing potion: One part rubbing alcohol and two parts water in doubled-up sealable plastic bags. When frozen, this concoction gets colder than frozen water alone. It was important to place a towel between my bruise and the ice bag to prevent frost bite and Jolene cautioned me to also limit the length of each icing session. Jolene also clarified what I could do and what I couldn't do to keep my skills sharp while I was sidelined. There wasn't much I could do defensively except toss a ball lightly to keep my throwing arm limber. Hitting practice was also severely restricted. I could bunt, but I couldn't stand in and take a full cut.

When I described these limitations to Coach, he devised a practice plan that called for me to spend a lot of time working on bunting while the rest of the team ran through all of their other drills. During the fielding drills, I would be the designated target for throws into Coach as he hit fungos to the infield and flies and line drives to the outfield. And I would be involved in all of the team huddles when Coach talked about strategy, explained new skills, and reminded us of the right way to perform the drills he'd introduced in the past.

Coach also suggested I take sit-down batting practice at home between team sessions, to keep my trigger and shoulder action in tune, while keeping my legs idle. My work with Curtis had made me an avid student of hitting and, before my injury, I would spend more than an hour almost every day working from the tee or taking soft toss from my Dad. In addition to standard two-handed swings, I used a short bat to hit balls with just my right hand and then with my left hand. These drills worked my hands and wrists and added some variety to the drills. Hitting from a chair wasn't the same as stepping into the batter's box and getting my hacks, but it gave me an outlet for my pent up desire to hit. To help with this drill, my Dad found an old armless swivel office chair and I sat in front of a net for hours in my driveway, hitting balls off of a tee. I hit so much and so hard, I wore holes in the hitting net.

Cheerleader

The week after my injury, we packed up my uniforms and other equipment and headed to the next tournament the same as any other softball weekend. I have to give my Mom and Dad a lot of credit for their support that season. They spent the money on hotel rooms and meals, sat through all of the practices and games, and let me go to team meals at Fazoli's and other restaurants, join my teammates at the movies, and take part in all of the other off-field team activities. I felt like I was still a teammate...even if I couldn't play on the field.

Sitting in the dugout was the hardest part. I was bleeding inside to take my spot on the field and my turn at bat. But all I could do was cheer my teammates on from the sideline. Coach had a rule, when our team was at bat, no one sat down in the dugout. He wanted us up at the fence and screaming softball cheers at the top of our lungs. If we had the third base dugout, he'd sometimes run over from the coaching box during an offensive rally, flapping his arms and screaming (yes, actually screaming!) at us to cheer more loudly. We had a lot of cheers and we sang them at the top of our lungs.

Since I couldn't play at all, my job during games was to stand at the dugout fence and cheer the entire game. This was more than a little ironic because, as an athlete, I had never aspired to be a cheerleader. That isn't because I have anything against cheer-leaders. Rather it's because, before the federal Title IX law paved the way for girls and women to participate on an equal footing with boys and men in school athletics, cheerleading at male athlet-ic events was the only way girls could participate in varsity sports. As we prepared to play high school ball, and dreamed of careers on college diamonds, my teammates and I were all about playing in the games, not cheering on the sidelines.

But a cheerleader I had become. By the end of the weekend I would be pretty hoarse. Still, it felt good to be contributing to the team, even if all I could add were yells of encouragement and high fives to teammates when they came back to the dugout. Later on in the season, Coach called the team aside and embarrassed me a little. He pointed out that, although he had worried an injured player could distract the team, I had proved him wrong. Even though I was hurt and couldn't play, I was keeping a positive attitude and helping my teammates win without me.

During practices, I bunted my brains out. I took my turn in the rotation as the coaches tossed us balls to bunt, working on my sacrifice bunt and my drop step or sneaky bunt. I would focus on placing the ball down the third and first base lines with surgical precision, making sure I squared and moved the bat and my head up and down in unison to make contact on the top half of the ball to avoid a pop-up. I worked on catching the ball with the bat, letting the bat absorb each pitch instead of stabbing at it. This allowed me to deaden the impact with the pitch and softly place the bunt on the ground in no man's land between the catcher and the other fielders.

When the other girls were swinging away off of live pitching, the machine or a tee, I was bunting some more, relying on a coach to soft toss to me and using a fence to stop each bunted ball. When no one else was available, Coach told my Dad he could toss pitches to me while practice went on around us. I have to admit, bunting for an hour or more a night can be a little boring, especially when I could only look on with envy as my teammates were doing all of the other hitting drills, or running the bases and working on fielding. But, as Jolene said, I had to be satisfied with what I could do and not think about what I was missing.

My recovery seemed to take forever as my family and I settled into our new routine. I'd start out the week with a session with Jolene, she'd begin by measuring my progress and I'd wait anxiously as she manipulated my leg and tested its range of motion. Progress came slowly. My question as Jolene tested my leg was always a simple one: "Can I play?" Jolene understood me well enough to never answer with a simple, "No." The walls of her office were lined with jerseys from the high school, college and professional athletes she had helped. Once their bodies were restored to full health, you might expect athletes to turn away from Jolene and her therapy room and never look back. But it was obvious Jolene's patients truly appreciated her ability to keep hope alive for injured athletes who had been deprived of the thing they loved most: the ability to compete on the court or playing field.

At each session, Jolene would focus on the progress I had made. She'd stress that I was moving steadily toward my goal and, although the gains were small at first, they were important because they showed we were on the right track. She never promised a specific timeline for my recovery. She couldn't predict how my body was going to react to the therapy. All she knew was, I would not be cleared to play if there was any chance I could cause further harm to my leg. Additional injury would not only deprive me of the rest of the season, but would also mean I couldn't participate in freshman basketball in the fall—I still loved basketball and playing on my high school team had been a personal goal for years. But most important of all, additional injury to my left leg could limit my ability to compete in softball, basketball or any sport requiring strong legs for the rest of my life.

As each tournament weekend drew near, my Dad would call Coach and update him on what Jolene had told us. Week after week for four weeks, he had to tell Coach I could not play. This helped Coach set up his lineup for the weekend, and I am sure he appreciated hearing from us in advance. But I also think he was beginning to become discouraged at my slow progress and wonder if I would be coming back at all. Like me he probably thought, if the bone isn't sticking out, what's the problem?

I was growing desperate and a bit impatient. Although my rehab was progressing steadily, I had been unable to crack the 80 percent mobility goal that Jolene had set. The season was winding down now with only two weekend tournaments left and then nationals. We had already qualified to go to the Pony Nationals in Sterling, Virginia, outside of Washington, D.C. While the prospect of traveling to the East Coast to play in a week-long tournament was exciting, I knew spending an entire week cheering from the dugout as my team played without me would be tough. Although they hadn't hesitated for a second in deciding that we'd continue to travel with the team, I knew it would be hard on my parents to travel to Virginia for a week, using the remainder of their summer vacations to watch me cheer while other families' daughters played.

Our next-to-last regular season tournament before nationals would be the ASA (Amateur Softball Association) State Tournament in Midland on the east side of the state. We were due to begin play Thursday evening so the *Blaze* families would be leaving town at about 2 p.m. to make the two-and-a-half hour drive to Midland. I was scheduled to see Jolene at 1 p.m. that afternoon and would be leaving for Midland right after the appointment. I put on my uniform and we packed the car so we could make a quick getaway after the appointment.

I was cautiously hoping that this would be the week Jolene would say I was ready. I had been close to the 80 percent goal the previous week but unable to reach it. Jolene greeted us in the office lobby and we walked into the therapy room together. I sat on the examination table. After examining my leg and poking and prodding at the hard lump that had formed underneath my bruised skin, Jolene had me turn over on my stomach for the moment of truth. She slowly pulled my foot back toward my butt. Before my injury, I could touch heel to backside. We weren't expecting that today. I just needed to get within 80 percent of my normal range.

Jolene eased up her pressure on the leg and paused for a moment before slowly repeating the exercise. She relaxed pressure again, this time letting the leg fall back to the table. Then she said, "It's close, but you made it!" I couldn't believe it. "You mean I can play?" I asked in disbelief. Jolene said yes, I could hit, I could run, I could slide, and I could play in the field.

But she also said I had to be careful. I couldn't put myself in harms' way. If I felt pain, I needed to be smart and take myself out of the game. Jolene said the worst thing I could do would be to get hit in the same spot again. That's when she gave me a present: a football thigh pad she had obtained from the *Rampage* trainer. She said I needed to wear it for all sports activities until my leg was completely normal again, which might be another six months or even a year. She also said I would still need to do my stretches and see her once a week for the rest of the summer to keep regaining mobility and get ready for fall basketball. I have to admit, while my parents listened intently to Jolene, all I heard was, I could play ball!

The Comeback Kid

I felt like I was floating on air during the entire drive to Midland. I couldn't wait to tell Coach and my teammates that I was ready to go. We pulled into the softball complex in Midland right on time, two hours before game time, and just as Coach was pulling out to lead a caravan of families to the practice fields a short drive away. We stopped next to Coach's car and I called out to him that I had the green light to play. He broke into a smile and said "That's great, kiddo, let's go get warmed up!"

We filled Coach in on the details when we arrived at the practice field. He had me run a little bit so he could see how much I still limped. I moved pretty well, but still had to drag the leg behind me. I couldn't lift that knee up high enough to run normally. But I could still cover ground. I also worked on a few ground balls to my right and left and realized that there was no way I could bend the leg enough to get down to ground balls hit to either side. That meant I wouldn't be playing shortstop or third base. I was exclusively an outfielder for the time being.

I joined my teammates in every drill as we warmed up. Then, about 40 minutes before game time, we loaded up our cars and headed for the tournament fields. As usual, Coach's thorough pregame practice routine had us all warmed up and ready to go. But the official team pregame warm up at the fields put the finishing touches on our preparation. Then the home plate umpire called out "play ball" and my days as a cheerleader were officially over. I was back to being a softball player again.

Coach didn't play me in the field right away. I understood. While I had been rehabbing, my teammates had stepped up and earned their spots on the field and in the batting lineup. But I was ready to contribute. The game was a tight one and both teams were having trouble scoring runs. Finally, we had runners on first and second with no outs and coach called for me to pinch hit. I expected him to signal the bunt. After my long layoff it was unlikely I would drive the ball through the infield in my first at bat. I might even be overly aggressive and pop up or strike out. Besides, bunting was all I had practiced for four weeks. I should be able to get one down now and move the runners. Perhaps I could even limp out a single!

I squared on the first pitch but bunted it foul. Strike one. The next pitch was a ball and I let it go by. The third pitch looked good, but I was over anxious and bunted it foul. Now I had two strikes and another foul bunt would be an automatic out. I might have to swing away after all. But then coach gave me the bunt sign again. He must have a lot of confidence in my bunting, I thought as I stepped into the box. I decided I did, too. Positive thinking had helped me get through weeks on the sidelines, I wasn't about to start doubting myself now.

The next pitch was a fastball, right down the pipe. I stayed on top of it, cushioning the pitch on the bat and laying down a picture-perfect bunt between the pitching rubber and the third base line. I admired my hit, giving the ball plenty of time to clear my path to first base, before I took off like a gimpy rabbit. Even though I squared and showed I was going to bunt as the pitcher took her wind up, the short ground ball seemed to take the infielders by surprise. I hobbled through first base with a single and saw my teammates pause just past second and third base. They weren't there for long. Slow to react to my bunt, the opposing third baseman fielded the ball and hurried a late throw to first base. The wild throw allowed our lead runners to score and I was able to hobble over to second before the right fielder could get the ball back into the infield. We had our first runs. It was the beginning of a big inning and we won the game handily.

We were off to a great start in the biggest tournament of our season. Although the National Softball Association (NSA) and the United States Specialty Sports Association (USSSA) also held state tournaments, the ASA State Tournament always attracted the best teams from across the state. The Detroit area powerhouses and teams from Lansing, Saginaw, Kalamazoo and Grand Rapids were all there. We had never won a state championship. Winning the ASA State Tournament would give us considerable bragging rights. But we'd have to play our best to have a chance.

As the weekend progressed, we continued to win. One-by-one, teams were eliminated, some by us, others at the hands of the other strong teams in the tournament. In the semifinals, the last of the Detroit area teams was sent packing and then it was down to just two teams playing for all the marbles: The Grand Rapids *Blaze* and the Kalamazoo *Klash*. My playing time had increased with every game and I was now set as the starting center fielder, gimpy leg and all. I was quite a sight dragging my leg around the broad expanse of centerfield, but I still had good range and a strong arm. I wasn't handicapping the team. I knew Coach would not have played me out there if I was a liability.

Our opponents for the championship, the *Klash*, were also from West Michigan and we were familiar with their lineup. We had played them several times in 12-and-under ball and even earlier in this season and had never come out on the winning side. Now, we'd be facing them with the state championship trophy on the line. It was Allie's turn to pitch and she was on her game from the start, holding the strong *Klash* hitters at bay as our lone rally gave us a one-run lead. The lead stood up into the bottom of the seventh and final inning. The *Klash* were the home team and would have one more shot at Allie before we could claim the championship trophy.

By then, Allie was getting tired, but still throwing hard strikes. The *Klash* managed to get a runner on first, but Allie was able to retire two batters as the runner moved to second and then third base. With the tying run on third, a short sprint from home, I watched from centerfield as Allie carefully pitched to one of the *Klash* power hitters. The hitter was patient until she saw a pitch she liked. At the crack of the bat, I knew it was hit well. It was headed on a high arc into the left center gap. Instincts honed in hours of "Say Hey" practice, not to mention two years of working with Coach, gave me a quick first step in the right direction.

Now it would be all about speed. How fast could I drag my leg into that gap? The ball was hit deep, so I had to race to my right and back to the fence. If it hit the ground, the runner on third would score, the game would be tied, and the winning run would likely be sitting on third base.

I knew if I reached up too soon, it could slow me down and keep me from reaching the streaking ball in time. This was no time to overestimate how far I could reach, I needed get under the ball and it would take all my speed to get there. Then I could see the fence out of the corner of my eye. It was now or never. Legs still pumping, I stretched my left arm and glove hand as far as I could across my body and snared the ball in the webbing just as my foot came down on the warning track. One stride more and I arrested my momentum with both elbows against the fence. Grinning from ear to ear, I turned and gimp-sprinted toward the infield where the celebration had already begun. The game and championship were ours. We were state champs, and I was back!

Time to Reload

After winning the state championship and coming off a good performance in our last weekend tournament, we headed to the national tournament filled with confidence. We made a strong showing in Virginia, getting into the quarterfinals before we were eliminated. I wasn't back at full strength yet, but started in center field and contributed on defense and at the plate. All too soon, though, we lost for the second time in the double elimination tournament brackets, which put an end to my abbreviated season.

After the season I continued to see Jolene and worked hard on my own to try to regain full mobility in time for the girls' high school basketball season, which at the time was still held in the fall. (Today in the state, girls and boys both play in the traditional winter basketball season.) As school began, I tried out for the East Kentwood High School freshman basketball team. East Kentwood has one of the largest high school enrollments in the state, so surviving the final cut was no small feat. Despite the lingering stiffness in my leg, I could still shoot, handle the ball with both hands and box out in the paint. I was excited when the coach announced that I was one of the girls to make the final roster. Basketball was still a real passion in my life.

Although I had played point guard throughout middle school, the coaching staff decided my defense, rebounding and ability to produce offense from the outside and the post made me a good candidate for the three and four spots. I had good size for a freshman, but one look at my 5'7" Dad and 5'3" Mom and you could tell I wasn't going to grow to be a force in the paint on the varsity squad. Still, I enjoyed my first season of high school basketball, and—if playing time, rebounds, steals and points are any indication—I had a fairly successful freshman year.

The start of my high school hoops career didn't reduce my focus on softball. A couple of weeks after school started, it was time for *Blaze* tryouts again. After missing most of the prior season, I was anxious to get back on the field with my teammates. Then the unexpected happened. Several of my teammates decided to move up an age group to play on the *Blaze* 16-and-under team. A couple of other girls also made the decision to leave for other teams. I was too loyal to Coach to even consider making such a move, but I now realized that, for some girls my age, travel softball was already more than just a game. They saw it as a means to an end, with that end being the opportunity to earn a scholarship to play college softball.

I'd be lying if I said I hadn't already added college recruitment to my list of athletic goals. I had seen the college coaches watching the older girls at the biggest tournaments we played in. But at age 14, I wasn't worried about college yet. First I wanted to win a spot on the *Blaze* 14-and-under squad for next season, and then I'd try to win a spot on the high school varsity softball team as a freshman. I figured if I continued to work hard, improved my skills, performed on the field, plus earned good grades in school, college would take care of itself.

Although a lot of my teammates would not be returning, Coach and his daughter, Katie, plus Deanna and Ashley, would be coming back. Coach would have to assess a lot of new talent to fill out our roster, which meant our tryouts this year would be wide open. Fortunately, when we pulled into the parking lot at tryouts on the first weekend, I could tell we had a big turnout. There'd be plenty of talent to assess.

It soon became apparent that the Grand Rapids *Blaze* was going to be the West Michigan *Blaze* in the coming season and our rivalry with the Kalamazoo *Klash* the previous summer was going to produce an unusual outcome. During tryouts, several players immediately stood out as strong competitors for our many openings. They included two players from the *Klash* team we had faced in Midland: Amanda and Simone, both of whom lived on the outskirts of Kalamazoo, about 45 minutes south of Grand Rapids.

Amanda was a strong pitcher who, like me, could also play all of the infield positions and the outfield, too. Simone was a great catcher and infielder. Both were also good hitters. Coach offered them positions almost immediately.

Also at the tryouts was a pitcher and first baseman, Molly, from the Benton Harbor area in the southwest corner of the state, about 90 minutes from Grand Rapids. Molly had been our teammate on the 12-and-under *Blaze* squad. She could throw a rise ball in addition to the more common drop ball, changeup and fastball combination and she had played for a one of the leading Detroit area teams the previous summer. We had lost two pitchers from last year's team so Coach quickly made Molly an offer.

The next two players Coach invited to join the team were Meghan and Sarah, twins out of the same part of suburban Kalamazoo as Amanda. Meghan was a pitcher and outfielder and Sarah was a catcher and infielder. Next to join us was Becky, a pitcher from Lowell, east of Grand Rapids. Becky also had the talent to play in both the infield and outfield. That gave us nine versatile players and left room for more in case another great prospect or two came along in the coming months.

We were a team again, but a very different team than the previous year's *Blaze*. I sensed that my new teammates were as competitive as I was and that all would benefit from Coach's teaching and his disciplined but positive and enthusiastic approach. Only time would tell if we would come together as a team to continue the winning tradition set by a different group of girls a few short weeks earlier. I didn't know it at the time, but not only would we win, we would enjoy a special season together.

Choices

As my first high school basketball season wound to a close, off season softball practices were in full swing. In addition to my weekly sessions with Curtis at his hitting club, we practiced for three hours every Sunday with Coach in a school gym. I was also playing AAU basketball, chasing my hoop dreams with a passion that now matched and even exceeded my desire to be a great softball player.

Basketball was a love I hadn't been able to shake, even though softball now consumed so much of my life. In the course of my childhood athletic career I had had many passions and my goal was always to be the best, whether the sport was softball, basketball, soccer, ice hockey, or sandlot football. Over time, I had to make choices. There were only so many sport seasons in the year! My Dad and Mom helped me make some of the decisions. For example, my Mom wouldn't let me suit up with all of the boys and play pee wee football. And my Dad said boys' ice hockey was out because he was sure my excellent skating skills would not spare me from the fate of other girls on boys' teams: play goalie and find myself on the receiving end of slap shots and large bodies crashing into the net.

After my travel soccer career ended with a sprained knee, basketball and softball were the two athletic passions left to fight for my heart and my parents' time and financial support. Since he'd begun coaching me, Curtis had razzed me almost nonstop about basketball. "When are you going to quit spending time doing that?" he'd say. "You need to focus on softball and train year round to be the best." I listened to Curtis, but my basketball coaches and teammates…and my heart…were telling me something different. My parents didn't discourage my two-sport passion either. My Dad said he thought basketball and soccer helped me develop speed and agility I wouldn't gain from playing softball alone. Besides, he knew I still harbored a good-natured grudge over my involuntary retirements from football and hockey. He wasn't about to make me stop playing basketball, too.

Then, one winter day as we were leaving the gym after a Sunday practice, Coach Greenman called to me to wait. He wanted to talk. Coach took me aside in the hallway and gave it to me short and to the point: "You're the best young third baseman I have ever seen," he said. "Is anyone saying that about you in basketball?"

Coach left it at that. But he had given me a lot to think about. As much as I loved to play basketball, I knew he was right. I was a classic hardworking "tweener" on the basketball court...too slow to be a college point guard and not big enough to play down low. I got by on desire and attention to detail, plus my ability to defend in the open court, box out beneath the basket, grab rebounds, and dish quick outlet passes to teammates streaking up court. I didn't quit playing basketball there and then. But I soon let my AAU coach know that I would have to miss some practices and games because softball now had to come first.

For the next two years, a continued to play high school and AAU basketball, but the time I once might have spent practicing basketball I now devoted to working on softball skills. Coach had helped me set a big new goal in my athletic career: I wanted to play NCAA Division I college softball.

Best Softball Friends

The story of my career in softball would be incomplete without describing the close bonds between teammates and the great times I had practicing, playing, and just hanging out with the girls on my youth travel ball teams. We traveled together, won and sometimes lost, and shared the special years that are the bridge between girlhood and womanhood. I didn't become close friends with every player on every team, but I shared a lot of good times and enjoyed close friendships on every team I played on, from KBL to college.

I have already mentioned Deanna, Melissa, Brooke and Kristi, my softball buddies from KBL. In my later years of travel ball, I also had a lot of laughs and good times with Nicole, my first close friend on Finesse and the teammate who helped keep me sane during the craziness of recruiting. Later on Christina, from Rockford north of Grand Rapids, joined Finesse and we shared some great long drives to practices in Detroit and a much longer ride to Oklahoma City for the ASA Gold Nationals. And in high school ball, I had a ton of fun with Julie, Kayla, and a bunch of other girls.

But there is one team and a single season that stands apart in my memory from all of the rest—the year Amanda, Simone, Molly, Sarah, Meghan and Becky joined Katie, Ashley, Deanna and me on the *Blaze* for 14-and-under travel ball. It was the closest team I ever played on. The addition of two more teammates—Amber, and Amanda's younger sister, Alexis—early in the season, made this special group complete.

Looking back, I can see now that one of the reasons we became so close was our age. At fourteen going on fifteen, we were not yet driving or as independent from our parents as we would be in a year or two. But we were independent enough to prefer the company of our friends to spending time with Mom and Dad.

Although many of us had boyfriends, we were still more into hanging out with close friends than "going out" exclusively with one guy.

Most of us were multiple sport athletes, but each of us had decided softball was our greatest passion. Coach's intense approach to coaching and the way he worked to bring out the best in each of us also brought us together. We were united in our desire to make him proud and to become the best softball players and the best team we could be.

I didn't know it at the time, but as college recruiting became an increasingly important part of our softball lives, things would become more competitive. The passion that drew us so close as 14-year-olds would strain the relationships between teammates and families. Plus as we grew older, we would become more independent and expressive as individuals. Boyfriends would become more serious. And we would naturally gravitate toward strong individual friendships, which would replace the group bonds that attracted us in our younger years. But that was all in the future. For one magical year, we became the closest of friends and teammates and had the time of our softball lives.

I entered winter practices glad that I would be playing with Deanna and Katie again. De had been my teammate and close friend for as long as I could remember, and Katie and I had become close in the two years I had played for Coach. What I didn't know was, how good a team would we be? We had lost our two top pitchers, Allie and Ali. And two of our sluggers, Kaprice and Amber, were gone. We had also lost valuable utility players Shannon, Jenna and Amanda.

But as the now familiar rhythm of winter practices settled in, my questions about our on-the-field strength began to be answered. This team could pitch, field and hit. Also answered was any concern about how we would all get along on the same team. Our nucleus of returning players was not a majority. The Kalamazoo contingent outnumbered us and they were already close as a group. But old alliances and geographic origins soon began to break down as Coach's non-stop teaching, shouts of encouragement, and equally strong corrections when we needed it made comrades of us all.

The nicknames Coach gave to each of us helped to loosen us all up. I was already "North", Katie was "Punk", Deanna was "De" and Ashley was "Ash". Soon, Amanda became "Jags", Simone was "Sammy", and Meghan became "MT". Sarah was now "Tommy", Molly was "Langer", and Becky was "Plum". When they joined us, Amber quickly became "Mattie" and Alexis was "Lexi". Before long we were calling each other by the same nicknames. When you call someone by a nickname, you can't help but feel closer to them. Pretty soon, we were razzing each other, offering help as we worked to refine new skills, calling out encouragement, and conspiring to get our parents to take us all out to dinner together after practice.

It's not that we all had similar personalities. I probably seemed pretty intense to some of my teammates and Sarah, Becky and Katie also wore their intensity on their sleeves. Fortunately, others were more laid back, or at least softened their own considerable inner drive with a more relaxed outward personality. Without this mix of personalities, the team could have been a mixture of gasoline and jet fuel, ready to explode at the first sign of adversity.

I think that's why I became especially close to Amanda and Simone. There is no question they shared my passion for the game and for achieving the dream of a college softball career. But their unique brands of humor loosened me up and made me laugh a lot. I think I made them laugh, too. We definitely had our share of fun. Simone was a fan of the old British comedy group, Monty Python, and my Dad had introduced me to the same offbeat humor when I was younger. Pretty soon we were singing the lumberjack song and trading Monty Python insults back and forth constantly.

Amanda was a total extrovert. She and her younger sister, Lexi, would often break into spontaneous song, including show tunes (*Annie* was a favorite) and musical cheers. At a tournament near Cincinnati, Jags and Lexi dragged us all on stage in an open air concert facility on the main street of Oxford, Ohio, home of Miami University. We locked arms and sang and danced at the top of our lungs. People stopped on the sidewalks and just stared, but we were laughing too hard to care what anyone thought of us. We even attracted the attention of the local police, two of whom joined us on stage to find out what was going on. Jags did her best to convince the officers to join the show. They declined but soon were laughing and joking with us. We came away with their business cards, and, to the immense relief of our parents who witnessed the scene from the lawn in front of the stage, we received no citations for disorderly conduct or disturbing the peace.

On a rainy afternoon a year later, Jags and Lexi led our team in a chorus line song and dance routine on the curb outside a restaurant in Raleigh, North Carolina. We had just been eliminated from a national tournament and had shared a last team meal before starting the long drive home. Jags and Lexi felt just as bad about losing and having to say goodbye as the rest of us, but they wouldn't let us dwell on defeat or the end of the season. They got up from the table and lured us all out into the pouring rain to perform for the heavy traffic swishing by on the wet pavement. By then our parents were used to this. They just watched us through the restaurant windows, shaking their heads and laughing as traffic slowed to a crawl to take in the scene.

Amanda and Simone were more than just funny and capable of making me laugh. They were also articulate and thoughtful friends with a serious side when the occasion called for it. A one-on-one conversation with either one of them could help you keep things in perspective, whether the topic was softball, school, boyfriends, or just life in general.

Together my teammates and I competed strongly in every tournament on the schedule. Unlike the previous year when we often overwhelmed opponents with our talent, we were less dominant this year. But Coach prepared us well. If we executed to the best of our ability, we were hard to beat on the field.

As tough as we were to play against, nobody could beat our team spirit. In fact, when we traveled to the national tournament in Virginia at the end of the summer, we became a featured attraction wherever we played. We cheered far louder and more enthusiastically during our games than anyone else. Other girls must have decided they were getting too old to just let their guards down and laugh out loud. Not us. We didn't hold anything in. Even our families got in on the act with my teammates' brothers painting their bodies and acting as cheerleaders for an equally boisterous group of parents and other relatives.

Soon our own fans were joined by crowds of other spectators attracted by all of the excitement. The games on adjacent fields were as quiet as funerals compared to ours. It wasn't long before total strangers were walking up to us and our parents and saying how much they enjoyed watching us play. We didn't win it all...but we played our hardest, not just for ourselves, but for each other.

I'll probably remember that season forever. Someday if I have a son or daughter of my own, I'll encourage them to try team sports in hopes they can experience the kind of great friendships I made during my athletic career, especially the ones in that special 14-and-under season so many years ago.

Aiming for College

I stayed with Coach for another season of ball and it was an eventful year. Most of us moved up together to 16-and-under ball, staying together for a second year. A few of our teammates moved on to new teams. Two girls who had left a year earlier returned to play with us again. Then Coach had a falling out with the *Blaze* and we left as a group to form a new club, the *Michigan Force*. At the same time, we stepped up the quality of our play and the level of competition on our schedule.

My teammates and I were really excited to be moving up to 16-and-under ball as the *Michigan Force.* Jon Greenman was still our Coach, almost everyone on the team had played together at least some time in the past, and we were deep in pitching and hitting talent. We didn't think things could get any better.

We practiced hard all winter before most of us went off to play high school ball. Then in May we began to meet on weekends for some warm up practices to get ready for the travel ball season, which would begin right after our high school teams were eliminated from the state tournament.

In early June, it was time to play ball. As much as we had enjoyed high school ball, we were anxious get started in our first season wearing our new *Michigan Force* uniforms. We had all voted on the name and our team colors, which were borrowed from the North Carolina Tar Heels. We felt like the *Force* really was <u>our</u> ball club.

We had a successful season, culminating with a long road trip to Raleigh, North Carolina, to play in a national tournament. But it wasn't a repeat of our dream season of the year before. Although we had added more talent in the offseason, the chemistry of the team wasn't as close. Looking back, the older girls on the team and their families were probably thinking ahead to the college recruiting process which would kick into high gear once our junior year of high school began. Even the girls who were a year younger were thinking ahead.

Having lots of pitching and a deep lineup of talented hitters and fielders had seemed like a recipe for great success in the pre-season. But instead, it led to unhealthy levels of competition within the team. Coach couldn't keep everyone happy. There were times when he, too, seemed to get caught up in the competition among teammates, leading to the first fractures in the trust that made us such a close team in the past.

At our year-end picnic, we were already making plans for a fall tryout and to apply to participate in the prestigious Colorado tournaments the next summer. Held over the Fourth of July in the Denver suburbs and in neighboring Boulder, these tournaments attracted the best travel ball teams in the country as well as hundreds of college softball coaches. You had to apply early to gain a berth in one of the tournaments and acceptance was not a sure thing. The first order of business at the picnic was to get commitment from the families so we could raise the money to submit our entry. But when Coach floated the idea in the parent's meeting during the picnic, many of the families were unwilling to make a firm commitment. Nobody said "No". But they didn't say "Yes", either.

Later that week, it became clear why families were holding back. Four players called Coach and said they would be joining other teams. Suddenly, at the beginning of the most important year of travel ball I would play, my team was beginning to disintegrate. Because we were an independent team, the *Force* didn't have a pipeline to new talent like the *Blaze*, which attracted hundreds of girls to its tryouts each fall. Those of us who had not decided to leave waited for Coach to tell us how we could rebuild a strong team and continue with our plan to compete at an even higher level the next summer. We still wanted to step up to play in bigger tournaments in front of the college coaches who would decide where we would play when our high school days were done.

But the loss of our teammates had taken Coach by surprise and without a backup plan. He called the remaining players and said we'd probably have to pick up players from local high school teams and, because many of them would probably be unwilling to make extensive travel commitments, we would play in more local tournaments and scale back our plans to compete on a bigger stage.

A Difficult Decision

For my younger teammates, including Coach's daughter, Katie, scaling back for a year would be disappointing, but not really a barrier to college recruitment. They were still a year away from the all-important junior year of high school. Those of us who were entering our junior year could not afford to scale back. It was now or never for us. Fall tryouts for travel ball teams across the state were starting. We had to make a decision quickly and with no margin for error. Since many tryouts would be held on the same weekends, choosing one opportunity meant turning our backs on others.

As my desire to play Division I college softball had grown stronger, my Dad and I had talked about how to make sure college coaches would see me play before they made their final decisions about which girls to recruit. My Dad had done some research into travel ball clubs that offered good coaching, plus had a track record for getting players recruited. But in the past, whenever he had asked if I thought I should join a more prominent team to gain more exposure, I had answered quickly and emphatically: "I'm not leaving my Coach!" End of discussion.

But now I had no choice. Coach and the *Force* could not take me where I needed to go to attain my dream of playing college softball. For the first time since I had joined the *Blaze*, I would be trying to earn a spot on someone else's team, for coaches who didn't know what I could do, and in front of players who would view me as an outsider and perhaps even a threat to both their playing time and their plans to earn a spot on a college team.

My parents and I decided we would not let distance dictate where I would try out. We knew the best programs in Michigan were in the Detroit area. One club was at the top of our list: *Finesse*, which was headquartered in the west suburbs of the city. *Finesse* had been a frequent opponent of the *Blaze* and the *Force* and always seemed to be in the running for tournament championships.

Over the years, we had talked to *Finesse* coaches on the sidelines and had learned that they were not parents of players. This meant they were able to put personal relationships aside and judge talent impartially. Since the coaches stayed on after players moved, their primary focus was building and maintaining a strong club so they could provide maximum exposure to every girl who played for them. Finding a team that was coached by non-parents was an important factor in choosing a team. It would be too easy for parent-coaches to favor their own daughters over other players when awarding positions and playing time.

Many of the *Finesse* coaches had been with the club since its origins as a women's slow pitch club. The founder of the club, Denny Schlimgen, was a sales representative for a company that made hair care products, including a product called Finesse, which is how the club got its name. The coach I wanted to play for had coached against my teams for several years and had once served as an assistant college coach. He was known for his ability to coach the fundamentals and get his teams prepared to play against top competition. And, he had a reputation for getting players recruited to play college ball. His name was Donny Dreher, coach of the *Finesse* 16-and-under team.

When I made the decision to try out for *Finesse*, I was deciding not to try out with other clubs whose tryouts would be held on the same weekends in September. Once I set my sights on becoming a member of *Finesse*, my softball career depended on the judgment of Donny and the other *Finesse* coaches who would select the team.

Tryouts with Finesse

I was not alone among my *Force* teammates in needing to find a new team. De and Ali were in the same boat. After discussing their options, they also set their sights on playing for *Finesse*. It was a bright and sunny September morning when we arrived at the Wayne-Ford Civic League, a working class social club in the west suburbs of Detroit where the *Finesse* tryouts would be held. Since the drive from home would take more than two hours, my Dad, Mom and I had left early to make double sure we would be on time.

We were the first to arrive at the fields, but soon De and her family arrived, followed by Ali and her family. To kill some time, the three of us began tossing a ball to warm up our throwing arms. Gradually the parking lot began to fill with cars and soon there were dozens of girls and their families waiting for the registration tables to be set up.

Finally, the coaches arrived and we began lining up to register and get our player numbers. Newcomers like me would remain nameless as tryouts began. Our numbers would be our only identities as far as the *Finesse* coaches were concerned. It would be up to us to display enough skill to attract the coaches' interest. If we looked "special" enough to warrant a closer look, they might take time to look up our names on the registration list.

There must have been a hundred and fifty girls at the tryouts, which was more than *Blaze* tryouts had ever attracted. *Finesse* was a top program, and the Detroit area had a lot more softball players, so the turnout was not surprising. Compounding the competition, and increasing the challenge before me, was the fact that there were a lot of players returning to both the *Finesse* 16- and 18-and-under teams from the prior season. Many had played for *Finesse* teams since 12-and-under ball and a core of players had played for Coach Dreher from the beginning. Although travel ball tryouts are supposed to be open competitions, it's only natural for a coach to be loyal to players he knew and who had proven themselves in the past. In this case, Coach Dreher had almost an entire team returning.

When we registered, our age dictated which team we were permitted to try out for. Although 16's and 18's would work out together during tryouts, *Finesse* had a policy of not allowing players to play up except under special circumstances. This was the only reason I had hesitated to play for *Finesse*.

In other areas of the country, and on many other clubs in Michigan, coaches moved the most promising players up to the 18-and-under team in the belief that college coaches would only recruit from the 18-and-under age group. The Finesse coaches viewed things differently. They believed that most 18-and-under teams were filled with high school seniors or recent graduates who had already been recruited. Therefore, college coaches would pay closer attention to 16-and-under teams where players were still un-committed to a college program.

On the West Coast and in the South, girls as young as 14 played on 18-and-under squads. But in the Midwest, that trend had not yet taken hold. Clubs protected the competiveness of their younger age groups by making playing up an exception and not the rule. Today, kids are making unofficial commitments to colleges in their freshman years of high school, so things have changed a lot. But back in 2004, things were different. When I moved up to Finesse 18-and-under ball and played in two consecutive Amateur Softball Association (ASA) 18-and-under Gold tournaments—the top level of travel ball—a glimpse at opposing rosters made it clear that the *Finesse* policy was unlike those of clubs from other parts of the country.

I knew if I played for *Finesse's* 16-and-under team, I would be gambling that college coaches would take me seriously, even though I was not playing against 18-and-under competition. But it came down to coaching and my belief that the *Finesse* coaches would not only help me get the exposure I needed to get recruited, but would also make me a better player, just as Coach Greenman and Coach Youtzy had done earlier in my career.

The three-hour tryout went by in a blur. We were divided into groups and split up onto three fields for simultaneous outfield, infield and hitting workouts. Ali and De joined the other pitchers and catchers on a fourth field to show their stuff before joining the fielding and hitting drills. As practice continued, I went about my business the way Coach Greenman had taught me. Going all out to catch fly balls, diving for grounders during infield practice, and using my strong right arm to make long, accurate outfield throws and to throw darts to the bases. There were a number of coaches putting us through our paces, but Coach Dreher was definitely running the infield. When it came my turn to take grounders, he seemed to take extra joy in sending me to my right and left with hard grounders. I dove for every one, stopping my share, never quitting, but mad that I couldn't get to every ball hit to me, no matter how hard and wide they were hit. I hadn't been perfect, but maybe I had impressed him with my effort. I couldn't be sure.

During outfield drills, my Dad heard one of the coaches at the registration table turn his attention from the Detroit Lions' football game on the radio to say quietly under his breath, "Look at that arm!" as I came up throwing on a hard ground ball. Of course, I didn't hear it. Even if I had, it wouldn't have made any difference. I was going to put every bit of effort I had into every drill. I felt I was literally fighting for my softball life.

When I moved over to another field to hit off the pitching machine, the assistant coach of the 18-and-under Finesse squad, Kevin Kilburn, was running the machine. I hit the ball hard during my turn at the plate, but hitting is one part of the game where effort doesn't necessarily translate into results. If you tighten up or try to do too much, it affects your swing, depriving you of that extra power that can be the difference between a hard ground ball and a line drive in the gap. In this case, I was a little overanxious, getting out in front and pulling the ball sharply down the left field line more than I normally would. Curtis had made me an all-fields hitter, but on this day, Coach Kilburn was right when he commented, "I can see you're a pull hitter!"

When practice was done for the day, we lined up to return our numbers and find out when we should return for the next tryout. As I was standing in line, a felt a tap on my shoulder and turned to see Coach Kilburn. He asked my name and then said, "You're a good player." Although I was confident in my abilities, for the first time all day, the coach's comment gave me a glimmer of hope that my skills would be enough to crack the *Finesse* roster.

We learned that there would be a second tryout a week later on the same fields. My Dad and Mom walked over with other parents to talk to the coaches and see if coming back for a second week made sense. If we were not going to make the team, we needed to see if we could find another tryout the next weekend. Ali learned that the 16-and-under team already had four pitchers but the 18-and-under needed one more pitcher. The club was willing to break its age rule to fix the vacancy. They offered her a spot on the team. Coach Dreher said he had already selected 13 players, one more than he would typically keep. But he made it clear he liked what he saw in De and me and would add us if he could find a way to make it work.

On the drive home, I replayed the day's workouts in my head and wondered if there was anything I could have done better. I decided I had done my best. I had no regrets. We didn't know if it would take another tryout to convince Coach Dreher to make room for me on the team, but my parents and I decided we would go to the second tryout regardless. We had confidence that, if I continued to go all out, there was no way I would not make the team.

One evening in the middle of the following week, the phone rang. It was Coach Dreher, calling to speak with me. He said he was going to expand his roster and asked if I wanted to play. There was no doubt how I would answer. I said "Yes", but said I'd also like my Dad to talk to him if that was alright. My Dad just wanted to know where I fit into the team's plans. After hearing that I'd get the chance to earn a spot in the lineup, despite the number of returning players, he said that's all we wanted to hear. I was a member of *Finesse*. The same night, De also received her invitation to join the team. For the first time since 12-and-under ball, we had earned a place on a new team. Now we'd have to earn the respect and, hopefully, the friendship of our new teammates.

Playing with Finesse

The first thing I learned from my new coach was, he wanted us to call him "Donny", not Coach Dreher. It felt strange at first, and I called him "Coach" just about as often as "Donny" for the first few weeks of fall practices. My first chance to get to know my teammates came at the fall team players' and parents' meeting a couple of weeks later in Wixom west of Detroit. During the meeting, Donny laid out the rules for the team. His comments were addressed to both the players and the parents.

The most important rule was, parents would not be helping out at practices or during games. That meant, unlike the *Force* and *Blaze*, where my Dad and other parents routinely helped out, they'd be in the bleachers with the other fans this year. Dad had no problem with that rule. He had figured out several years earlier that for me to fully develop my skills, I needed the best coaching we could find. We valued all I had learned from Coach Youtzy, Coach Greenman and Curtis. And we chose to try out for *Finesse* because of Donny. My Dad said he'd gladly take a seat and watch me chase my dream of playing college softball.

Parents would also not be allowed to talk to the coaches about their daughters' playing time, game strategy, or anything else about the team at the field during tournaments. Donny said he was always willing to talk to parents about their own daughters off the field, but never about other people's daughters.

Donny's reasoning was simple. For the team to have a successful season, we would have to maintain team unity. Having parents involved in coaching the team could lead other families to believe some girls would be favored over others. Donny wanted to be sure everyone on the team (and their families) knew that players would all have an equal chance to earn playing time and that the best player at each position would play that position. There would be no politics to undermine team unity if he could help it.

He also knew letting parents criticize and complain right before or after games when emotions were highest could lead to heated words and rash decisions. Given time to cool off, there was a better chance he could have a calm discussion with a parent or player and, hopefully, reach a meeting of the minds.

Donny felt confident he could manage the ups and downs of fifteen competitive girls, but he knew that what those girls heard from protective and equally competitive parents off the field could upset the team chemistry and even small resentments could tear the team apart. The high stakes of college recruiting would magnify things even further. As Donny explained, every player on our team was good enough to play college ball and he would do everything in his power to make sure every one of the high school juniors on the team was recruited. But he said players and their families would have to put aside their personal goals and let him make decisions that were best for the team. After all, if we didn't play well together, we were not going to win on the field. Early elimination from tournaments would limit our exposure opportunities and turn off college coaches who didn't want selfish players any more than Donny did. If we didn't win, we also would not earn a berth in the prestigious ASA National Tournament, which would be attended by dozens of coaches and would be the biggest showcase for our talents that season.

Donny's final argument for excluding parents from helping out with the team was probably the most compelling of all. College coaches would rarely, if ever, permit parent participation on their teams. *Finesse* parents might as well get used to sitting in the bleachers and cheering for the entire team because when their daughters went off to play in college, that's as close to those teams as they would probably get.

Donny outlined an ambitious fall practice schedule and said we would play in some fall tournaments to get some practice time under game conditions. Playing in the fall would be a new experience for me and De. Coach Greenman was an assistant high school football coach so we never practiced in the fall until the high school football season ended in early November. We didn't play any games in the fall.

While my parents were listening as Donny told them about the cost of participating on the team, the availability of team rooms for girls whose parents could not attend tournaments, team fund-raisers, winter practice facilities, and other details, De and I hit some balls in the batting cages next door and began to get to know some of our teammates. We knew making close friends could be difficult. Most of the girls were from the eastern part of the state and many had played together for years on *Finesse* teams. Several were close friends. We were sure some were not looking forward to having to earn playing time in competition with newcomers. And with 15 players, there would be a lot of competition.

My Quest Begins

That fall marked the beginning of my quest to become a Division 1 college softball player. I was excited to get started and a bit anxious to find out how it would all turn out. I was still in awe of players from our area who had earned a spot on a top college team. I was confident in my abilities, and Donny obviously felt I was worthy of a spot on his team, but I didn't know if college coaches would see in me what Donny did. Of course, part of my personal quest would be to keep getting better, to be the most complete player I could be. I also wanted to be part of a special team. A team that won games the right way: with solid pitching, fielding and hitting, and with an aggressive, take no prisoners attitude.

If I had any doubt about joining Donny and *Finesse*, they were gone less than a week later. We received a call from Donny saying there was a skills camp the next Sunday afternoon at Indiana University in Bloomington. The new assistant coach at IU, Stacey Phillips, had once played for Donny on *Finesse* and he wanted to help her build her program while also helping his current players achieve their college softball dreams. Donny had mentioned to Stacey that he thought I had the skills to play at IU and she wanted to see me at the camp. Just that fast, I was on the radar of at least one Division 1 college coach.

My Dad, Mom and I made the 11-hour round trip to Bloomington the next Sunday so I could attend the camp. Knowing Donny gave me instant recognition with Stacey. I knew I would still have to prove to college coaches that I was good enough to play on their teams, but having a coach who could open doors wouldn't hurt my efforts to get noticed. It was an exhausting day, but I went home satisfied that I was on the right path to achieve my dream.

Finesse met the next Saturday at the Wayne-Ford Civic League fields for our first team practice, then climbed into our cars to make the long drive at dusk to Rochester, Indiana, where we were scheduled to play in a Sunday tournament hosted by the *Indiana Magic*. To get to Rochester, we drove through the outskirts of South Bend, Indiana, a town I was to get to know a lot better in the next several months. But South Bend didn't hold any allure for me yet. I was napping in the back seat of the family van as we drove south on U.S. 31 through the flat darkness of the Indiana farmland.

After a night in a local hotel, we were up at dawn and driving to the fields on the outskirts of Rochester. We played four games in the round robin tournament format. In the first game against a team from Indiana, Donny started me at shortstop. As it turned out, that put me right in the firing line. Our pitchers served up a steady diet of drop balls that resulted in seven innings of ground-balls, most of them headed my way. I did my job, fielding balls hit sharply up the middle, in the hole behind third, as well as right at me, helping the *Finesse* defense halt several rallies in their tracks. I also had a chance to demonstrate a little of my "Say Hey" talent. On a pop fly over my head, I ranged back down the left field line, called for the ball and made the catch. In the dugout, Donny let out a laugh while shaking his head. Just because I had range, didn't mean he wanted me calling off outfielders to turn their easy catches into Willie Mays highlights.

I also managed a couple of hits in the game, and *Finesse* went on to win. As we lined up to shake hands with our opponents, their head coach called out, "Nice game short!" It was just one game, but as a *Finesse* rookie, it felt good to start strong. There was no time to savor our first win, though. We were due to start our second game right away. During the brief wait between games, the Indiana assistant coach I had met the week before arrived at the field. Donny had encouraged her to make the drive from Bloomington to see us play. Now everyone on the team was suddenly aware of her presence.

We played three more games that day and Donny juggled the lineup to be sure all fifteen of us had a chance to play our best positions. I played some outfield, more at short and some third base. I didn't field as many balls on defense as I did in the first game, but I handled all of the balls hit my way. I felt loose and comfortable in the field. At the plate, I wasn't as loose. I began to press as the afternoon went on, the first indication that trying my hardest in every at bat could work against me. Tension of any kind is the enemy of quick hands and a fluid swing...both essential elements in success at the plate. After seeing what I could do in tryouts and in practice, Donny's frustration grew as I tied myself up repeatedly one at bat after another. But the more I failed at the plate, the more I pressed. My debut performance in front of a Division I college coach wasn't going as well as I had hoped.

Thankfully the afternoon ended before I could fall into a total funk. During the drive home that night I had plenty of time to process the events of the day. Overall, I felt good about my first day in a *Finesse* uniform, even if it was someone else's spare uniform from the previous year.

Two weekends and one practice later, we were off to Chicago to play another one-day round robin tournament at the University of Illinois Chicago in the shadow of the city's famous Loop. Donny used these games to further evaluate the team under game conditions. I played short, third and outfield again and had a solid day in the field and at the plate. The big highlight for me was in my last at bat of the day. We were tied in the bottom of the seventh and had runners at second and third. I worked the count and then went with an outside pitch to drive a hard ground ball past the first baseman for a run scoring, walk-off single. It was another late ride home, but I felt I had done a better job of staying within myself and performing to my full capabilities.

A New Level of Winter Practice

After our second tournament we settled into our winter practice routine. Donny had made arrangements to hold practices at an indoor training facility in Ypsilanti, Michigan, about two and a half hours from home. He had reserved the batting cages in the facility for most of Sunday afternoon and we had the main floor playing surface for about three hours starting at 4:30 and ending at 7:30 p.m. Assistant Coach Bill Martin was on hand each week to help Donny run the drills with help from coaches from other *Finesse* teams.

In addition to team hitting and on-the-field practice, Donny also offered individual training sessions before the team sessions. Of course, I immediately signed up for the individual training, too. Every Sunday at about 1 p.m. my Dad and I would head out for Ypsilanti. We'd get back home Sunday night between 10:30 and 11 p.m., just in time to head to bed.

Donny and the other coaches ran a tight practice. There was no wasted time. Since individual training sessions ran back-to-back before team practices began, you had to be standing beside the cage and ready to go as soon as your session began. Donny closely supervised as we bunted and swung away while he fed the pitching machine. We also worked on a technique that Donny called the "power slap". You presented the bat as though you were going to bunt, but then triggered by pulling the bat back into the normal ready position as the pitcher wound up. Then you swung away... the goal was a line drive in the gap or, at the very least, a hard ground ball through a hole in the infield.

Donny took the time to call Curtis and talk about the swing techniques I was working on back at home. We tried to build on the platform Curtis had given me rather than going off in an entirely new direction. One thing I had learned in my years of training with Curtis was not to get too high or too low after a session in the cage. The purpose of training was to work on my swing. That meant working on keeping my hands inside the ball and perfecting a short compact swing to meet the ball in my power zone out in front of the plate. We also continued to work on driving inside pitches to left center and sending outside pitches to the right field gap.

Of course, none of the fine points would work without continued work on the timing of my trigger, stride and swing, and constant reminders to keep my natural aggressiveness in check so I would stay back on every pitch and focus on staying on top of the ball to drive it on a line. Donny's mantra was, "Make a mistake on top of the ball." We heard it from him constantly. Fortunately, Curtis and his assistant, Sean, were big on hitting with a strong top hand. They knew that to avoid the dreaded pop-up in critical situations, it was essential to hammer the ball with the right hand the same way a carpenter drives a large nail into a plank. Curtis had even taught me to shrug my shoulders a little bit to stay on top of the rise ball so I could drive the high pitch, which would give you fits if you tried to make contact with an uppercut home run swing. Donny also reinforced another essential skill I worked on with Curtis: be ready for the fastball and adjust to off-speed pitches, going after the "ham" in right field.

After the first several practices, Donny told us he would schedule time with each of us to put together a recruiting video to provide a preview of our skills for college coaches. I arrived early on the Sunday we had scheduled for my taping and, with my Dad behind the camera, Donny orchestrated the workout. We started in the cage with each bunt in my arsenal. Then we went into a round of power slaps. I rattled a couple of those off the frame of the screen that protected Donny, a nice dramatic touch for the camera that was punctuated by a yelp from Donny who called out,

"Chuck and duck!" before serving up the next pitch. Finally, Donny had me hit away and I focused on driving the ball hard into the back of the cage.

Once I'd finished demonstrating my abilities with a bat, we moved over into the indoor playing surface where Donny hit grounders to my left, to my right, and right at me. Fly balls were next. Donny had me running all over the field, tracking down short pup-ups, fly balls to both sides and even a few "Say Hey" balls over my head. The practice facility was an air-inflated dome, designed as an indoor golf driving range, which meant there wasn't room for a full-size field inside. Lighting was provided by banks of lights in the corners because the inflated roof would not support ceiling lights. The lighting posed a challenge as the ball would rise up above the lighting then come back down again out of the shadows. But I made it through the filming session without any serious flubs. Those same lights would give me more trouble a few weeks later, resulting in an injury that would make me glad my afternoon in front of the camera was already behind me.

Early in the fall, Donny called us together with our parents to outline how we should approach our quest to earn a spot on a college softball team. He told us that every player on the team was talented enough to play college ball. He urged each of us to make a list of universities or colleges that we wanted to focus on so he could review our list and weigh in with his opinion. He wanted us to pursue our dreams, but he also wanted to be sure our goals were realistic based on the types of players the coaches were looking for and our own skills and academic qualifications.

By this time, the players who had completed their junior year of high school had either taken or were in the process of taking the SAT and ACT standardized scholastic tests. Scores on these tests would be considered by college coaches in combination with high school grade point averages to assess whether players would qualify for entrance to their universities and whether they would succeed academically if the university accepted their applications.

My hard work in the classroom was an asset. I scored high on both of the standardized tests and was a straight A student with additional advanced placement credits on my high school transcript. Donny said I wouldn't have to worry about qualifying academically for any college I wanted to attend. I had to prove I could play at a high level first. But after that, coaches made it clear it could come down to academics as well as character and attitude. The best softball programs knew they could attract great players. But players who couldn't remain eligible to play because of bad grades, or who were constantly in trouble off the field and difficult to deal with on it, were no help in building a winning team. The universities themselves had their reputations to protect as well. The academic standings of student athletes are compiled and reported publically by the NCAA. A poor team grade point average (GPA), insufficient athlete progress toward graduation, or a pattern of bad team behavior could cost a coach her job.

I knew it was important to consider how well a university matched up with my academic needs. Donny and everyone else I talked to reminded me that it would be a mistake to choose college based entirely on playing softball. After all, very few players have the opportunity to make a living playing professional softball or can expect an invitation to play on an Olympic team after they graduate. For most girls, college softball is the final chapter in their softball careers. As important as the game would be while I was actively playing, the degree I earned would have a far greater impact on my life in the long run than what I accomplished on the softball diamond.

My tentative career plans had a big influence on the schools I included on my list of targets. I was a math whiz in high school, earning the math faculty award when I graduated. Although I wasn't sure what I wanted to do when I graduated from college, I was seriously considering the engineering field. This immediately narrowed my list of schools. A lot of schools don't have a college of engineering. I decided a school that had an engineering program would rank higher on my list than one that did not.

At 15, I wasn't that certain I was cut out to design cars or even running shoes or hula hoops for that matter. So I also wanted to find a school that offered a range of academic fields. That way I could put off making definite career plans until I got a taste of college life and could explore all of my options.

As I composed my list of target colleges, I started with the University of Michigan at the top of the list. U of M had the top softball program in the Big Ten Conference and, in many people's opinion, the best program east of the Mississippi River. They had been to the NCAA College Softball World Series several times and there was no reason to believe the Wolverines' success would not continue.

Michigan was also where Jessie Merchant played. Jessie grew up and played high school ball just down the road from Grand Rapids in Wayland. She was the starting shortstop for the Wolverines and had once played for the *Blaze*. Coach Greenman and Katie knew Jessie through the Wayland high school softball program. Katie went to school there and Coach would sometimes invite Jessie to practice with them when she was home for the summer. I had the chance to join them once or twice. I really wanted to follow in Jessie's footsteps. She was proof that a kid from West Michigan could play and star for a big time Division I softball team.

Also on my list were several other Big Ten universities, and several more from the Mid America Conference. I had set my sights on playing Division I softball, so I didn't include any of the smaller college programs. After some soul searching, I decided that I wanted to go to school reasonably close to home. Choosing a college no more than a day's drive away would mean my parents could come to see me play and I could occasionally come home during the school year. As recruiting progressed over the next several months, the coaching grapevine expanded the possibilities to several schools in the Ivy League on the East Coast, but my original list didn't extend much past Penn State in the east, Iowa in the west, and Indiana University to the south. Central Michigan University in Mount Pleasant marked the northern extent of my target recruiting area.

I didn't know if my targets were realistic or not. One Sunday before practice in the dome, one of the *Finesse* coaches approached me in the small lobby of the training facility and asked me where

I most wanted to play ball in college. Somewhat tentatively, I said I wanted to play for Michigan, thinking that that was probably the response he'd hear from nine out of ten *Finesse* players. But instead of raising his eyebrows or questioning my sanity, he said simply, "Why not you?" It was clear he didn't mean it as a question. He thought it was a perfectly normal and realistic goal. From that day forward, whenever the slightest doubt crept into my thinking, I'd just say to myself, "Why not me?"

Donny agreed with my list of schools. But he also said to keep an open mind, because during recruiting other great college programs might also express an interest. He cautioned me never to close a door until I had a firm offer in hand from my final college choice.

Donny recommended that we attend as many softball camps as we could over the winter and the next summer to get as much exposure as possible in front of college coaches. To cast a broad net and uncover additional opportunities, my Dad helped me put together a mailing to about 35 Division I college coaches. We enclosed my video in packages to about fifteen of the top schools on my list, sending letters offering the video and my resume to the rest. We received a lot of mail from coaches in the next several months, inviting me to their camps, asking me to fill out their application forms, and requesting our game schedule for the upcoming season. I knew the letters didn't necessarily mean the coaches were interested in recruiting me. It was too early in the process for that. But, each package was a reminder that the recruiting process was in full swing. For the next several months, going to the mailbox was a pretty exciting part of each day!

Showcasing My Talents

Over the Christmas holidays I attended a two-day softball camp at Michigan State University. Jacquie Joseph, the MSU coach, held the holiday camp every year and the *Finesse* coaches said it was one of the best in the Midwest. Since my family would be visiting my grandmother in Royal Oak outside of Detroit, my Dad and I decided to commute from her house to the camp both days.

The first day of the camp was a preview of how competitive recruiting could be. There must have been 150 to 200 girls at the camp, most of them looking to be recruited by a big time softball program. In addition to the MSU staff, coaches from other Big Ten and Mid America Conference schools were on hand to run us through the camp drills. As we sat in the indoor practice facility waiting for the camp to begin, I heard someone call out my number from across the room. I looked around and saw one of my *Finesse* teammates. I didn't know her well, but she called me over and we began to talk. Her name was Nicole and she was funny and bright. As we talked I realized that I had played against her for years when she played on *Compuware*, *Finesse's* chief rival for state travel softball supremacy. She had joined *Finesse* a year earlier. By the time our season began, Nicole would be my closest friend on the team.

The MSU camp was as good as advertised. The camps are described as skill-building opportunities, but everyone who attends also knows the college coaches use them to "discover" potential recruits and to gather additional information about girls who are already on their radar. I was glad to attract Coach Joseph's attention during fielding drills. She gave me a few tips and complimented me on my aggressiveness. In the batting cages, I hit the ball hard, attracting the attention of the coaches again. But the highlight of the camp for me came during the walk from the hitting building back to the indoor practice facility on the first day of the camp.

As my Dad and I walked through the light wet snow between buildings a voice behind me called out, "North!" I turned around and saw Jessie Merchant walking toward me. She was helping out at the camp as a favor to Coach Joseph. Jessie asked how I was doing and we traded small talk as we walked together the rest of the way to the indoor practice field. It was just a brief conversation, but talking to Jessie seemed so natural, I felt even closer to being a college student and softball player.

Over the next few weeks I attended camps at Purdue University in West Lafayette, Indiana, Eastern Michigan University in Ypsilanti, and a team camp at Central Michigan University in Mount Pleasant. Former *Finesse* athlete Rachel Gillespie, a member of the Purdue Boilermaker softball team, introduced me to Coach Carol Bruggeman at the Purdue camp, further proof that the *Finesse* network could help gain the attention of college coaches.

One Sunday, Donny invited college coaches to observe our *Finesse* team as we practiced in the dome. We were excited to see Michigan Assistant Head Coach Bonnie Tholl in attendance along with coaches from nearby Eastern Michigan University and other schools. I felt good about practice that day. I was solid on defense and hit well off the machine. Then Donny had us line up to hit live off of the *Finesse* pitchers. When my turn came, I stepped into the box and waited for the pitcher to toe the rubber. I sprayed a couple of shots to both sides of the cage, then drilled the next pitch like a rifle shot straight back off the shin of the pitcher. She went down hard, bringing practice to a halt.

As good as it felt to hit the ball hard and gain extra attention from the coaches, I didn't feel good about hurting a teammate. I hoped she wasn't seriously injured. I knew what it was like to be sidelined and how quickly a season can be ruined by a freak injury. Fortunately, the pitcher came away with just a bruise. The next day I received this email message from Coach Tholl: "Way to take out that pitcher!" It was funny to hear her say that because the pitcher was the younger sister of Michigan left fielder Rebecca Milian.

A few weeks later, I attended Michigan's one-day winter camp in Ann Arbor. By this time, if Michigan was sponsoring a camp of any kind, I was attending it. My Dad and I had walked around the Michigan campus a few times and I had remarked that I felt like I could really do great things at U of M, academically as well as on the softball field. Michigan was definitely my first choice in college softball programs.

About a week before we headed to Ann Arbor for the Saturday camp, Ali said I should also go to the Notre Dame softball camp in South Bend on Sunday. Ali and her family were big time Notre Dame fans...they felt the same about ND as I did about Michigan. I didn't know much about the Fighting Irish except that they had come close to qualifying for the NCAA Softball World Series in a couple of recent seasons but had fallen short. Still, my Dad and Donny had both said not to close any doors until I signed with a school. So, we signed up for the Notre Dame camp. It would be a busy weekend, with about 440 miles of driving punctuated by two four-hour camps and a night in a South Bend hotel.

Attendance at the Michigan camp equaled the numbers I'd seen at Michigan State. After an introductory talk by head coach Carol Hutchins, we split into groups and began working through the hitting stations set up around the walls of the football practice building. As I worked through the stations, my hitting really felt like it was on. I did well off the tee, hitting wiffle balls, at the bunting stations, and at soft toss. Then I went into the batting cages where Wolverine assistant coach Jen Brundage was running the pitching machine, a sophisticated unit that could replicate most of the spins you could expect to see from a live pitching.

Coach Brundage started me out with a few bunts, then gave me some swings at balls pretty much down the middle. I was connecting solidly. Then the coach began to work the inside corner and I made the timing adjustment necessary to meet those pitches out front and pull them solidly into left field. After the first few pitches I noticed Head Coach Hutchins was standing behind the cage watching me work. Meanwhile, Coach Tholl had introduced herself to my Mom and Dad and joined them as they watched me hit. Coach Hutch gave a subtle signal to Coach Brundage to start working the outside corner, the part of the plate the best college pitchers would use to get hitters out without giving them anything good to hit.

I was used to hitting for hams at Curtis' club. I knew how to wait for the outside pitch and drive it into right field. I proceeded to show the Michigan coaches what I could do. When I stepped out of the cage I hoped they had liked what they saw. A few minutes later, the camp ended and we started to pack up to leave for the long drive to South Bend. Just then, Coach Tholl walked up and said she wanted to introduce me and my parents to Coach Hutchins. We walked over and before I knew it, I was talking to the coach I most wanted to play ball for when high school was done. Afterwards, I didn't remember much about what we talked about. I was too excited to worry about the details. But I did remember she invited me to come and observe a team practice before the college season started a few weeks later. That was a date I was definitely going to keep. Then it was time to head for South Bend, 180 miles to the southwest.

First Glimpse of the Golden Dome

The Upper Midwest was in the throes of a brutal winter, with snow piled up more than a foot deep and temperatures hovering in the single digits. Fortunately for us, it wasn't snowing and the roads were relatively safe as we drove across the southern part of Michigan. By the time we arrived in South Bend it was dark. It took some doing, but we found our hotel and hunkered down for a fitful night's sleep. We had an early wakeup time because the Irish camp was scheduled to start at 8 a.m. the next morning.

As we drove onto the Notre Dame campus, I saw the landmarks that Ali had told me to look for: Notre Dame Stadium, Touchdown Jesus, and of course, The Golden Dome. But I was more focused on getting fired up for the camp. I felt I had performed well at Michigan and I wanted to do equally well at this camp, even if I wasn't sure where Notre Dame ranked on my list of prospective softball and academic destinations.

We found the Notre Dame indoor practice facility and moved quickly through the cold to get inside. We were greeted by a scene similar to the one in Ann Arbor: hundreds of girls ready to refine their softball skills and hoping to be noticed by the Notre Dame coaching staff. We signed in and I prepared to take the field. The coaches signaled that it was time to start and we were split into groups. Pitchers were sent to the far end of the facility to work out in front of Head Coach Deanna Gumpf. The rest of us were ushered through the nets and onto the near half of the field. As in Ann Arbor this would be primarily a hitting camp. Coach Gumpf's father, Larry May, who was the head coach of Gordon's Panthers, a legendary Southern California travel ball club, started things off with a talk about hitting and equipment. Then we were assigned to groups to begin working our way through the hitting stations that lined the outer edge of the practice area.

Irish assistant coach Charmelle Green was running the hitting camp, but Irish players were joined by members of the nearby Saint Mary's College team to man most of the hitting stations. Coach May was helping Coach Green run the hitting machines in the two batting cages at the end of the field. As I worked my way though the stations, I quickly found my groove, driving the ball off the tee, smacking wiffle balls off the perimeter netting, and executing all of the bunts. When I finished the last of the stations I prepared to enter the cages.

I was ready to hit when I stepped into the cage. I started ripping balls to the left and right sides as well as back up the middle and didn't stop until my turn in the cage was over. I helped pick up the balls and grabbed my bat to leave the cage. Just then Coach Green stopped me and asked my name. When I responded she said, "Let me have your name tag," pointing at the sticker I had been assigned when I registered at the beginning of the camp. I peeled the label off of my shorts and handed it to her and she stuck it on the leg of her Notre Dame Softball shorts. We chatted for a couple of minutes and then it was time to go. I began to walk over to where my Mom and Dad were standing with my equipment bag and the sweats and winter coat I'd be wearing on the drive home.

Before I reached the gap in the netting, Coach Green called me back and asked if I would be willing to hit a few live pitches thrown by Coach May. I was already pretty excited that the Notre Dame coach wanted to know who I was, but now I was really pumped up. Coach Green trotted over to Coach May and asked him if he would throw some pitches to me. Meanwhile a small crowd began to gather around the cage and I heard one girl say to a friend as they were leaving the practice field, "Wait, watch this. This 'chika' can really hit."

I stepped up to the plate again as Coach May loosened up his arm tossing balls into the net at the other end of the cage. Then he stepped up behind the pitching screen and began throwing me a variety of pitches with speed and a lot of movement. I fouled off the first few, but then started making solid contact, sending them to all fields. I hit for a while longer before Coach Green ended the session, apparently satisfied with my performance. Coach May also seemed satisfied.

As I prepared to leave the field again, Coach Green asked me if I would be willing to take a few ground balls and catch some flies. Of course, I said "Yes". She asked a volunteer to hit me grounders at short while she positioned herself at first base to take my throws. Since I had not had a chance to warm up, she said to just lob the ball to her. I began fielding grounders and making my throws as the volunteer hitter gradually stretched my range from side to side and picked up the velocity of the hits. Although I heeded Coach Green's advice and threw lightly at first, before long I was throwing harder...probably at about 75 percent of full speed, to give the coach a chance to judge the strength and accuracy of my arm.

After the grounders, Coach Green had me back up and began to hit me short fly balls and pop-ups. The practice area would not allow me to play deep enough to chase really long flies. We used every inch of the available space, though. On a couple of longer hits, I became tangled in the net at the far end of the practice field. Except for a couple of late breaks on balls I had trouble finding in the lights, I felt good about my fielding. Coach Green seemed to like what she saw. She called me in and introduced herself to my Mom and Dad who had been watching my extra practice session. The coach said she was impressed with my skills and asked what kind of grades I was getting in high school. I knew Notre Dame was very selective in its entrance requirements and that the academic performance of the university's student athletes was a source of pride across the campus. I told her my grade point was above 4.0 and also shared my test scores. She was excited to hear that I was a good student as well as a good athlete.

To cap off the day, Coach Green asked me to stay in touch with her by email and to send her my summer travel ball schedule so she and the rest of the Notre Dame Softball staff could come and see me play. Then it was time to bundle up and begin the drive home.

As we drove home through the snowy farmland, I reflected on the events of the weekend. I had started out focused on making a great impression to the staff at Michigan and I thought I had succeeded. I had decided to attend the Notre Dame camp out of curiosity but came away very impressed with Coach Green, the Irish softball program and the school. ND was now definitely on my short list of prospective schools. After that weekend, I almost couldn't contain my excitement. It seemed like the summer season, conversations with college coaches, official visits to their campuses, scholarship offers, and signing day would never come.

A Close Call

As the winter moved on, we had settled into our Sunday practice routine. With a busy school schedule, Saturday mornings with Curtis, and plenty of homework, I would try to use Sunday morning to catch up on my sleep and enjoy a leisurely breakfast. But by 1 p.m. we were in the car and headed to practice. We often car pooled with De and her Dad and we did homework or listened to music in the back seat while our Dads took care of the driving.

One Sunday in late winter Donny decide it was time to add some infield drills to our Sunday practice routine in the dome. We had finished our hitting drills and some of the basic throwing and fielding drills that had become a staple of our Sundays together. Donny set up a plate and three bases on one corner of the artificial turf playing surface and positioned infielders around the infield. We were going to work on throws to the bases so it would be clear which fielder had coverage responsibility under different game situations.

Donny told me to go to shortstop. He positioned De at catcher, and had other girls take the field at first, second and third base. One of our pitchers toed the rubber at the center of our makeshift diamond and Donny said the first drill would be a throw from catcher to gun down a runner stealing second. As the shortstop, my assignment was to sprint from my position between second and third and arrive at second base as De's throw would arrive. As the pitcher released the pitch I broke for second. As I arrived at the bag my eyes were up looking toward De for the throw that should be on its way.

At that moment I was stunned to discover that I was staring straight into the bright glare of the pod of spotlights that stood behind the plate illuminating that corner of the dome. I hesitated for a split second, trying to pick up the ball. Then, out of nowhere, my face took the full impact of De's throw and I went down to the floor as my face exploded in pain. I reached up to my nose and my hand came away covered in blood. I tried to get to my knees, and could see the red liquid pouring from my face like water from a hose. "I'm bleeding, a cried," stating the obvious. I was surrounded by teammates and I heard Donny try to relax me by saying, "Don't worry kid, you've got plenty of blood."

The next thing I remember, my Dad was kneeling at my side with his arm around me to keep me calm as one of the other dads, a retired emergency medical technician, wiped my face and began applying ice wrapped in a white towel. The towel quickly turned crimson with my blood. My poor Dad. He was the guy who had perfected the ability to teach me to play catch without endangering my "pretty little face" so many years earlier. Now all he could do was say my name softly over and over again while I bled all over the turf.

I was crying pretty hard at first...if you have ever been hit hard in the nose, you know tears come with the territory. But as Donny and Dad told me I was going to be OK, I began to calm down. The adults asked me questions about how I felt. Was I nauseous or dizzy? That would be a sign of concussion. I was in pain, but my stomach was fine and I wasn't dizzy.

Could I see clearly? I had been hit square in the nose, lucky that both my eyes had been spared the impact. I could have suffered serious damage and possibly loss of vision if the ball had struck my face an inch to the right or left. I had two black eyes (the area below them was actually a nasty combination of black, yellow, purple and green) but I could see fine once my tears were wiped away. I was relieved that the ball had also spared my mouth. I could have suffered a broken jaw, shattered teeth or other serious injuries that could have meant painful oral surgery and led to other complications.

It was fortunate that the ball had not hit me in the forehead or either temple. I had once turned on an inside pitch in a tournament and lined a shot off of a third baseman's forehead before she could get her glove up. That girl went down to the ground like she had been shot and everyone one on the field and in the stands had held their breath while she regained her senses and was guided on wobbly legs to the opposing dugout. I was in better shape than that.

Getting the bleeding to stop was another story. There was no turning off my twin faucets, no matter how much ice we applied. I heard Donny asking how I had missed the throw but then he looked up into the lights from where I lay on the floor and saw immediately why I'd caught the ball with my face instead of my glove. "Poor kid", he said. "She never had a chance." By then, I was getting a little embarrassed at all the attention I was getting. My teammates were all staring at my face and De was pretty upset. I told her later not to worry about it. She had made a perfect throw...it was hard and right on target. It wasn't her fault I couldn't find it before it found me.

As my Dad helped me to my feet, I told Donny he needed to get back to practice, that I would be alright. The adults walked me to the chairs that lined the spectator area outside the netting of the dome and I took a seat. The dad who had been attending to my wounds packed my nostrils with gauze to see if that would stop the bleeding. It slowed the flow somewhat, but we had to change the packing every ten minutes or so as it became saturated. He told my Dad that I should probably be seen by a doctor. But it was Sunday night, we were more than two hours from home, and any trip to a nearby hospital emergency room could mean hours of waiting before a doctor would see me.

My Dad decided that, as long as my symptoms did not appear serious, we should start driving home and decide when we got there if we should call our family doctor then or wait until morning. After arranging for De to drive home with Ali, whose 18-and-under team was also practicing that night, we grabbed a clean towel and some gauze and headed to the parking lot and my Dad's car. We reclined my seat and I put the towel under my chin to catch any stray blood that might leak from my nose. Once on the freeway, we drove to a convenience store where Dad bought some ice and sealable sandwich bags so I could apply ice to my throbbing and swollen face during the long ride home.

As I lay back in my seat with the ice on my face, I began to sing my favorite country songs softly under my breath. It took my mind off my injury and the fact that the practice I had looked forward to all week had been unexpectedly cut short. We stopped about every half hour on the way home to change the gauze in my nose, finally arriving home at about 9:30 p.m. By then, the bleeding had stopped and I was feeling well enough that we decided to wait until morning to call the doctor.

The next day our doctor quickly determined that I was OK except for my broken nose. He referred me to a specialist who would have to rearrange my facial features. The surgeon literally took matters into his hands and painfully straightened my nose. Then he sent me to a special department in the hospital where other specialists would make a plaster mold of my face and create a clear shatterproof plastic mask to protect my face from further damage during all sports activities. It would look similar to the masks worn by pro basketball players like Richard Hamilton of the Detroit Pistons, but I wasn't thrilled with the prospect of looking like a freak on the softball field.

The technicians who made the mask had some fun with the project, taking digital photos of me with my face covered in plaster...I looked like a mummy lying motionless on the bed as the plaster dried. I later emailed the photo to Bonnie Tholl, the assistant head coach at Michigan, along with an account of the accident. She responded that I looked pretty "scary". Although the actual mask was clear plastic and not white plaster, it would make me look pretty scary for the rest of my spring practices with *Finesse* as well as for my entire junior year of high school softball. I returned to *Finesse* practice the weekend after the collision between my face and the ball, wearing my mask and ready to resume training for the season ahead. I managed to make it though the rest of the winter without further damage.

The Biggest Season of My Life

In early April, high school softball season began. Our high school team was going to be pretty good. There were five of us who had played on the East Kentwood High School varsity as freshmen and again as sophomores. Now we were entering our junior season and we had some talented seniors on the team as well as other juniors who were coming up from the JV team.

Fielding a good softball team at any level always starts with good pitching. We were lucky to have Ali, who had been my travel ball teammate in the past. She had pitches most high school players could not hit—especially a wicked drop ball that she liked to throw just off the outside corner of the plate—which really gave us an advantage. Of course, you also had to have a catcher who knew how to catch a drop ball. We had De. De had been catching Ali and other talented pitchers as long as we had played travel ball. We were strong behind the plate.

Conventional wisdom says a good ball team is also strong across the infield. A third member of our talented junior class was Julie, a great second baseman. I held down the other middle infield spot, my third year at shortstop. Rounding out the infield were Meghan, a senior third baseman who was starting her fourth year of varsity ball, and Tricia, also a senior and a former Youtzy's Angels teammate, who gave us a solid glove to field throws at first.

In centerfield, we had Melissa, Greg Youtzy's daughter and my old Angel's teammate. Melissa had great speed and a strong arm to anchor our outfield. Our coach rotated several girls in right field and left, but Mallory, a junior with blazing speed, usually played one of the corners. Cheryl, who was also a junior and a talented pitcher, and Sabrina' another senior, usually cycled in at the other corner.

We fulfilled our promise by compiling a 27 win, 5 loss season, winning our district, regional, and the state quarterfinals. Along the way, I had a painful run in with an opponent's forearm. I had decided part way into the high school season that I was tired of sweating under my face mask and having infield dust caked beneath it, rubbing my skin like sandpaper. I threw the mask in my team bag before one of our conference games and took the field free to enjoy the breeze in my face. I was liberated! That great feeling lasted about three innings. Then I ran from my position at shortstop to third base to take a throw from a teammate on a bunt play. The throw came in high as the base runner rumbled in from second base and as I reached for it she hit me with a hard forearm "shiver". I let out a howl and bent over in pain. You guessed it, she got me right across the nose.

The faucets were open again as blood flowed from my nose onto the stone dust at my feet. Apparently, the base runner thought clocking my tender nose was pretty funny. She was laughing it up with her third base coach as the umpire called time and my coach and the school trainer ran out on the field to take a look at the mess that was my face. Fortunately, the flow of blood slowed to a trickle pretty quickly. The trainer stuffed gauze up my nose and handed me my mask. I resumed my position at short before the next batter came to the plate, looking scary again with face protection in place and now with white tusks of gauze sticking out of my nose. I'm happy to say that the base runner's joy at wounding me was short lived. She didn't score and we beat her team soundly that day. I wore the mask the rest of the season to protect my re-broken nose. I decided against further surgery. It's still a bit crooked to this day.

Although we had a great season, our high school campaign ended one game too soon. We ran into a buzz saw in the state semi-final game. Playing in Battle Creek in front of Coach Hutchins and Coach Gumpf, plus coaches from other leading Midwest college softball programs, we came up against Nikki Nemitz, a left-handed riseballer from the east side of the state. I had faced Nikki and her Michigan Bulldogs travel ball team for years, but now she was the ace pitcher for Harper Woods Regina. She would go on to a very successful career at the University of Michigan.

Long story short, Nikki threw a perfect game against us. Most high school players don't see many left handed pitchers, never mind one throwing a rise ball in the 60's. There were plenty of strikeouts. The more our team swung at the high pitch, the higher the ump's strike zone crept. Once balls at the eyes became called strikes, we were toast. Laying off the rise ball was no longer an option. All credit to Nikki, though. She did what great pitchers do: convince hitters to swing at her pitch instead of waiting for something they could drive. Ali was nearly as effective, holding the Regina team scoreless until they finally pushed a run across on a close play at the plate in the sixth. That 1-0 loss in the state semifinals spelled the end of my junior season of high school ball. We had rolled up 27 wins with only a handful of losses, but our final defeat was a heart breaker as Regina went on to win the state championship we thought would be ours.

We didn't have time to feel sorry for ourselves, though. The next day I took the field for the first time that spring with *Finesse* at the big Compuware tournament held every year in Canton just west of Detroit. High school ball was over for the year, but the most important season of my travel softball career was suddenly underway.

The Compuware tournament was sponsored by a large software firm, which also sponsored one of the leading travel ball programs in the state. In addition to attracting more than a hundred teams in four age groups, the tournament was also a magnet for college coaches who came to see talent from Michigan, Ohio, Indiana, Illinois and even more distant states.

I arrived emotionally spent from our disappointing loss in Battle Creek but also excited to start performing in front of the college coaches and help *Finesse* win tournaments. I was a bit over-anxious in the beginning, chasing pitches I should have let go by. I was also over-thinking my approach at the plate. My awareness of all those coaches and my new *Finesse* teammates made me try to do too much. As the weekend wore on, I began to relax and grow more comfortable, but our team underperformed as a whole and we were eliminated on Saturday. We would have to perform better if we wanted to be considered one of the top teams in the Midwest.

The next weekend we headed to Barberton, Ohio for an ASA qualifying tournament. We wanted to qualify for the ASA 16-and-under national championship in Bloomington, Indiana, later in the summer. We were anxious to prove that we were better than we had looked in our first tournament. Barberton is located near Akron, southeast of Cleveland. We had traveled farther for travel ball tournaments, but this was still a long, six-hour drive from Grand Rapids. Our drive paled in comparison to the distance traveled by the two California teams in the tournament. Although the ASA offered more qualifying berths in California than in other states, the competition was so intense that teams from the Golden State would show up all over the country trying to win the single berth offered in a state like Ohio or Michigan.

The importance of pitching in softball can't be overstated. Our *Finesse* squad had a strong pitching staff, with a normal starting rotation comprised of three hard throwing right-handers: Elizabeth, Keri and Stacy. Few teams could match the strength and depth of our pitching. As long as we hit and played defense, we should contend to win every tournament we played in.

We came out strong, winning our first couple of games including a game against one of the California clubs before landing in the loser's bracket with a close loss to the other West Coast squad. We kept fighting but eventually lost a second close game to an Ohio team. I rode home disappointed that we had not earned our qualifying berth. I also had a swollen right hand. I had been jammed on a hard inside pitch and the bat handle had slammed back into the meat at the base of my thumb. It would prove to be a nagging injury for the rest of the summer, the kind you learn to live with if you are going to play softball. Although hitting was painful, the hand became so swollen I also had trouble gripping the ball to throw. In mid-tournament, Donny had to switch me

Impossible is Nothing

from shortstop to centerfield so I wouldn't be called on to throw as often.

The good news was, I had relaxed and begun to hit the way I knew I could. I didn't like losing and I wanted to get to Nationals, but there was reason for optimism. We had beaten some good teams. Now we had to put together a winning streak and take home some championship hardware. During the long drive home and the next week, I iced the hand constantly to get ready to take the field for the next tournament.

I had learned in four years of travel ball that, once the seasons starts, the tournaments come and go unbelievably fast. Many tournaments start on Thursday night and finish on Sunday. By the time you get home Sunday night, you have barely three days before you are packing up to drive to the next tournament. Wedge a midweek practice in between tournaments, and you have a really compressed schedule for six or seven weeks in a row. This year was no different except there would be two four-day college softball camps—one at Michigan, the other at Notre Dame—to fit into the schedule as well.

- 95 -

Camping in Ann Arbor

On the way home from Barberton, my parents dropped me off at the University of Michigan in Ann Arbor. While college camps are opportunities for girls to learn new skills and refine the ones they already have, they are also an important opportunity to be seen by college coaches. Coaches will tell you, they not only want to see your skills, they also want to see how well you practice, if you accept coaching well, if you hustle, and if you are a leader. I hoped my drive to be the best—along with the skills I'd brought with me—would convince the Michigan coaches that I was worth an offer at the end of the summer.

I had been attending Michigan camps for a couple of years so the coaches knew me pretty well. Assistant Head Coach Bonnie Tholl had been corresponding with me by email for several weeks and I knew the Michigan staff was expecting to see me at their summer camp. Watching me for four days in a row was an important part of the talent evaluation the coaches put prospective recruits through. Seeing me perform in games gave them glimpses of my skills. But a four-day camp would allow them to study me at close quarters in a controlled setting.

I wasn't the only one they were watching. There were plenty of prospects at the Wolverine camp. My Notre Dame experience the previous winter proved that coaches were always looking for new prospects that might materialize at any moment. Prospect or not, once we arrived at the camp, the coaches treated us all the same. After all, every one of the dozens of girls at the camp shared the same dream...to someday wear the maize and blue uniform of the Wolverines and play ball for Coach Hutchins and her staff.

We checked into the West Quad dorm and got ready for four days of non-stop practice, team building activities, and competition.

Of course there were breaks for dorm food, evening entertainment and time to just hang out with friends at night.

The Michigan camp was my opportunity to get a taste of campus life. It was also my chance to interact with some of the Wolverine players who were working as instructors. I had already gotten to know Rebekah Milian, who was helping out as an assistant to Donny on our *Finesse* team. Rebekah's sister Elizabeth was a *Finesse* pitcher and Rebekah was the Michigan left fielder. Jessica Merchant was also working the camp. And, I got to know several other players before the week was over.

The Michigan camp proved to be a meeting place for softball friends, past, present and future. I spent more time with current *Finesse* teammates, caught up with past travel ball teammates whose dreams were leading in the same direction as mine, and I even got to know girls who had been rivals in the past. Spending time with Nikki Nemitz turned out to be a lot more enjoyable when we were fellow campers than when I faced her in the state high school semifinals earlier in the year. Overall, it was a preview of what I imagined college would be like. I liked being on my own, away from home; spending time with girls who shared my passion for softball, competition, and being the best players we could be.

The week went by quickly and I listened, worked hard and, I hoped, made a good impression. For the most part I did well defensively and at the plate, bruised hand and all. Even when I messed up, there was a silver lining. How many 16-year-old short-stops are repaid for a rushed offline throw to first with encouragement from an All American who calls out, "Relax Beth, you've got a gun. No need to rush it!" Jessie Merchant's comment was a small thing, but it turned a defensive misfire on my part into a moment of encouragement. I learned a lot about softball that week, but Jessie's words reinforced an important lesson in leadership: don't overlook an opportunity to pick a teammate up. I have no doubt that that type of leadership from the senior shortstop played a big part in the Wolverines' triumphant march to the NCAA College World Series Championship the following spring.

Another Wolverine player shared some more serious thoughts about the recruiting process and my potential as a future Division I college athlete. One afternoon late in the week she took me aside out of the range of others and told me I was definitely a Division I athlete and that I could play just about anywhere I wanted to. Then she turned serious: "Don't make playing here at Michigan your only goal. They may make you wait until the last minute and then not make you an offer. By then, a lot of the other schools will have used up their scholarships and you could end up without a spot in a good program."

Then she said something else: "No matter which school you choose, it will become your home." She listed several Big Ten schools and said I should keep an open mind and consider any of them. It was a valuable reality check. College softball is a numbers game. On a team like Michigan with lots of talent, there might only be one or two spots available in my recruiting class. Donny had said I needed to keep my options open. Now I was getting an insider's perspective that seconded that opinion.

To understand the numbers game behind Division I softball, it is important to understand that, unlike some sports, softball rosters are not composed entirely of athletes on full scholarships. The NCAA only permits each Division I team a total of eleven and a half scholarships across a roster that may range from 15 to more than 20 deep. While pitchers often receive full scholarships each of the four years they are in school, and sometimes a catcher or elite infielder will receive a full ride, there are also a lot of partial scholarships distributed across a school's roster. Many players play without any athletic financial aid for a year or two and some play their entire careers without receiving athletic aid.

While some of my travel ball teammates had said they were going to play college ball for whichever school offered the most money, my parents and I had decided that I should try to play ball for a topflight program at a school with great academics and a diverse curriculum that would allow me to choose from a wide range of majors. We knew that once my softball career was over, I needed to walk away with a great education. If I had to turn down a full scholarship "ride" at one school to accept an offer to play for less at a school that was a better academic fit, we were willing to take on the financial burden necessary to make it happen. Still, an offer of financial aid would signal that a coach had serious plans for me.

Despite the dose of reality from one Wolverine, my desire to play softball at the University of Michigan was at an all time high when my parents came to pick me up on Thursday afternoon. Michigan was still my dream. But my eyes were open. I realized that if I had more than one dream, it would increase the odds that one of them would come true.

Our Season Heats Up

Our next tournament was the ASA state tournament in Midland. After our stumble in Barberton, this was a second chance to qualify for the ASA national tournament. It would also be a chance to test ourselves against the best teams in the state. As an added bonus, the Team USA Olympic Softball team would be playing an exhibition game against a local 23-and-under team as part of their nationwide tour prior to the 2004 Olympics in Athens. We had already made arrangements to attend the game, which would be held on Friday night after the first day of tournament play.

So far since joining *Finesse*, I had begun to accept that my dream of playing Division I college softball was realistic. Now, in the third tournament of our season, I was going to watch a team of women who had not only achieved the dream of playing college softball, but were fortunate enough to extend their careers as members of Team USA, representing the United States in the Olympics and the annual World Softball Championships. Many of them also played professional softball in the National Pro Fastpitch League.

Playing for Team USA, or for a team in the fledgling professional league, was a more remote dream for most travel ball players. We knew that dream would only become realistic if we were successful as collegiate players and none of us had been offered a spot on a college team yet. Donny and our parents reminded us constantly of the importance of academics both in high school and in college. Very few players would go on to play after college and an even smaller number would ever earn enough money from the sport to support themselves. Our job was to perform at the highest level on the field and in the classroom to earn a spot on a college roster. Then we would need to continue to excel in both areas to help our college teams win and prepare ourselves for the careers we would pursue after our playing days were over.

But a girl can dream, can't she? That night we watched with awe mixed with admiration as Team USA warmed up for their exhibition game. Lisa Fernandez, Jennie Finch, Crystal Bustos, Jessica Mendoza, Lovie Ann Jung, Natasha Watley and all of the rest of the Olympians were there as the stands filled with travel ball players, their families and friends as well as local residents. Team USA's opponents would be the Midland Explorers, comprised of college and former college players from across lower Michigan.

As much as we were fans of Team USA, we were even bigger fans of the Explorers' left fielder…the University of Michigan's Rebekah Milian, who was also our *Finesse* assistant coach. It would be nice to say the Explorers went on to pull off an upset that night, but it was not to be. Rebekah played well, but the Explorers were overmatched as Team USA won handily in a run-rule shortened contest. There was certainly no shame in losing to the best softball team in the world. It was good for all of us who witnessed the game to see how high the bar was set for participation at the highest level of our sport. I am sure if any members of the Explorers hadn't already come to terms with the limits of their softball dreams, that mercy-rule loss to Team USA delivered the message loud and clear.

We didn't have much time to wipe the stars from our eyes because day two of our tournament was scheduled to get underway early the next morning. On day one, we had gotten off to a good start, but our deep pitching staff suddenly had been hit with a rash of injuries. First Elizabeth came down with a bad back, then Kari began experiencing pain in her forearm. Our third starter, Stacy, was also hurting after being hit in the hand by a pitch. Elizabeth was hurting too badly to pitch, but Kari and Stacy gave us the best they had as we worked our way through the early games of the tournament.

Unfortunately, we couldn't get our bats untracked. We made it to a semifinal game where we faced off against *Compuware*, our big rival from the Detroit area. Hurting or not, our pitchers kept the game close into the late innings before *Compuware* pushed a run across. We were unable to respond and, just like that, we'd fumbled our second shot at a nationals bid.

Orland Park

The next weekend we headed to suburban Chicago to the Orland Park tournament sponsored by the *Sparks* travel ball club. It was a big tournament that attracted a lot of local 'Chicagoland' teams as well as the best teams from downstate Illinois, Michigan, Indiana, Ohio, and Wisconsin. Also in attendance were college coaches from the Big Ten, Mid America, Horizon and other Division I, Division II, Division III and NAIA conferences. Even the Ivy League was represented since Chicago was prime recruiting territory for girls who were great softball players and outstanding students.

I had enjoyed some of my most exciting moments as a travel ball player in earlier Orland Park tournaments. One year our *Michigan Force* team was playing the *Indiana Magic* in the tournament semifinals when our game was interrupted for over an hour when the field's lightning detection alarm went off. We were locked in a scoreless tie with Ali on the mound against an equally tough *Magic* hurler. Just before the delay, the *Magic* had a runner on second when the next hitter connected on a drop ball and drove it deep into the left center gap. I was playing centerfield and began to sprint with the crack of the bat. We were playing under the lights on a field without outfield fences.

As I chased after the deep drive I ran into the near-darkness out beyond range of the lights. Still traveling at full speed I made a final desperate lunge for the ball, catching it backhand in the webbing of my glove as I crashed to the grass in a heap. I was up in a flash and threw as hard as I could to second base, hoping to double up the base runner who had already rounded third on her way home. We missed the double play by a couple of steps.

Meanwhile, the author of the long out had stopped between first and second and I saw her throw her hands up in the air in disgust as she turned to receive an exaggerated "What can you do?" shrug from her first base coach. In the heat of competition, some moments really stand out. That catch was one of them. Ali got the next batter to retire the side and I was greeted in the dugout by a lot of slaps on the back and a "Nice catch, North!" from Coach. My Dad said a college coach who watched my catch from the stands immediately turned to others and mimicked the ESPN *Sports Center* theme…"da da da, da da da!"

When play resumed, we eventually lost to the *Magic*, 1-0 in extra innings, but we stuck around to play in the consolation game, taking home the third place trophy with a win in front of bleachers populated by our families, a handful of umpires moonlighting as college talent scouts, and the assistant coach for the University of Wisconsin. We arrived home dirty and exhausted at 2 a.m. Monday morning. At least I got to sleep-in when the sun came up. Dad had to get up at 7 a.m. and go to work.

This year, we expected to see a lot more college coaches in the tournament and we were not disappointed. Although the tournament fell well behind schedule due to rain, Coach Green from Notre Dame came to watch us play and ended up spending a lot of time with Donny during one of the delays, cultivating a relationship that would help bring *Finesse* talent to the attention of the Notre Dame Softball staff in the future. I hoped Donnie was spending some of the time pointing out what made me special as a player.

When the weather cleared and we finally had the chance to play an entire game, Coach Hutchins and Coach Tholl from Michigan showed up to watch. They already considered *Finesse* to be a prime source of talent in the state of Michigan, so they didn't need to get acquainted with the team or our coach. But they stayed for almost the entire game, a significant investment of time for a leading college program during a major Midwest talent showcase tournament. They were scouting several of our players, including Roya, one of our catchers, Kari, a hard throwing pitcher, and me. Since Roya and Kari were a year younger, they would not be part of the current year's recruiting class.

I managed a couple of hits and had an opportunity to demonstrate my base running skills in front of the Wolverine coaches, a performance that I'm told caused Coach Hutchins to remark, "She's faster than she looks." Maybe I wasn't a typical "speed burner", but I prided myself on being alert and aggressive. I also worked hard at rounding the bases efficiently, hitting the inside corner and taking a direct line to the next sack. I guess I could be considered "softball fast". I could steal, take the extra base and beat out a bunt or other infield hit. I was flattered that Coach Hutch had noticed my hidden asset.

Our pitching staff was still not healthy and we ended up being eliminated before the championship round but, due to all of the rain delays, it was still late Sunday afternoon by the time we drove away from the fields. It hadn't been my most memorable tournament in terms of softball action, but I'd had another chance to perform in front of the college coaches.

Camping in South Bend

The only thing good about our early elimination in Orland Park was the head start it gave us on the drive to South Bend where I was going to participate in the four-day Notre Dame summer camp. Like the coaches at Michigan, the Notre Dame staff was expecting me to attend their camp. It was part of the evaluation process that would determine if I would be recruited to play ball for the Fighting Irish.

We arrived in South Bend at about 8 p.m., about the same time Ali arrived with her parents. Ali was being considered by the Irish staff for a spot on their pitching staff and Notre Dame had always been her dream school as Michigan had been mine. We learned we would be roommates in the dorm, which would be great since I wouldn't know as many players at this camp as I had in Ann Arbor. Once we were settled into our room, we were walking out of the dorm with our parents when we heard someone call out our names. We turned and were greeted by Gessica Hufnagel, a Notre Dame catcher and one of the instructors at the camp.

Gessica volunteered to take Ali and me on a tour of the most famous landmarks on the Notre Dame campus before the camp counselors would signal lights out in the dorm. We quickly said goodbye to our parents and set off on our private tour. Gessica was from nearby Middlebury, Indiana, and was absolutely passionate about the Irish and Notre Dame. Our whirlwind tour reinforced Ali's already strong feelings for the university and it lit a fire in me. Seeing the Golden Dome, the Grotto, the Basilica, the mosaic of Christ the Teacher—better known as "Touchdown Jesus"—on the library tower, Notre Dame Stadium, the Joyce Athletic and Academic Center, the Stonehenge sculpture...the beauty and magic of the place revealed itself to me in new ways at every stop.

This was a different kind of college campus from the bustling urban environment of the University of Michigan. It seemed to touch me in a spiritual way. I could see how this special environment could provide a place away from the crowd where a student athlete could focus on achieving her full potential on the field, in the classroom and socially. It wasn't that I liked it better than Michigan; I liked both places for different reasons. If in the end I had to choose one of the two campuses over the other, I would certainly have two very different places to choose from.

As far as softball went, Michigan had enjoyed more success than the Irish if success is measured by trips to the NCAA College World Series. The Wolverines had been to eight of the championship tournaments in Oklahoma City while the Irish had yet to qualify. But Notre Dame had come close and they were definitely a team to be reckoned with each year. Like Michigan, the Irish also played an aggressive preseason schedule against the top teams in the country. While Michigan was a power in the Big Ten Conference, Notre Dame was traditionally the team to beat in the Big East Conference. A recent expansion of the Big East would make Notre Dame's road to conference championships, and the resulting automatic berth in the 64-team NCAA Tournament, more difficult in coming years. Joining the Big East were perennial softball powers DePaul and Louisville as well as the rising program at South Florida.

The four days of softball at the Notre Dame camp were every bit as much fun as I'd had at Michigan. I got a taste of the coaching styles of Head Coach Deanna Gumpf, and her assistants Charmelle Green and Kris Ganeff. The drills were run with the same precision and discipline as those I'd experienced at Michigan. The campers had come to Notre Dame from all over the country, reflecting Notre Dame's standing as a national university. In addition to Ali, Simone, my teammate and friend from earlier travel ball days, was there, along with dozens of others players.

The coaches ran us through a full range of infield and outfield drills, which gave us a chance to demonstrate what we could do, how willing we were to learn something new, and the attitude and leadership qualities we had to offer. Coach Green was the coach of my team during the daily competition sessions and I enjoyed her intense and aggressive coaching style. I had been coached hard by Curtis, Jon Greenman and Donny. A little yelling and constructive criticism didn't bother me a bit. I went all out for all four days and tried to show all of the coaches that I had what it takes to succeed at Notre Dame. At one point in an outfield drill I pulled up short and took a short fly ball on the first bounce. The ball no sooner hit the ground when I heard Coach Green shout, "Beth, you can get to that ball!" It made me feel I was back with Coach Greenman or with Curtis in the cage. They never cut me any slack either. I felt like Coach Green recognized my potential and cared enough to push me to greatness. That feeling was reinforced later when she promised, "If you come here, we'll make you better."

In four short days, I came away from Notre Dame convinced that, perhaps as much as at Michigan, Notre Dame *could* make me better…as an athlete, as a student, and maybe even as a person.

Keeping it Light

As we entered the last two weekend tournaments of the summer season, the excitement and tension of recruiting was becoming almost unbearable. Every week presented a new opportunity to demonstrate to coaches that I was worth a spot on their short list of recruits. At Chelsea near Ann Arbor, we played in a small "exposure" tournament in front of many of the college coaches in the state. At this point, we were used to playing in front of the Michigan coaches, but in Chelsea the Michigan State, Eastern Michigan, Central Michigan and other coaching staffs were also there to check out the talent.

In the first game we played I hit a low line drive down the left field line with runners on base. As the ball hit the grass in fair territory the left fielder tried to short hop it on the backhand side. She reacted slowly and missed, tacking a two-base error onto my two RBI double. It wasn't pretty, but I wasn't complaining about getting the chance to show Michigan's Coach Tholl that I was still faster than I looked. I hoped the other coaches looking on got the same message.

Unfortunately, it turned out to be another weekend where we underachieved as a team. Donny became so frustrated during one game, he left the dugout and sat in a chair far down the left field line as we failed to execute the fundamentals he had had worked hard to reinforce all winter. We missed out on the championship hardware again, making us 0 for 5 on the season with just one more tournament to go.

We also had not yet landed a berth in the ASA national tournament, which was our team goal. With no more qualifying tournaments available to us, Donny had to take a less conventional approach to getting us a berth. Fortunately, Donny's talents included a knack for salesmanship. He started working the phone with the

ASA officials in charge of assembling the tournament field. He highlighted our second place finish in Midland, our strong performance against California teams in Barberton, and our overall won-loss record. Even though we hadn't won a tournament championship, we had won a lot of games on our way to losses in semifinal and championship games.

The week after Chelsea my Mom and I made an exhausting overnight trip to Madison, Wisconsin, to attend a one-day camp. The Badger coaches had asked if I could be there and I wanted to see Madison and get a close up look at the Wisconsin softball program. To be honest, the trip was so exhausting and our drive home through a torrential rainstorm was so harrowing that I didn't really get a chance to relax and enjoy the visit. I knew I'd have to see more of Madison and the Wisconsin campus to really appreciate them. For the time being, I had to catch up on my sleep and get ready to head to our final tournament in Toledo.

When we arrived in Northern Ohio a couple of days later, Donny was still working the phone to try to get us a spot in the national tournament. He was also focused on coaching us hard. This was our last chance to win a weekend tournament and he was tired of watching us fall short of our potential. We started out with a couple of wins and then went on a roll, working our way through the first two days of the tournament without a loss. Best of all, Donny called us together on Saturday and said his persistence on the phone with ASA officials had paid off. We'd been granted an at-large berth at Nationals based on our overall record and quality wins against good teams. That was a load off our minds. Now we could really relax and have some fun!

Although the coaches and many of our Detroit area teammates were commuting from home that weekend, the drive back to Grand Rapids was too far to allow my Dad, Mom and me to shuttle back and forth. It was also too far for Nicole, my teammate and buddy, to commute home to the Flint area.

Nicole joined us for dinner at a restaurant across the parking lot from our hotel and as we were leaving the hotel Donny and other *Finesse* coaches walked in to have dinner before heading home for the night. After a quick hello, we headed out the door and began the short stroll across the parking lot back to our room. We hadn't gone far when we saw Donny's car. Nicole and I instantly hatched a plan.

We knew Donny never carried his car keys with him. He left them in the locked car and used a keypad code to get back in when he returned. Earlier in the season he had shared the code with me so I could get team equipment from his car. I was sure he didn't remember giving me the code.

Our plan was simple. We knew Donny had a long drive ahead of him and it was getting late. So, we decided to throw him a curve by stealing his car and moving it around to the other side of the building. He'd panic when he didn't find the car where he had left it and we planned to be on hand to see the expression on his face.

We unlocked the car, grabbed the keys and pulled the car around the building to its new parking space. We left the keys inside and locked the doors. Then we grabbed my Dad's video camera and hid in the bushes near where Donny had originally parked the car. Before long, Donny and company came out of the restaurant and headed for his car, only to find that it wasn't there. Meanwhile, Nicole and I were in the bushes cracking up. We were laughing so hard, we couldn't hold the camera still.

Donny knew in an instant who the culprits were. He let fly with a few choice words as we came out of hiding acting all innocent. But it only took him a few minutes to break down our attempts to keep a straight face and we told him where he could find his car. I guess it was a good thing we were winning that weekend because Donny got a good laugh out of it and he didn't hold it against us the next day.

Maybe it wasn't the best prank in the world, but it was a lot fun at the time. Just because we were trying our hardest to win the tournament and land a spot on a college team didn't mean we couldn't forget about all that and just share a few laughs. At the end of the season, I passed Donny's security code over to Lauren, a younger teammate who would be playing for him again the next year. I hoped stealing and hiding Donny's car would become an annual *Finesse* tradition.

On Sunday we wrapped up the tournament championship in front of several college coaches from Indiana, Ohio, and Illinois. It was a great victory and we celebrated in a team dog pile after posing for a team picture with the trophy. Finally...we were over the hump with first place hardware in our hands and a berth at Nationals.

Team Building

Donny strongly believed in team unity and, with an oversized squad comprised of 15 girls from all over the state, he knew it would be difficult to build and maintain the chemistry necessary to compete against the best teams. Donny had been coaching softball long enough to know that great athletes can be self-absorbed...so focused on achieving their own goals that they aren't sensitive to the needs of people around them.

Giving girls a chance to showcase their talents and earn spots on college softball teams was one of the stated goals of the *Finesse* organization and that was bound to lead to tension among both players and parents. We needed to succeed as a team, but each of us also had individual goals. With a large roster, several girls were going to have to watch the action from the bench. Although Donny had tried to make sure each girl and her parents understood their role before they accepted his offer to join the team, we were all competitive enough to believe we could earn a spot in the starting lineup. What's more, it soon became apparent that some team members would not be satisfied unless they started at specific positions on the field.

Donny made it clear that he would make all of the decisions about playing time and positions. But he also understood that his decisions would not necessarily settle the issue among the players and their parents. He couldn't do much to alter the opinions of the parents, but he was determined to do everything he could to get us to play together as a team. If he could build team unity, we would perform better on the field and we would be less likely to let any complaining from our families and friends undermine our loyalty to each other.

Instead of just encouraging us to cheer for each other and giving us team pep talks, Donny decided the best way to make us come together as a team was to involve us in activities that forced us to get out of our personal comfort zones and interact positively with others. The first activity was a chance to volunteer at a mid-week field day for under-privileged children in the Detroit area. I was unable to attend the event due to a conflict, but my teammates who participated said they had a lot of fun and enjoyed brightening the lives of kids who weren't as fortunate as we were.

The week before nationals, Donny arranged a second team-building event that brought us together in an entirely different way. We met in Ann Arbor at a "ropes" course on the North Campus of the University of Michigan. There we spent the day under the supervision of counselors who guided us through a number of physically and mentally challenging team activities. Each of the activities was designed to force us to rely on each other to successfully complete our tasks.

We helped each other climb over walls, cross rope bridges, complete relay races, and cooperate to solve problems that required a close group effort. The challenges we faced forced us to deal with frustration, physical exhaustion, and emotional situations. Most of all, they forced 15 alpha females to place individualism on hold for an afternoon as we worked through each challenge as a team.

We were pretty sore and more than a little tired when the day was over. But we felt good about what we had accomplished. We also understood and respected each other even more as teammates and individuals, which is what Donny had in mind. Now it was time to show how well our team spirit could serve us at the ASA Nationals in Bloomington, Indiana.

Two Weeks in the Spotlight

We headed off to Bloomington the next weekend ready to do our best to win the ASA 16-and-under championship. Of course, dozens of other teams heading to the tournament had the same goal. Bloomington is about a six-hour drive from home, so we hit the road early. We finally pulled into the town in the middle of the afternoon, checked into our hotel and then headed over to the Indiana University campus to pick up my player credentials.

As we drove across the campus and turned into the parking lot outside of the university building where check-in would occur, we began to see how big the tournament would be. The town and campus were filled with softball players and their families. We negotiated the line to the tables where I would show my identification, have my age and team affiliation confirmed, and pick up my player pass and other materials. My parents also picked up their passes to the fields.

Like most national tournaments, this one would start with a parade and an opening ceremony. We gathered at the hotel that evening to caravan to the IU soccer stadium where the festivities would begin. Donny took the team aside as our families headed for the grandstands. A few minutes later, teams began to assemble and the parade began. The stands were filled with families, friends and other spectators as we filed, team by team, onto the field. Some of the teams really got into the spirit of the event, tossing strands of colored beads and candy into the stands. We were a little more subdued, anxious to get the parade and speeches out of the way and begin playing ball. At last the speeches were done and the tournament was declared officially underway. We filed off the field and Donny called us together to review our practice schedule and pool game times to be sure we were all on the same page. Then it was off to dinner and an early curfew.

The next day we got down to business. Donny had reserved practice time on the official practice fields and he had arranged a couple of practice games to get us warmed up. Once those preliminaries were out of the way, we started pool play. We would play three pool games and then be seeded into the double-elimination brackets. We wanted to do well in pool play, winning every game if we could, but it was absolutely imperative that we do well in bracket play. If you lost a game in bracket play, you were sent to the losers' bracket. Once you were in the losers' bracket, you had to play several games a day to stay in the tournament. One more loss and you were done.

I wish I could say that we swept through the tournament like a team on a mission, but the truth is, our performance in the tournament mirrored the way we'd played most of the season. We won a couple of our pool games but when bracket play began, we won just enough to stay in the tournament until Friday night before losing our second game and joining the ranks of eliminated teams.

At the time, winning it all was the most important thing on our minds. I was upset that we'd underachieved on the biggest stage of the season. But the silver lining was, we had played in front of the coaches of most of my target schools...including my short list of preferred schools: Michigan, Notre Dame, Indiana and Wisconsin. Along the way, the coaches from Northwestern happened upon one of our games and saw me play. They talked to Donny and expressed an interest in me. If we couldn't win the national tournament, at least I would be leaving Bloomington with a good shot at getting offers and opportunities to make official visits to some excellent universities.

After we were eliminated, I had originally thought I'd be driving home with Mom and Dad. During the week Donny received a call from Kevin Kilburn, coach of the *Finesse* 18-and-under team, which was leaving for Atlanta for the ASA Gold Nationals as our national tournament was wrapping up. Kevin invited me, De and

Roya to join his team in Atlanta. So we split up as a family. My Dad went home with De's family so he could return to work. Meanwhile my Mom, De and I headed out for Atlanta. Roya and her family would meet us down there. It looked like we might be playing in our second national tournament in two weeks. As it turned out, we learned that ASA rules would not allow us to compete in a second tournament that year. But my Mom and I had a chance to talk with several of the coaches in the stands and get to know how seriously they were considering me. Not long after we arrived home, the coaches would make their intentions even clearer.

Getting Down to Business

Back at home, things began to happen quickly. I received a call from Coach Gumpf at Notre Dame and she asked if she could visit us in Grand Rapids to outline an offer. She didn't have to ask twice. We arranged a meeting for the following week. Next I received a call from Northwestern. Coach Kate Drohan wanted to know if I wanted to make an unofficial visit to see their campus. We arranged to drive over to Evanston, Illinois, a few days later.

My Dad took a day off from work so he could go with me and Mom on our unofficial visit to Northwestern. The Northwestern campus is just north of Chicago, about a three-and-a-half hour drive from home. Wildcat Head Coach Kate Drohan and her twin sister, Assistant Coach Caryl Drohan, had seen me play in Bloomington and had reached out to Donny to see if I was interested in Northwestern. They had made it clear they didn't have a scholarship to offer but wanted to know if I would be willing to walk on.

Like many private schools, Northwestern's high tuition made it difficult to afford if you didn't have a scholarship. But the Wildcats had an up and coming softball program and Northwestern was an academically elite university. If Coach Drohan thought I was good enough to crack their lineup and earn scholarships in my second, third and fourth years with the program, I would seriously consider walking on as a freshman.

When we turned off the Edens Expressway and drove through the tree-lined streets of Evanston, I was curious to learn more about the school and to meet the coaches. Northwestern had been among the schools I had sent my recruiting tape to but, unlike just about every other program on my mailing list, I had not received an information package from them in return. I assumed it was because they did not have a lot of open spots on their roster and were not actively recruiting very widely that year. When the Northwestern coaches showed up on the sidelines to watch us play in Bloomington, I had thought they just wanted to spend time with the other Big Ten Conference coaches who had congregated there.

We met Coach Drohan and her sister in the temporary softball office outside of the football stadium. Northwestern was constructing a new athletic office building near the Drysdale softball field so several of the teams were headquartered in temporary quarters. The coaches were easy to talk to as they asked questions about me and what I was looking for in a softball program. The conversation quickly turned to academics. The coaches made it clear that getting accepted to Northwestern was difficult. I would probably qualify for admission but my grades and test scores would be nothing special among the high caliber freshmen Northwestern would attract.

The coaches had arranged a meeting with a professor in the engineering department because I was considering applying my math skills in that field. I also met with the academic advisor for the softball team who further described what would be expected of a Northwestern student athlete. Nothing I heard discouraged me. I was looking for top flight academics in addition a great softball program. I wanted coaches who liked my skills and could make them better. My interest grew still further during my walking tour with the coaches around the campus. The place was beautiful and, for a girl from Grand Rapids, the location a short El ride from Chicago's North Side and the Loop made Northwestern an almost exotic place to study and play ball.

But, Northwestern would be a risk. The coaches seemed impressed with me as a player and I had the academics they needed. They said they expected me to compete strongly for a spot in the line-up, either in the infield or the outfield. And they said they were committed to their athletes. Coach Drohan said she felt it was their duty to help me improve each year and that they were so confident in their abilities as teachers and coaches that they would not recruit girls behind me to take my spot. But, when all was said and done, I would have to walk on, pay the entire cost of tuition and room and board for the first year, and take my chances that by my sophomore year I would earn a scholarship.

No matter where I ended up playing ball, there would be some risk. It is a little known fact that NCAA Division I scholarships are awarded one year at a time. Coaches do not have to provide athletes with more than a one year commitment when they recruit them. Offer letters are given to athletes and signed each year and the amount of the grant can vary year to year. That means there is a chance a student athlete could lose her scholarship a year or two after committing to attend a university. A debilitating injury, a change in coaching staff, or just a change of mind can leave an athlete on the outside looking in right in the middle of her college career.

At a state-supported school like Michigan, I could afford to continue my education if I did not receive an athletic scholarship. But that would be far more difficult at a private school with much higher tuition like Northwestern or Notre Dame, or at a state school like Indiana or Wisconsin where I would have to pay higher out-of-state tuition rates. I was not looking for a risk-free athletic opportunity. Playing a sport is all about taking chances, putting everything on the line, and having enough confidence in yourself to risk it all in the pursuit of personal excellence and team victory. Still, it was clear that I would have to carefully listen to the coaches as they outlined my opportunities at their schools. I would have to read between the lines to gauge their level of commitment to me. A missed signal along the way could be costly.

That gave me plenty think about on the long drive home. My Mom and I decided the best way to decompress and mull over all we had learned that day was to take in some of the shopping on North Michigan Avenue in downtown Chicago. Ever the jock, I really wanted to check out the new athletic "kicks" at the Nike store. We asked my Dad to drop us at the curb so we could shop while he cruised for a convenient parking space. Right! Like that was going to happen along the Magnificent Mile. He ended up circling the block over and over again while Mom and I had fun checking out the shoes and fashions.

When we finally hit the road for home it was late afternoon. As we were navigating the Dan Ryan Expressway through Chicago's South Side, I decided I should return a call I'd received earlier in the week from the coach at Dartmouth in the Ivy League. She was wondering if I would consider attending the prestigious college in New England. I was flattered that they wanted me. But I had also received correspondence from Harvard and Cornell earlier in the summer and had decided that the distance from home and the shorter softball schedules played by Ivy League teams were not a good fit for me. After my brief conversation with the Dartmouth coach, I hung up and realized that the phone call represented a milestone of a new kind. Dartmouth was the first school I had given a definite answer to. I had said "No". It was the same answer I would have to give to every school who was interested in me except one. The day when I would have to make that final choice was drawing closer.

Notre Dame Comes Calling

Back in Grand Rapids, we had a date with the Notre Dame coaches who had called and asked if they could visit us in our home to present their offer. We provided driving directions and prepared to host our first home visit. When the big day arrived, Coach Gumpf and Assistant Coach Kris Ganeff drove up to our house and we welcomed them in.

We sat in our living room and listened as Coach Gumpf described the history of Notre Dame Softball, their high hopes for the future, and the steps they were taking as coaches to help Notre Dame build on its past accomplishments to achieve new levels of success. Coach Gumpf outlined the support Notre Dame athletes receive on and off the field to ensure their success as students and as athletes. And she showed us a highlight video that continued the inspirational work that Gessica Hufnagel had started when Ali and I joined her for a tour of the Notre Dame campus during the Irish camp earlier in the summer.

Then the coaches described what they liked in me as a player. They said I clearly had the talent to perform at the next level and they thought I could compete to start in the infield or the outfield. But Coach Gumpf said they were especially impressed with my aggressive approach to the game. They expected me to bring that same all out approach to Irish softball and help the team win Big East Championships and get to the NCAA College World Series.

Coach Gumpf outlined the opportunity she wanted me to consider: she said her challenge in recruiting was to make 11-and-a-half scholarships stretch across her entire roster, a challenge she shared with every other D-I softball coach in America except those in the Ivy League where athletic scholarships were not offered at all. I had learned from Donny that top pitchers and catchers were the recruits most likely to receive full ride offers as freshmen. A top infielder or an elite hitter might also receive a full scholarship as a freshman. Donny didn't want to discourage me, but he wanted me to go into the recruiting process with my eyes open. Both he and my parents agreed with my decision to try to play college softball at the highest level possible at a university that also offered strong academics. Money was a consideration, but it would not be the top consideration.

By setting my sights on an elite Division I program, I knew I might be giving up a shot at a full scholarship at a less prestigious school. I expected to begin as a freshman with whatever my travel ball performance had earned me, and then let my performance on the field earn me additional scholarship aid over the rest of my college career. What Coach Gumpf said next surprised me.

The cost to attend Notre Dame without a scholarship or other financial assistance would be beyond the means of many players and their families, so Coach Gumpf said she felt compelled to provide a four-year financial plan that she said she would honor as long as I met my commitments academically and as a member of the Irish softball team. She said the plan would also be honored even if I was injured and could not play softball.

Coach Gumpf's plan for me included little athletic aid as a freshman. But as a sophomore I would receive an athletic scholarship equal to about two-thirds of the total cost of tuition and room and board. In my junior and senior years, I would receive a full ride. The plan was appealing because it leveled the playing field between the cost to attend Notre Dame and the expense of attending the University of Michigan in my home state with no financial assistance. It also made Notre Dame more affordable than attending an out-of-state public university like Wisconsin or Indiana.

But more important, it told me that Coach Gumpf and her staff believed in me and my ability to help the Irish win games and get to Oklahoma City. NCAA rules required no more than a one-year commitment, but the Irish staff was willing to commit one of their most precious assets—one of their few athletic scholarships—to me for two years and part of a third.

Coach Gumpf said she was sorry she couldn't offer me more but she hoped her plan would earn my serious consideration. She also reminded me that I might be eligible for needs-based aid from Notre Dame. Notre Dame does not offer academic scholarships, because virtually every incoming freshman graduates from high school with a high GPA and has earned a high score on the standardized tests. However, a high percentage of all students who attend the university qualify for grants, loans or other aid due to financial need. With annual tuition and room and board costs of more than $40,000, even middle class families like ours might qualify for such aid. Coach Gumpf encouraged us to complete the government's FAFSFA financial aid application online before the February deadline and let Notre Dame consider if we qualified for needs-based aid.

The coaches were very open in responding to my questions about their program and their plans for me if I decided to attend Notre Dame to play softball. I felt like I had gotten to know Coach Gumpf and Coach Ganeff pretty well during their summer camp and our conversation in my living room confirmed my earlier impression: the Irish coaching staff was committed to winning and to helping their players achieve their full potential on and off the field.

Before their visit ended, Coach Gumpf had one last question for me: would I like to come to Notre Dame for an official visit? The NCAA only allows softball players to make five official visits, so getting me to accept their offer to visit Notre Dame for a weekend would signal that I was seriously interested in joining the Irish. I quickly said "Yes" and we set a date.

As we said goodbye to the coaches, I was excited and relieved all at once. I had my first offer from the short list of colleges I really wanted to attend. Over the coming weeks, I would receive a call from Coach Hutchins outlining her offer to join the Wolverine softball team and inviting me to make an official visit. I would also receive invitations to make official visits to Indiana and Wisconsin. My dance card for the next six weeks was filling up and I was getting closer to making the decision that would set the course for what would be, in all likelihood, the final four years of my softball career.

Official Visit in South Bend

My first official visit would be to Notre Dame. My parents and I started from Grand Rapids early Friday morning to make the two-hour drive to South Bend. The plan was to meet Irish Assistant Coach Charmelle Green at the hotel where my parents would be staying. When we arrived, Coach Green and three other recruits were already waiting for us. The other three girls had flown in from Southern California the night before.

It was a beautiful autumn day in South Bend. The sky was blue, the trees were showing some fall color, and temperatures were in the high sixties. If you wanted to recruit Sun Belt or West Coast athletes to the upper Midwest, you couldn't ask for a nicer day. For a kid like me from America's "North Coast", it was the kind of day that made the Golden Dome shine especially bright.

Coach Green introduced me to Brittney Bargar, Linda Kohan and Alex Kotcheff, who were also weighing offers from the Irish. They would join me in spending the next two days deciding if Notre Dame was the right place to spend their four year college careers. We piled into a university van and Coach Green drove us to our first stop, a local restaurant where we were joined by several Irish players for breakfast.

While I had met some of them during Irish camps, I quickly saw that this weekend would be a lot more relaxed than a sports camp. The Irish players now treated us as potential teammates instead of as mere camp participants. I listened as the players joked around with the coaches and each other. As recruits, we were on our best behavior at first. But we soon relaxed and joined in. It didn't hurt that I knew Gessica Hufnagel from the Irish summer camp and Linda and Brittney had played travel ball with some of the current Irish players in California.

After breakfast, Coach Green took us on quick driving tour of the campus before we met the Irish players who would take us to class with them. This would give us a taste of the academic environment that set Notre Dame apart from many Division I universities.

Notre Dame is known for its focus on undergraduate education. With fewer than 9,000 students overall, the university requires that all incoming freshmen, including student athletes, participate in the demanding First Year of Studies program. There is no easing into college life. Every student is challenged by course work designed to provide a foundation for the remaining three years of their college careers. By exposing students to a variety of courses, the First Year of Studies also helps students choose their college major as they enter their sophomore years.

Among NCAA Division I schools, Notre Dame perennially ranks in the top five in athletic graduation rates, which is remarkable considering the school's high academic standards. While it is not uncommon for student athletes at other top schools to use a 'five-year plan' to obtain their undergraduate degrees, Notre Dame athletes are expected to graduate in four years. Even a very high percentage of football players graduate from Notre Dame in four years, almost unheard of in major college athletics. That means taking more classes each semester, long evenings in study halls, the discipline to study while traveling to games, and, in many cases, attending summer school to earn additional credit hours. Although Notre Dame offers a diverse curriculum and a lot of academic majors, missing are the less strenuous majors offered by larger schools. That means there are no hiding places for student athletes. They have to attend the same rigorous classes and study alongside all the other students at Notre Dame

The four of us split up to go to different classes. I went to class with Irish junior Meghan Ruthrauf. Although it was the first time I had attended a college class, I wasn't surprised by the level of student involvement and interest in the class. It was what I expected at a university known as "highly selective" in its student admission policies. I was looking for a challenge in the classroom and on the softball field. My glimpse of Notre Dame academic life didn't disappoint me.

After class, we met our parents who had taken a walking tour of the campus, visiting many of the landmark attractions on the tree-lined campus. We stopped at the Coleman-Morse athlete's study hall, known as "Como", where we met with academic advisors who described what would be expected of us as Notre Dame student athletes and the kind of support we would receive from tutors, study groups and support staff whose mission was to give student athletes every opportunity to be successful in the classroom.

After lunch in the South Dining Hall, we walked over to the University's Alumni Center for a presentation by the director of alumni relations. We were shown the "Domer" coins we would receive as graduates of Notre Dame and learned about the nationwide network of Notre Dame alumni and the power of that network in helping us achieve our career dreams and maintaining fulfilling social relationships with fellow alumni after graduation.

Then we headed to Notre Dame Stadium where we were given a tour of the press box and watched the University of Washington football team in their walk-through drills in preparation for the next day's game against the Fighting Irish. Then it was on to the Joyce Center and the Monogram Hall where we viewed displays depicting the storied history of Notre Dame Athletics and highlighting the accomplishments of current teams. Extending around the perimeter of the hall was a chronological roster of everyone who had earned the Notre Dame Monogram as a varsity athlete. By this time, all four of us were picturing the day our names would join athletes like Joe Montana, Ruth Riley, Jarrah Myers and hundreds of others on those walls.

Coach Gumpf led us into the Irish Softball office where she met with each of us individually to review our offers, answer any questions we might have and ask us if we were ready to commit to Notre Dame. Although I knew Brittney, Linda and Alex were on the verge of committing, I wasn't ready yet. Linda and Brittney had already visited other schools and had decided that Notre Dame was number one on their lists. Alex also seemed to be leaning toward the Irish. This was my first official visit, though. I wanted to visit Michigan, Indiana and Wisconsin before deciding. I had one question for Coach Gumpf before telling her of my decision to wait: would Notre Dame Softball wait for me to make a decision, or would she extend an offer to another player instead? Coach Gumpf told me she understood and said she wasn't going to offer my spot to someone else. That was a great relief to me. I don't know what I would have done if she had asked for my decision right then and there.

We went to Coach Gumpf's house for dinner and then went to a team get-together at the off campus apartment of one of the seniors on the team. I spent most of my time talking to Gessica Hufnagel, Kenya Fuemmeler and the other girls to get a feel for the team chemistry and campus life at Notre Dame. It was clear that academics were on the minds of most of the players, even on the weekend. An Irish athlete was very much a student athlete.

The next morning, we attended the softball tailgate party on the lawn in front of the Joyce Center, then we headed into the stadium where we were allowed to stand on the field while the teams warmed up. Just before kickoff, we took our seats in the boisterous student section of the stadium to cheer on the Irish. Only we didn't really sit down. It is tradition that Irish students stand for the entire first half. Then after a short break at halftime, they stand for the last two quarters of the game as well. There was no way we were going to sit down, surrounded by Irish students who were singing and cheering along with the band, the Leprechaun mascot, and the cheerleaders. There wasn't a quiet minute all game long. The Irish handled the Huskies easily on the field and we held up our end by cheering our lungs out in the stands.

After the game the formal part of our visit was over. We said goodbye to Coach Gumpf and headed back to the dorms for a second night with our hosts. Gess, Kenya and several other girls took us to Rocco's, a local Italian restaurant. After dinner we dropped in on football and lacrosse parties. But I could tell my hosts needed to get back to their studies and Coach Green had reminded us that

NCAA rules required the weekend to end before 8 a.m. Sunday morning. The other recruits had even earlier wake up calls to catch flights to California, so ending the night early was not a bad idea. I couldn't complain about getting up early Sunday morning because Coach Green was up performing shuttle duty at about 4 a.m. to get the other girls to the airport. The sun was actually up and shining when she picked me up in front of the dorm and dropped me at the hotel to rendezvous with my parents for the drive home. Still, I was asleep almost before we crossed the state line into Michigan. It had been an exciting and exhausting 48 hours.

Decisions, Decisions

I was scheduled to hit the road again a week later to Indiana and we would also be traveling to Wisconsin before my visit to Michigan. There was a chance that I would also be invited to make a fifth official visit, but I had delayed confirming those plans until after my trip to Notre Dame.

In the days after my weekend at Notre Dame, I came to the conclusion that, although I knew Indiana and Wisconsin were great schools, my choice now really came down to two schools: Michigan and Notre Dame. In fairness to the coaches at the other schools, I felt I should cancel my plans for official visits to Bloomington and Madison so they could turn their attention to other prospects and I could focus on making the very difficult decision between Michigan and Notre Dame. I made the two phone calls and the coaches seemed to appreciate that I was being honest with them and not taking advantage of their hospitality to enjoy a weekend of entertainment.

Now I had to wait. My visit to Michigan was still three weeks away. Meanwhile, I had learned that the six other girls who had received offers from Coach Gumpf this fall had committed to Notre Dame. I was the only one who was still undecided. Holding out was beginning to feel a bit awkward, especially when I traveled to the Chicago area to watch the Irish play in a fall tournament on the Orland Park fields where I had played so many times in my travel ball career. Between games, the Irish coaches used one of the contacts permitted under NCAA rules to talk to me and Coach Green razzed me good naturedly to try to get me to commit on the spot.

As we drove back to Grand Rapids that afternoon, I couldn't wait for my visit to Michigan so I could finally make my decision one way or the other. By now, everyone knew I had narrowed my choices to Michigan and Notre Dame and it seemed everyone had an opinion. When it comes to Michigan and Notre Dame, there is no middle ground. The two schools have been bitter rivals in football for decades and over the years that rivalry has extended to other sports including softball. Die hard Notre Dame fans despise Michigan and Wolverine fans "hate" the Irish just as much. I was probably one of a handful of people in the country who liked both schools and it was hard to find anyone, outside of my Mom and Dad and Donny, who understood how hard my decision would be.

I had earned a spot on the *Finesse* 18-and-under team during fall tryouts and would be playing under Coach Kevin Kilburn, a Michigan graduate, coach of the U of M club softball team and an ardent fan of Michigan softball. One of Kevin's players had accepted an offer from Michigan the year before and Kevin lobbied hard on the Wolverines' behalf at every *Finesse* practice that fall.

Although he shared Kevin's strong feelings for Michigan, Donny was less biased, in part because he had talked to both the Notre Dame and Michigan coaches about me and felt both schools would give me an opportunity to play. He acknowledged that the four year commitment outlined by Coach Gumpf would be hard to turn down. Besides, Donny's mentor and good friend Denny Schlimgen, the founder of *Finesse,* was a member of Notre Dame's "subway alumni", the legions of fans nationwide who hadn't attended Notre Dame but who gave their total allegiance to the school. Denny was thrilled that I was the first player in *Finesse* history to receive an offer from the Irish. He had filled Donny's ears with Irish lore while accompanying our *Finesse* team to nationals in Bloomington.

My high school coach wasn't a strong Michigan fan (she was a graduate of Michigan State), but she knew Coach Hutchins and made it known that she felt I should choose the Wolverines. Of course, relatives on my Dad's side of the family were also in the Michigan camp, since they were all Michigan alumni. Except for Ali, most of my travel ball teammates had, like me, always dreamed of playing for Coach Hutchins who had the best team in our state and the Midwest. They would probably consider me crazy to turn my back on an offer to be a Wolverine.

But my Mom and Dad, Donny, and my closest friends understood my feelings about wanting to go to a great school and the place where I had the best chance of earning a spot in the starting lineup. I was now convinced that both programs had quality coaches and solid programs where I could contribute to a winning tradition and become better as a ball player. Academically, both Notre Dame and Michigan were top flight universities that would prepare me for success after my playing days were over. My choice was going to come down to intangibles. I hoped my visit to Michigan would give me the final information I needed to decide, in my heart, which university would become my softball "home".

A Weekend in Ann Arbor

We started out for Ann Arbor early on a Friday morning to arrive by about 8 a.m. We parked a short walk from the athletic department offices where we would meet Head Coach Hutchins, Associate Head Coach Bonnie Tholl and Assistant Coach Jen Brundage. Once inside, we were greeted by Coaches Tholl and Brundage and reviewed the plans for the next 48 hours.

Coach Tholl explained that there would be one other recruit on campus that weekend and that Coach Hutchins was meeting her at the airport. To get things started, Coach Tholl would take my parents and me on a driving tour of the campus and visit Michigan's North Campus, located apart from the main campus. The North Campus was home to the school of engineering. I had told the coach of my interest in putting my math skills to work by pursuing a degree in engineering.

Unlike Notre Dame, a compact pedestrian campus, the campus of the University of Michigan is a part of the city of Ann Arbor, with university buildings mixed together with businesses and residences along city streets. As the campus has expanded, new classrooms, laboratories, athletic facilities and offices have all been built along and within a few blocks of State Street, the main road through campus. Although students travel by bus from the main campus to the North Campus, they usually walk to class on the city streets of the main campus.

Coach Tholl pointed out campus landmarks as we made our way over to North Campus where I was scheduled to meet with an academic adviser in the engineering department. During the meeting, I learned what I could expect as an engineering student. She outlined the classes I would take as a freshman and the time commitment required to keep up in the demanding classes required by the engineering school.

I wasn't intimidated. I already knew balancing athletics with academics would be challenging no matter where I went to college and I was determined to excel both athletically and academically. We drove back to the main campus where we arranged to meet Coach Hutchins, my fellow recruit, and the players who would serve as our hosts for the weekend. Coach Hutchins took us on a walking tour of the law quad with its distinctive courtyard and library. Then we strolled over to the famous "Diag" and Angell Hall where we dropped off the tour to go to class with our hosts while our parents continued on their walk with the coaches.

We met our parents and the coaches later that afternoon for individual meetings with Coach Hutchins so she could discuss her offers with us, describe how she saw our roles with her team, and allow us to ask questions. My offer from Michigan was similar to the one I had received from Notre Dame, but it was also different. Coach Hutchins wanted me to come to Michigan as a preferred walk on. Walk ons receive no athletic financial assistance. But unlike other walk ons, a preferred walk on is assured a place on the team. In effect, her offer of support for my freshman year was the same as the one Coach Gumpf was offering at Notre Dame.

Coaches in softball use preferred walk on status to recruit girls who might receive athletic scholarships from other schools. The NCAA does not allow Division I universities to offer enough scholarships to fill a softball (or baseball) roster. Even when full rides are split into partial scholarships, coaches can run out of money before their roster needs are met. When a girl has a strong desire to play for a program, money is often a secondary decision factor. A preferred walk on offer lets an athlete know she is wanted and has a place on the team, even if there is no money involved.

A preferred walk on offer can be attractive to an athlete who is considering a school in her home state because in-state tuition is low compared to the expense of attending a private school or a public university in another state. In my case, the cost to attend Michigan for four years would be less than the cost of two years at Notre Dame, even if I never received an athletic scholarship from Coach Hutchins. What Coach Hutchins was really offering me, in addition to the chance to earn playing time on her softball team, was the opportunity to attend Michigan, an elite academic institution that the vast majority of top students in the state of Michigan cannot attend because of the university's highly selective admission standards and limited annual enrollment capacity. There was a chance I could qualify for financial aid at Michigan to reduce my cost to attend. But even without a scholarship, a preferred walk on offer from Michigan was very attractive.

What was missing from Coach Hutchins' offer was a detailed four-year plan like the one Coach Gumpf had outlined. The high cost of attending Notre Dame made Coach Gumpf's long-term promise a more important consideration than it would be at Michigan. My parents and I could afford to pay my way at Michigan if I was injured or never received financial aid. Paying for four years at Notre Dame would be a lot harder. Still, Coach Gumpf's offer demonstrated a lot of confidence in my ability to contribute to the success of the Irish softball team during my four-year career at Notre Dame.

Coach Hutchins knew how much I liked Michigan and that playing for the Wolverines had been my longtime dream so she may have expected me to accept her offer that day. But when I explained that I was going to choose between Michigan and Notre Dame the week after my visit, she said she hoped I would choose to play for her but that she was willing to wait a week for my answer.

After the meetings, we joined most of the Wolverine team for dinner before I left to spend the night with my player host, Lorilyn Wilson, a Wolverine pitcher. We had a good time just hanging out watching movies and a standup comedy DVD. We also went to a team event where I got to spend time with the other members of the Michigan team. I felt relaxed and comfortable with them and could tell the team chemistry would be a great fit for me.

The next morning I met my parents at the U of M athletic department tailgate on the university golf course across the street from "The Big House" as Michigan Stadium is known. It is the largest college football stadium in the country and home to the nation's winningest college football team. As we sat at a table under the large white tent, I had a chance to ask Coach Hutchins what she felt I needed to work on to get better as a player and break into the Wolverine line up.

She said she expected me to compete for a spot in the lineup. In her opinion, most players aren't ready to play until their junior and senior seasons and, with a deep line-up, it was clear that she was not going to mislead me into thinking a freshman was likely to become a full-time starter right away. She said she liked that I was disciplined, coachable and that I knew how to play the game. When I asked her what her top priority for me would be, she said the coaching staff would focus on making me physically stronger to withstand the rigorous demands of college softball.

Finally, Coach Hutchins emphasized that she is loyal to the players she recruits. I took that to mean that, even if I didn't get to play immediately, I would receive a fair chance to compete for playing time throughout my career. For a preferred walk on, the loyalty of the coaching staff would be important. Every year, new scholarship athletes would join the team with their own aspirations to break into the starting lineup. I didn't want the coaches to see me as a 'has been' part way into my four-year career.

We walked with the coaches over to the stadium and rode the elevator to the press box to view the crowd of over 100,000 filing into the vast stadium. NCAA rules said we had to leave the press box before kickoff, so our visit was a brief one. We soon headed to our seats for the kick off against the Minnesota Golden Gophers in the battle for the famed Little Brown Jug, one of the oldest trophies in college football.

It turned out to be a great game for the home team. The Wolverines fell behind early but then rallied to beat Minnesota at the end. In the middle of the game, the other recruit hung the 'hold out' label on me again by giving Coach Hutchins her verbal commitment. By now I could only hope my deliberate decision-making process wasn't going to be held against me when I finally accepted an offer. So far, it seemed like every recruit who had joined me for a campus visit had arrived with her mind already made up. I had always thought of myself as a decisive person, able to make good decisions quickly, but I wasn't going to hurry now. This was the biggest decision I had ever faced. I was going to take my time and get it right.

After the game, we spent our second night with our player hosts. I arrived back at my parents' hotel just before the NCAA mandated time limit. After only two official visits, meeting that crack-of-dawn deadline was getting to be a real pain! Ordinarily I would have jumped in the car and, after getting almost no sleep all weekend, caught up on my rest during the two hour drive home. But my *Finesse* teammates were playing a practice game against the Michigan club softball team at Alumni Field, home of Michigan's varsity softball team. So, we made the short drive to the field and I played a groggy seven innings of softball before finally calling it a day. Now I could get some sleep. I woke up as we pulled into our driveway that evening and I knew it was time to start making my decision.

Decision

The next few days were some of the hardest of my young life. Certainly having to choose between Michigan and Notre Dame to play softball and get a great education wasn't the worst thing I had ever faced. It was nothing like having my Grandma and Grandpa on my Mom's side pass away, hearing that my cousin had died, or losing my Grandpa on my Dad's side. But those were events I could not control; they happened to me and my family but were not the result of any decisions I made. This was hard in a different way. It was hard because I had complete control over my decision and I didn't want to have any regrets once I made my choice.

At first I just tried to think through what I liked about both schools, about their coaches and my prospective teammates, and the softball programs I might be joining. But before long my brain was mush and I knew I'd have to organize my thoughts and weigh my options more deliberately. I started to make lists of the advantages of each program.

On the Michigan side, the first advantage was my long-standing desire to be a Wolverine. I loved Ann Arbor and the school. I would definitely get a great education at Michigan and the Ann Arbor campus was an exciting, cosmopolitan environment where I would probably live off campus in an apartment for three of my four years of college.

I also knew Michigan would be a strong contender every year for a Big Ten Conference championship and for a berth in the NCAA College World Series. Coach Hutchins and her staff were not likely to leave Michigan during my four years of college, which meant I probably would not have to win the confidence of a new coach in the middle of my playing career. The Michigan coaches had a strong reputation as teachers who made their players better. I wanted to learn and improve, so I considered that a real plus.

I also had friends on the Michigan team, even though some would graduate before my college career would begin. There was Rebekah Milian, the starting left fielder and former *Finesse* assistant coach who had become a good friend during my recruiting season of travel ball. Also on the Michigan squad was Jessica Merchant, the player whose footsteps I had always wanted to follow from West Michigan to Ann Arbor. I also knew several of the other Wolverine players from the Michigan softball camps. And then there was my family background. On my Dad's side everyone had graduated from Michigan or was a Michigan fan. Most of my friends were also convinced Michigan was the place to play ball. I'd be bucking popular opinion if Michigan was not my choice.

I couldn't think of any negatives associated with Michigan. Sure, some of the classes were large, and many of them would be taught by graduate assistants and not professors. But Michigan was ranked as one of the most highly regarded public universities in the country. It was a "Public Ivy" with nearly the same academic standing as the prestigious schools in the Ivy League. Really, the only reason I hesitated to just say yes to Coach Hutchins was actually a positive: Michigan had a really good team with a deep line up of returning players. They were a good bet to be one of the eight teams to make it to the College World Series every year of my college career.

As an athlete who can't stand to sit, I wanted to make sure I picked a school where I was going to get every opportunity to play right away. I had a lot of confidence in my ability to break into the Wolverine line-up eventually, but I knew that my chances of playing as a freshman were slim. Coach Hutchins had hinted that she saw me as a role player who might not start regularly but would end up getting playing time because of my versatility and overall athleticism and work ethic. This was worrisome to me. I only had four years left to play softball, I didn't want to spend it sitting on the bench. As I told my Dad, I didn't want to just make it to the College World Series, I wanted to *play* in the College World Series.

Michigan had a lot going for it, but Notre Dame had also captured my heart and I had a lot of positives to weigh on the Fighting

Irish side of my list. First, there was the beautiful, spiritual atmosphere of the campus. I loved the place. While Michigan's campus was part of the town of Ann Arbor, Notre Dame's campus was a sanctuary away from the bustle of the outside world. Although I hadn't grown up dreaming of attending Notre Dame, the more I learned about the university, the more I admired and respected its academics and athletics. Notre Dame was now definitely right up there with Michigan in my estimation.

My family decided that, if I might attend Notre Dame, we should learn all we could about the school, the educational opportunities it offered, and its guiding principles and traditions. We learned that, with only about 9,000 students, Notre Dame is a lot smaller school than many people realize. But unlike many larger universities, Notre Dame places its primary focus on undergraduate education. This translates into smaller classes, most of which are taught by professors. While the school has a growing standing as a research institution, it does not allow research to overshadow the education it provides to undergraduate students.

As a Catholic university, Notre Dame strongly emphasizes personal ethics and service to others as part of the educational experience. Although I wasn't going to choose a college specifically for religious reasons, I was attracted to Notre Dame's emphasis on character and personal accountability. The obvious loyalty of Notre Dame's alumni to the school and to their fellow alums made me feel that if I attended Notre Dame, I would become a part of something bigger than myself, a member of a family stretching across generations and extending from coast to coast and around the world.

While Notre Dame's coaches had not been at the school as long the Wolverine staff had been at Michigan, the coaching staff appeared to be stable and I thought there was a very good chance Coach Gumpf would be the head coach throughout my four-year college career. Coach Green had stressed during my visits to the campus that the Irish coaching staff was committed to improving the skills of its players. Like Greg Youtzy, Jon Greenman, and Donny Dreher, not to mention Curtis Morgan and his assistant

Sean, the Notre Dame coaching staff would help make me a better player.

I didn't know any of the Notre Dame players as well as some of the Wolverine players, but I had enjoyed their company on my official visit. I felt confident they would be great teammates and I would have no trouble making friends or sharing in team camaraderie. Early in my athletic career I had decided I liked playing team sports more than competing in individual contests. It was why my early talents in track and swimming never went beyond participation in middle and high school intramurals. It was also why I treated tennis and golf as recreational escapes and not serious competitive activities. Becoming a member of the Irish softball team would satisfy my desire to be part of a close knit group of competitors united by the desire to be the best.

Notre Dame was always a contender for the Big East Conference championship and had come close to getting into the NCAA College World Series. I thought it would be great to be part of the first Irish squad to earn a place in Division I college softball's Elite Eight and compete for a national championship. Notre Dame had a roster full of great athletes just like Michigan. But Coach Gumpf's plan gave me extra confidence that I could earn a place in the Irish lineup and begin contributing immediately. Bottom line, I really wanted to play.

While I was weighing the pros and cons of the Wolverines and Irish, I was also busy with classes and homework as my senior year of high school began to gain momentum. I had told both coaches that I would let them know my decision within a week of my return from the Michigan visit. But by the middle of the week after my trip to Ann Arbor, I was still struggling to decide. I would wake up in the morning convinced I was going to be a Wolverine, and by noon, I was just as strongly convinced I had Irish in my blood. I was running out of time. By then I had stopped listening to everyone who offered advice. My parents did a good job of letting me decide on my own, although one night my Dad grew a little impatient with me and, in frustration, expressed a strong opinion. As politely as possible under the circumstances, I asked him to let me decide for myself.

This went on for another day and a half until finally, late in the week, I came into the kitchen and told Mom and Dad I was ready to call the coaches. I said I had decided to accept Coach Gumpf's offer because, when all was said and done, I could not resist the mystique of the Irish, the opportunity to blaze my own trail as a student and a softball player, and to become a part of the Notre Dame family that had opened its arms to me. I picked up the phone and made the easy call first. As soon as I heard Coach Gumpf's voice I knew I had made the right decision. She was excited to hear that I wanted to come to Notre Dame and do my best to make the Irish a force to be reckoned with in Division I softball during the next four years. I think she was a bit surprised that she had managed to lure me away from my Michigan roots, which, given the huge rivalry between Michigan and Notre Dame, may have made my acceptance even sweeter for her.

After talking to Coach Gumpf, I immediately dialed Coach Hutchin's number. I knew this call would be difficult. I had a lot of respect for Coach Hutchins and her staff. After attending so many camps and getting to know them so well, I felt like I was as close to being a Wolverine as you can be without actually wearing the Maize and Blue Michigan uniform. I choked up a bit as I told her what I had decided. She was very kind and wished me luck in my career and, that quickly, my decision was official.

After a moment of reflection on how much I liked Coach Hutchins and her staff, I felt filled with a relief and joy that the last hurdle had been cleared. I was on my way to living my dream of playing Division I college softball for an elite university. I was going to be a member of the Fighting Irish softball team!

Signing Day

When signing day came later that fall, I wasn't celebrating alone. The athletic director at our high school arranged a signing party for three of us who would be going on to college to play softball and an East Kentwood baseball player who was also signing to play college ball. In addition to my letter of intent with Notre Dame, Ali was signing with Central Michigan University and De was signing with Eastern Michigan. Our classmate, Ben Rodewald, was signing with Central to play baseball. Donny and Kevin from Finesse made the drive up from the Detroit area to attend and Greg Youtzy was there along with high school coach Sue Barthold and other friends and family.

In all, four of us from the same high school class would sign with Division I college softball programs. Julie signed with Indiana University several weeks later to cap a remarkable achievement for members of the 2005 East Kentwood softball senior class. The next spring, the Detroit Free Press featured the four of us on the front page of the newspaper's sports section as the East Kentwood softball "Fab Four". We were riding a real wave of excitement going into our last year of high school ball.

Although I had chosen a college and was enjoying the congratulations from classmates, friends and family, I was still working on my game at every opportunity. As fall turned to winter, I was hitting with Curtis on Saturday mornings, practicing with *Finesse* on Sundays, and my Dad and I were stealing gym time up at the high school to throw and field pop ups and ground balls.

One night in January my Dad and I started my throwing warm up routine in the balcony of the East Kentwood fieldhouse. There were basketball practices on the main gym floor, so we decided to get warmed up in this out of the way area behind the bleachers. From the earliest days of my softball career, my Dad had insisted on a slow careful warm up process to ensure my arm was stretched out and loose before I threw hard. Coach Youtzy and Coach Greenman had reinforced this habit with their own warm up routines and I had carried the discipline with me to *Finesse*.

As we began our warm up this day, something felt different, and not in a good way. My arm had been tight for a couple of weeks, but I hadn't thought much of it. But as we tossed the ball harder, all of a sudden I felt a stabbing pain in my right shoulder. I let out a yelp and grabbed my shoulder. Dad immediately asked what was wrong. He could hear the worry in my voice as I described the pain. He worked with me to try to stretch my shoulder and loosen it up. Then we tried a couple of soft tosses. No pain; so far so good. We stepped back a few paces and I let loose with a harder throw. I was brought up short by a stab of pain. By now I was really worried. I could tell my Dad was, too.

We decided that was enough for the night. We needed to call a doctor right away to see what was wrong. I was feeling frantic and began to choke up a bit. Dad tried to comfort me as we changed from our training shoes to boots and packed up all the equipment. There wasn't much my Dad could say to make me feel better as we made the short drive home. We called our doctor the next day and received a referral to an orthopedic surgeon who would evaluate my shoulder, decide what tests should be performed and then prescribe any necessary treatment. Meanwhile, I shut down all practice except my hitting sessions with Curtis. I didn't want to make a bad situation worse.

A few days later we saw the orthopedic surgeon. He listened as I described the pain I was experiencing and he manipulated my shoulder to see if he could detect any injury. He also tested my strength and said it appeared my right shoulder was weak compared to the left shoulder...the opposite of what you would expect from a right handed softball player. My Dad and Mom explained my situation. I was going into my last year of high school softball, had signed to play at Notre Dame, and was planning to play travel ball all summer. We told the surgeon we wanted to exhaust every test as quickly as possible so we could get to the bottom of the problem immediately.

In the days leading up to the appointment, my confidence in my softball dream had been seriously shaken. The start of my senior season of high school ball was a little more than two months away. After our near miss in the state semifinals as juniors, we expected to challenge for a state championship as seniors. I wanted desperately to be part of that. I was also intent on rejoining my *Finesse* teammates at winter practices so my game would be hitting on all cylinders when the high school season started. I wanted to have a great travel ball season to show the Notre Dame coaching staff that they would be getting a great player in the fall. Most of all, I wanted to arrive on campus filled with confidence and ready to challenge for a starting position on the Irish softball team. I'd be lying if I didn't fear that all of my dreams were about to be snatched away.

The doctor said he was confident that I had simply strained my shoulder and that a few weeks of physical therapy would help ease the damage and strengthen the shoulder to prevent further damage. I arranged to see Jolene again to get my arm back in shape. Although the doctor's assurance that I had a minor problem made me hopeful and lightened the dark cloud of doubt that had filled my mind, I had hoped he would arrange an immediate MRI of the shoulder to make absolutely sure there was nothing more serious going on. He said the test was not necessary and that I just needed to rebuild the strength in my arm.

Now that I had some idea of what was wrong with my shoulder, I needed to call Coach Gumpf and let her know I had a problem. I felt awful as I dialed the phone. I wasn't sure what she would say when I told her my "money arm", as Jolene called it, was hurt. I hated the thought that I might now be perceived as damaged goods and that Coach Gumpf might not want me on her team.

As I described my injury to her, I could tell Coach Gumpf was concerned. Then she told me that I was the third of the seven-player 2005 recruiting class to report an arm or shoulder injury in the previous several weeks. "Don't pull any punches," she said, "tell me what's wrong." I told her what we knew and what we were doing to make sure my shoulder was completely healed as quickly as possible. Before hanging up, I promised to keep Coach Gumpf informed of my rehabilitation progress.

Then I was left to worry about my suddenly uncertain future as a softball player. I had gone from the top of the world—recruited and accepted by a great university with an elite softball program—to the pits in a little over three months. But there was no time to dwell on my misfortune. I had just a few weeks to get my shoulder back in shape so I could get back on the field. I was determined to get through this setback and come back stronger than ever.

If there was a way to recover completely and get back to full strength, I knew Jolene would make it happen. She had helped get me when I had suffered the 'hematoma from hell' years earlier. I was sure if anyone could get me back on the field this time, Jolene was the one. Together, we attacked my rehabilitation with no holds barred. We stretched, manipulated, exercised and otherwise worked my shoulder carefully and as strenuously as we dared. We gave it all we had for six weeks. After a follow-up exam by the doctor showed my strength was improving and I seemed pain free, it was time to test the arm again with some real throwing.

I was hoping the change in my shoulder's condition would be like the difference between night and day, but the results after six weeks of rehabilitation were less clear than that. My arm felt stronger and there was less pain, but it wasn't 100 percent. We went back to the doctor and this time implored him to refer us for an MRI at a local hospital. I was running out of time before the high school softball season would start. Travel ball would begin right after that and at the end of the summer I would be leaving home to begin my softball career at Notre Dame. This was no time for a slow, methodical approach to treatment. Fortunately the doctor agreed to the test.

MRI

We took the first available appointment for the MRI. We were planning a trip to see family in Pennsylvania over spring break and wanted to get the test and the results before we left town for a week. I didn't think I could stand waiting that entire week to receive the results and to get the doctor's judgment about the next steps in repairing my broken wing.

An MRI, or magnetic resonance imaging test, is a type of medical imaging used like x-rays or other types of scans to see the internal structures of the body. While today, MRI equipment has been installed in many locations in the Grand Rapids area, back in 2005, there were few machines in town and those were booked solid for weeks in advance. I had to wait for an opening to get my test.

Most shoulder injuries are due to a problem with the soft tissue in the shoulder joint. MRI's provide a better view of the soft tissues of the body than other types of scans. Short of cutting my shoulder open and looking directly inside, the MRI would give the doctors the best view of my rotator cuff, labrum, biceps and other cartilage, tendons, ligaments and muscles that control the upper arm and shoulder joint.

Before entering the room where the MRI would be performed, an x-ray technician injected a dye into my shoulder and performed traditional x-rays for a preliminary look at my shoulder joint. My parents and I were able to review the results of the x-ray test as the radiologist described what he could see. The results did not show any specific damage to the tissue inside my shoulder.

The next step was the MRI itself. My parents waited outside the room where the MRI would take place as the nurses and technicians prepared me for the test. I lay on a flat surface and was positioned within the large scanning ring where I lay motionless as the scan was performed. It took forever.

When the test was finally completed, I got dressed and joined my parents for a brief meeting with the radiologist who said his initial review of the results did not detect a significant injury but that he would have to review the results more closely and allow my doctor to review them before he could say for sure if there was anything seriously wrong.

The test results were supposed to be delivered to my doctor's office that Friday, just before we were scheduled to leave for Pennsylvania. There was no way I was going to leave town for a week without knowing the results of the test. The suspense was killing me. My entire softball career seemed to hang in the balance. I had to know what was wrong so we could do something about it.

By Friday, we were on pins and needles. Our trip to Pennsylvania was planned, in part, to allow my Mom's large family to celebrate the signing of my letter of intent with Notre Dame. My aunt and uncle had rented a hall and there would be nearly a hundred people there to see me. We only saw my Mom's family once or twice a year, so it was going to be a big deal. I hoped the MRI results would give me some good news to make the ten-hour drive to Pennsylvania and the family reunion a lot more enjoyable.

My Dad called the doctor's office early Friday afternoon and, wouldn't you know it, the doctor had left on his own spring break trip earlier in the day and the test results were on his desk unread. Dad's emphatic request for information to help get us through the next week convinced the nurse to read the report to us but, without the doctor's interpretation, the written notes didn't tell us much. Seeing our family was a lot of fun, but the cloud of doubt hung over us the entire week we were away.

When we finally reached the doctor the following week, he said I likely had an inflamed rotator cuff tendon which was causing an impingement as the neighboring tissue was trapped and squeezed under the top of the scapula bone in my shoulder. He prescribed icing and more physical therapy to resolve the problem. I headed back to Jolene for additional therapy but I had the doctor's approval to begin throwing and playing with my high school team.

Senior Leadership

My high school coach had been following the progress of my arm and had made the decision to move me from shortstop to second base to reduce the length of the throws I would need to make to convert outs at first base. I had never been as comfortable playing second base as I was at shortstop. The ball seemed to come at me from the wrong direction, the throws to first were mostly short flips and tosses and it just seemed like alien territory to me after playing shortstop and third base for so many years. Julie, who had played second the previous year, took over at shortstop, completing the new look for our middle infield. I didn't know it at the time, but I had played my last game as a shortstop.

I continued to rehab my shoulder throughout the high school season as I grew accustomed to my new position on the right side of the infield. We began to rack up the wins as De, Julie and I led the team offensively and Ali provided us with strong pitching to keep our opponents at bay. Defensively, we were not flawless, but we were more than a match for most of our opponents.

Unfortunately our high school season did not last as long as we had hoped. We were eliminated in the state regional tournament by our West Michigan high school rival, Jenison. It was a bitter loss because we had chances to take the lead and win the final game but couldn't get the hits or make the plays in the field in clutch situations. It wasn't the ending we had dreamed of for our high school careers.

If there was a silver lining in the season, it was the opportunity I had to become friends with the younger girls on the team. I tried to help build team unity on a squad split about evenly between seniors and underclassmen. I wanted the younger girls to be comfortable playing with us and to enjoy being on the team. Just three years earlier, I had joined the varsity as a freshman. Although I had four freshman teammates to keep me company, it really helped that one of the seniors on that team took me under wing to help me relax and perform to my full potential.

As one of four team captains, I felt it was my responsibility to lead by example and to offer guidance and friendship to any teammate who wanted or needed help. I feel strongly that classism is the enemy of high school or college team unity, and without a strong, inclusive team culture, you can't be successful in softball, basketball, soccer or any other sport where everyone has to contribute to achieve team success. The old saying that a team is only as strong as its weakest link is true. It wasn't my job to singlehandedly improve my teammates' softball skills (although I would help in any way I could). As I saw it, my job as captain was to make sure that lack of individual confidence; awe of older players; the criticism of coaches, teammates or spectators; or other factors did not keep every girl on the team from realizing their full potential on the field. Just as important, I wanted my teammates to remember Greg Youtzy's most important rule: relax and have some fun. If we all remembered that rule, we'd play our best individually and as a team.

The single greatest byproduct of reaching out to my teammates—as a captain in high school, and less formally in travel ball and college—has been the friendships I gained in the process. You don't think about it at the time, but at the end of a sports career, you are left with a lot of memories. But memories really only exist in the past. In my experience the best thing you take away from the softball field are the friendships that live on after your playing days are over. In the end, softball really is all about the team and your teammates.

Back to Summer Ball

The end of our high school season brought with it the start of what we assumed would be our last season of summer travel ball. This season would be a bit of an anticlimax after the previous recruiting campaign. But anyone who has ever earned a college athletic scholarship will tell you earning a spot on a college team doesn't mean it's time to coast through your final high school and travel ball seasons. For one thing, you want to prove to everyone who watches you that you deserved the scholarship. You also want to let your college coaches know they made the right decision when they offered you a spot on their team. And, no one wants her last year of ball before college to be a bust.

My arm was feeling better and I was hoping I'd be able to play in my familiar third base or shortstop spots on the Finesse 18-and-under team. But Kevin Kilburn, our coach, decided to let returning college players play those two positions and plugged me in at first base. I was fine with the decision, even though I had never played first in my career. After limping through my senior season in high school with a weak wing, I was relieved that my shoulder was feeling stronger and I was looking forward to playing at full strength for the first time in months. Kevin could have probably put me at catcher and I would have gladly put on the pads and hunkered down behind the plate.

As it turned out, I took to playing first base pretty naturally. I wasn't convinced the position was permanent, so I didn't run out and buy a big first baseman's mitt. My small 11-inch middle infielder's glove would work just fine. I used the agility I had gained in my years as a middle infielder to quickly adjust position and snare errant throws from my teammates and to cover ground on the right side of the infield to ensure we were strong defensively down the line and seamless between first and second base.

The one play that took some getting used to was the bunt. I had fielded plenty of bunts at third, charging hard, fielding the ball and quickly releasing a strong throw across my body to first. But at first, the footwork and resulting throw were completely different. I still had to charge quickly and field the ball cleanly, but first base was no longer in front of me. It was directly behind me. I had to pivot 180 degrees and then get off a strong accurate throw to the second baseman who would be sprinting over to cover the bag.

I had to learn this skill on the fly because our season began immediately after the end of the high school campaign and, because of my injury, I had not practiced on the field with *Finesse* all winter. I didn't get tested until the second tournament of the summer. We were playing outside of Chicago and came up against a team that played small ball as if Jon Greenman was coaching them. It wasn't long before one of their hitters lay down a perfect bunt between first and the pitcher's circle, I was charging and fielded the ball without hesitation. I whirled and let loose a bullet, but the ball sailed over the outstretched glove of the second baseman and into right field. Dang! I hated making errors.

My screw up had not escaped the attention of the coach in the other dugout. The very next batter lay down an identical bunt. I charged and snatched the ball up, whirled and did exactly the same thing. Now I was really shook up. I had been playing softball for years. Sure I had played bad games before, but here I was at what should be the pinnacle of my travel ball career and all of a sudden I can't field the bunt.

My errors ended up costing us a couple of runs. But worse than that, they sent my self-confidence tumbling. My teammates' attempts to cheer me up couldn't bolster my spirits. Fortunately, Lauren, our shortstop, hit a bomb to left field to drive in the tying and go-ahead runs, allowing us to pull out the win. The next day as we warmed up before our game, Kevin took Julie and me aside for some extra practice on the short game. He laid down bunt after bunt as I charged from first base, fielded, whirled and threw. I hit Julie square in the glove with a bullet every time. Kevin called a halt to practice and, with my confidence restored, we trotted off the field to get ready for the umpire to shout, "Play ball!"

I was solid against the bunt the rest of the year. But I relearned a valuable lesson that weekend in Chicago. No one is perfect, especially when it comes to sports. The best hitters in baseball or softball get a hit an average of three to four times out of ten. That means they fail more often than they succeed at the plate. In the field, some girls manage to achieve a fielding percentage of 1,000. But that's a lofty goal if you play a position where you handle the ball a lot every game. Mistakes are going to happen, especially if you play the game aggressively.

The key is to keep your mistakes in perspective. Understand why they happen. Learn from them. Then forget about them. Making yourself miserable about an error by dwelling on it won't erase it, but it can distract you and shake your confidence enough to lead to more mistakes. There's an old saying about the right way to celebrate a great play or win: "Act like you have been there before." It's a great reminder to be dignified, gracious and humble in victory. But I think it's also a great way to keep an error, a strikeout, or a defeat in perspective. Every great athlete has experienced failure. When you think about it, sulking about an error is the same as thinking you are the first athlete in all of creation who is not supposed to ever make a mistake. Get over yourself!

I wish it was a lesson I didn't have to relearn again later in my softball career. But, as a perfectionist, I have a pretty thick skull when it comes to forgetting about my failures. Over the course of my career I got better at leaving them behind. But on more than one occasion it took some processing time before I let it go and was mentally ready to win again.

Leaving Home

My senior year of high school seemed like a nine-month whirlwind of activity, all aimed at the graduation ceremony in May. Summer wasn't a lot different. There were fewer months and the end goal was the trip to South Bend to begin my college career. But the whirlwind part was identical. In between the travel ball tournaments every weekend, my Mom and I took care of pulling together the wardrobe, bedding and other things I would need to move from home to the dorm to begin life without the built-in support system my parents had always provided.

There were also graduation open houses to attend, one for each of my senior friends. Some weeks we'd go to three or four a day. We had to plan well in advance to be sure I could attend as many as possible. The parties were a distraction from the knowledge that each of us was headed our own way and we would not be seeing each other almost every day now that high school was over. The string of open houses stretched through June and into July, which meant I had to miss several due to travel ball. All the preparations to begin the next chapter in my life made playing on weekends both a relief and a burden. I still loved playing, but racing off every Thursday to another tournament and getting home late Sunday evening meant cramming an entire week of college preparation into three days.

Still, I was excited to begin my Notre Dame career. I began to trade notes with the girl who would be my roommate in Welsh Family Hall so we could decide who would bring what to furnish our dorm room. It seemed like every day I would get some correspondence from Notre Dame itself covering one more detail to be managed before I started school, or with information about freshman orientation. There were lots of checks for my parents to write for this thing or that. Every day I was growing more and more anxious to get to campus and begin my college experience.

Then in the middle of the summer, I was reminded how quickly things can change in college softball. I received a note from Coach Gumpf announcing that her assistant, Charmelle Green, would be leaving Irish softball to accept a position in the Athlete Academic Development office of the university. I was stunned. Charmelle had discovered me at the Notre Dame hitting camp the winter of my junior year of high school. She had scouted me during my summer recruiting season. And she had pushed and encouraged me during my week at the Irish summer softball camp. I had been looking forward to getting to campus and having Charmelle make good on her promise to make me a better player.

The only thing that kept me from being totally shocked by the turnover in the coaching staff was the insight Donny had shared during the recruiting process. He had cautioned us that coaching changes are common in softball or any college sport. He advised us to choose a school we would be happy to attend even if the coach who recruited us was no longer there, or if our softball career ended early.

I felt bad that I would not get the chance to be coached by Charmelle, but Coach Gumpf was still the head coach and Coach Ganeff was staying on as one of her assistants. I had accepted their offer to play Irish softball because I wanted to play for all three coaches, not just Charmelle. The speed with which coaching situations can change in college softball was soon reinforced. I learned before the summer was over that the head coaches at Purdue and Wisconsin, two programs I had considered, were no longer with those schools. Indiana had experienced a coaching change the year before and would change coaches again three years later. Compared to those programs, Notre Dame had great coaching stability.

Later in the summer, while we were participating in the ASA Gold Nationals in Salinas, California, I was introduced to Charmelle's replacement, former Irish star Lizzy Lemire. Lizzy would coach the outfielders and serve as hitting coach for the Irish during the four years of my Notre Dame career. At the start, Lizzy seemed a little more quiet than Charmelle, but she brought with her a wealth of experience gained in her college career and an understanding of the challenges we all faced in balancing the academic and athletic demands at Notre Dame. She was as committed to winning and individual excellence as any Notre Dame coach in any sport. Lizzy would draw on her intense inner drive to push us to reach our full potential as players and as a team.

After the national tournament in California, our season was over and two weeks later I found myself in the car headed to South Bend for freshman move-in day. When we arrived on campus, the traffic and activity outside the dorms made the atmosphere a lot different than my earlier visits. It was a madhouse. We slowly maneuvered our car through the traffic and onto the lawn in front of Welsh Family Hall, which is located near the South Dining Hall in an area of newer dorms on the Notre Dame campus. I had already said my goodbyes to my boyfriend, A.J., my brother Andy and Gus, the family pooch. Saying goodbye to my Mom and Dad would take a little longer because we had a two-day orientation schedule set up by the academic and athletic sides of the college.

Although most colleges and universities have student dormitories, at Notre Dame dorms have a special significance. There are no fraternities or sororities at Notre Dame. Instead, most students establish an allegiance to their dorm starting in their freshman years and maintain that bond throughout their years at Notre Dame. Except in special circumstances, students at Notre Dame must live in the dorms for the first three years of their academic careers. If they maintain their grades at a high enough level, they are allowed to move into an off campus apartment or house in their senior year. Athletes have to meet a higher academic standard to move off campus as seniors.

I was to find that my busy schedule as a student athlete prevented me from participating in dorm life as fully as a non-athlete. But, unlike many of my friends at other universities who would treat dorm life as a temporary, one-year inconvenience, I was moving into the place that would serve as my home away from home for at least three years. Might as well get comfortable, I was going to be here for a while!

We made the trek up to the second floor of the dorm at least a dozen times as we moved my clothing and bedding into the dorm. My roommate was also there and we stacked our beds, set up our desks, and arranged the futon and television in the remaining floor space. I had to listen humbly to my Dad as he reminded me several times about his less luxurious college experience without a TV or a sofa. My parents and I went shopping at a local home center and bought a piece of carpeting for the floor and a mini fridge for snacks. At this point my Dad remarked that the only thing refrigerated in his dorm room had been the plain tile floor under his bare feet every winter morning. My Mom and I responded in unison with, "Give it a rest!" and Dad wandered off to buy a utility knife and some tape so we could install the carpet in my room. By the end of the afternoon, the place was transformed into a small, but comfortable apartment for two.

After setting up the dorm room, we walked over to the bookstore and picked up the books I had preordered for my classes. Dad and Mom bought some ND gear for themselves and a few souvenirs for relatives. The place was packed with others doing the same. With most of the basics taken care of, we were ready to relax. Fortunately, we were scheduled to attend a dinner hosted by Coach Gumpf for the freshmen and their parents. After a day of lifting and toting boxes and suitcases up to my dorm room, and shopping and searching for parking spaces among the throngs of families in town for move-in day, we were looking forward to some down time.

There were seven freshmen families, so Coach's deck was pretty crowded as we dug into the lasagna and pizza. The informal atmosphere gave us a chance to get to know the other freshmen players and their families. We also had a chance to talk with the coaches about the start of fall practice, which would begin right after physicals and team meetings. Coach Gumpf formally welcomed us to the program and set some basic ground rules for our parents so there would be no misunderstandings as we began our

Irish careers. The rules sounded a lot like the ones Donny had set for players and families at our first team meeting with him. The Irish softball team was Coach Gumpf's responsibility and, while she was available to talk with parents by appointment, she would only talk to them about their own daughter and not other players. Also off the table were discussions of playing time, player positions, or other coaching decisions. As Donny had predicted, the softball relationships that counted most to Coach Gumpf were the ones she would have directly with her players. We were now adults and on our own. Coach Gumpf expected to have our complete and undivided attention as she molded us into a winning team.

The next day, we attended orientation for Notre Dame's Freshman Year of Studies program, the rigorous academic coursework that every freshman at the school must complete. Then we headed over to the DeBartolo performing arts center for freshmen athlete orientation. The program shared a lot of information but also was designed to inspire us to embrace Notre Dame's long history of athletic excellence. We learned about the academic support programs the university would provide to ensure our success and the high academic expectations the university had for its student-athletes.

The program ended with a highlight video of triumphant Notre Dame performances across all sports in past years. The video was accompanied by a soaring female vocalist singling *"Here Come the Irish"*, a tune that is guaranteed to put a lump in your throat and bring a tear to your eye. For our parents, who were witnessing the culmination of their daughters' academic and softball dreams—and who were also about to say goodbye to us—the struggle to hold back the tears was especially hard. As players, we were starting out on the biggest adventure of our lives but our parents were going home to pick up the lives they had largely put on hold when our travel softball careers began. Mom, Dad and I hugged a little longer than usual when the time to say goodbye finally came. I have to confess, my eyes were leaking a little bit as I watched Mom and Dad drive away.

Notre Dame Life

With move-in day and orientation behind us, my freshman teammates and I quickly got down to business. We began attending classes and received our introduction to mandatory freshman study periods in DeBartolo Hall. We also received our physicals and the first of our "issues", the workout clothes, shoes and other equipment we would use for conditioning, workouts and practices during the coming year.

Notre Dame had a contract with Adidas for athletic shoes and apparel, so our sweats, shorts, tee shirts, training shoes, spikes, socks and other gear had the company's familiar three-stripe emblem. The softball team also had a contract with Worth, which supplied bats, fielders' gloves, batting helmets, and batting gloves. Notre Dame did not scrimp on equipment and apparel. Our issues included everything we would need to perform on the practice field and in games. When we received the first of our new gear, we began to feel like we were really part of Notre Dame Softball.

We absolutely knew we were part of the team when we began team workouts and conditioning sessions with Mike Joseph, our strength and conditioning coach. Mike made it his personal mission to exhaust us in his quest to make us stronger and fitter than we had ever been before. I had always worked hard to stay in shape and, at one time was ranked second in total weight lifted by a girl in our high school weight room. I believed I could handle just about everything Mike threw at us without throwing up or collapsing on the turf of the Loftus indoor practice facility. Still, running sprint after sprint up and down the field until my knees were weak and my lungs burned was like nothing I had ever experienced before. It seemed like a million years removed from the winter day a year-and-a-half earlier when Charmelle had discovered me at the Irish hitting camp in this same facility.

Earlier in the summer, each of us had received a thick book containing the workout plan we were supposed to follow before we arrived on campus. I spent a lot of hours at the high school working the plan. There was no way I was going to show up as the weak link in our seven-woman freshman team-within-a-team. Still, Mike and the coaches did their best in our first several weeks on campus to surpass the level of strength and conditioning work I had expected.

Practices were more of the same. In addition to team practices on the softball field or inside the Eck hitting facility, we had individual workouts with the coaches. The NCAA sets limits on athlete practice time, but within those limits, we accomplished a lot to prepare us to perform on the field. Some mornings our day would start at 6 a.m. with a team workout session. We'd then head to class or to study but later meet Lizzy or another coach for an individual workout. After more classes or study sessions, we'd have team practice in the afternoon. Then it was off to dinner in the South Dining Hall and study hall at DeBartolo before we headed for bed to rest up so we'd be ready to do it all over again the next morning.

The upperclassmen had been through all of this before. They knew the drills, which meant the freshmen had to get up to speed fast. It wasn't long before we were practicing like veterans. Or at least we felt like we were. But seven freshmen is a lot of newcomers for a softball team to absorb in one year. We outnumbered the seniors, we outnumbered the juniors, and we outnumbered the sophomores. And before long, it was clear that some of us might win starting positions at the expense of upperclassmen who had been patiently—no, make that *impatiently*—waiting their turn on the field.

No one who is recruited to play college softball lacks confidence. We all strongly believe we are good enough to start and become a star. You don't get this far in your athletic career without confidence and the skill to back it up. But, a softball roster can be 18 to 20 players deep and only nine players can take the field at a time. Even if you add in a second starting pitcher and a designated player (DP) who hits in place of the pitcher (the equivalent of a designated hitter in baseball), that still leaves almost an entire team 'riding the pine' in the dugout during the games. The competition for playing time can erode unity and eat away at the fabric of a team. The best antidote for the ultracompetitive mindset of individual athletes is respect. Each player has to respect her teammates and the coaches have to respect every player on the team. When you respect all of your teammates as your equals, you acknowledge that they all deserve to play.

Seen that way, winning a spot on the field becomes less about beating out your teammates and more about performing at your personal best and helping the team win. If you play your best and still can't break into the line-up, it's not your teammates' fault. Coaches can reinforce this mindset by treating everyone the same and showing they respect each player's ability. The last thing a coach wants is to create resentment or reduce motivation by favoring some players over others.

Even if you can't break into the starting line-up, every team needs role players to be successful. A player with speed and great base running instincts can contribute runs in a pinch running role that can mean the difference between wins and losses. A defensive specialist can enter a game in the late innings and make a great catch to preserve a narrow lead. And a relief pitcher can come in for a couple of innings and baffle an aggressive opponent with a steady menu of off speed pitches or "junk" while saving the arm of a starter who might be needed later in the weekend. Accepting your role, working hard to excel, and delivering in the clutch allow role players to contribute to team success and earn the respect of their teammates and coaches.

But on any team respect doesn't come automatically or overnight. On the 2005-06 Irish softball team, the upperclassmen probably thought the seven freshmen who joined them in the fall were arrogant brats who felt they were automatically entitled to start for the Irish while everyone else took a seat on the bench. Whatever first impression we made, some of the older girls clearly felt a little humbling was in order. On the practice field, in the weight room, and in our conditioning workouts, we received plenty of blunt criticism from our big sisters. They expected the seven newcomers to keep up. When we didn't, we heard about it from the team captains and the rest of our older teammates, all of whom were not going to let seven freshmen hold the team back. Coming off of our senior seasons in high school and a final year of travel ball, none of us were accustomed to life at the low end of the pecking order. Some of my classmates took it more personally than I did.

Each of us managed to really irritate our older teammates and coaches on at least one occasion in the first weeks of our Irish careers. My chance to earn my coaches' and teammates' ire came early one morning when the cell phone alarm I had carefully set the night before failed to do its job. The battery had lost its charge during the night. I awoke with a start as the conventional telephone on the desk rang frantically. I was confused at first. Neither my roommate nor I ever used that phone. Everyone we knew called our cell phones. I stumbled from my bunk and, lifting the handset, heard a teammate urgently ask where I was. I was still a bit groggy and not entirely sure where I was. But I quickly grasped that I wasn't where I was supposed to be...at the Loftus practice field where my teammates were already preparing to begin our scheduled 6 a.m. workout.

I looked at the clock and saw it was 5:55 a.m. I threw on my sweats and sprinted across campus on my bike, but, it was no use... I was about five minutes too late. As a result of my carelessness, the entire team had to do a punishment run that Friday. Believe me, they were not happy, especially the upperclassmen. I felt terrible. I never wanted to let my team down. The lesson stuck. I was never late for a practice or workout again during my Irish career. Say what you will about the harmful effects of peer pressure on the young, on the Irish softball team fear of disappointing your teammates or coaches was a powerful motivator and source of personal discipline for all of us.

It wasn't long until our teammates and coaches were referring to the seven freshmen as "the cult". We didn't purposely stay apart from the rest of the team. But as our elders on the team sent more than a few barbed comments our way, we naturally circled the wagons, gravitating to the classmates who shared our pain. That was one of the advantages of a seven-girl class. We had a built-in support system to lean on when our older sisters were displeased with us.

Fortunately, most Irish veterans and underclassmen were motivated to break down the barriers quickly. As our fall softball games drew closer and the coaching staff turned up the heat on the entire team, the divisions between classes began to dissolve. The daily routine of strength training, conditioning, individual workouts and team practices brought us closer together. With the coaches and training staff there to point out everyone's shortcomings and push us to do better, who had the time or energy to criticize teammates? It was hard enough to muster enough energy to complain about how Mike was dominating us in conditioning sessions or how the coaches were pushing us to pick it up during practices.

While we were getting whipped into shape by the softball program, our professors were also imposing academic discipline on us. We quickly understood why Notre Dame has invested so heavily in academic support for athletes. With so many sport-related activities to fill our days and evenings, it was all we could do to keep up with the boatloads of reading, practice quizzes and tests, group assignments, papers, and other work outside of the classroom. We also had to be sure to attend every class, every day. Attendance was an absolute requirement to remain academically eligible to play ball. None of us were academic slouches. Even athletes have to be good students to get into Notre Dame. But this workload was unlike anything we had ever experienced.

On a typical day, we'd be up for our early morning workout, head to classes for most of the morning, attend practice in the afternoon, and rush off for dinner, before resuming our studies alone or in groups. Three nights a week, those studies would mean heading over to DeBartolo for mandatory study hall from 8:30 p.m. until 10:30 p.m. We'd be back in our dorm rooms by around 11 p.m. and, unless we had some additional studying to take care of, fall into bed.

Despite all of the demands on our time we still found some free moments to hang out together. It wasn't long before we were making friends outside of the team—from the dorms, our classes, or other athletes we'd meet at DeBartolo during study halls. The freshman athlete study halls were on two floors of DeBartolo and teams were paired up. We ended up paired with the football team, which turned out to be a great combination. It gave us the chance to meet and make friends with athletes from diverse backgrounds who were also passionate about their sport and who, like us, were shouldering the workload and responsibilities that came with being a successful college athlete.

Softball and football players seem to both have a fun loving side. Ninety-nine percent of the time we were able to keep that impulse in check during study hall...we all chose Notre Dame knowing we needed to perform in the classroom as well as on the field. But occasionally, we would let loose. One time a baseball game of sorts broke out in the corridor outside of our study hall and football and softball players both swung for the fences using someone's umbrella for a bat amid lots of laughing and razzing.

We did have some free time and we began hanging out with our older teammates. There were soccer games and other sporting events to go to, not to mention the weekend celebrations that surround Notre Dame football. Football weekends not only brought us together as a team, they brought all Irish students—plus alumni, families, friends and fans—together to cheer the Irish on to victory on the gridiron.

Football Irish Style

When most people think of Notre Dame, they think of football. Notre Dame has one of the most storied college football programs in the country. While there are many schools with strong football traditions, not many have had movies made about them like the timeless "Rudy". Very few have launched acting careers that turned into presidencies like Notre Dame did for Ronald Reagan who starred in "Knute Rockne, All American". And no other school has a nationwide fan base consisting not only of past students and their families and friends, but also the famed "subway alumni" who have adopted Notre Dame as their team even though most have never set foot on campus.

Notre Dame football is also the team fans of other teams love to hate. This strong anti-Irish sentiment is often also extended to other Irish athletic teams. The fact that, in football, Notre Dame is an independent school that has its own national television contract seems to make Notre Dame a lightning rod for criticism. But the fact is, the TV network that pays the contract wouldn't do so if it wasn't good business. Notre Dame Football is a national brand that puts butts in the seats, both in front of television sets as well as at Notre Dame Stadium (and other schools' stadiums when the Irish are on the road). Advertisers looking for an ardent audience of college fans can't do much better than sponsoring a Notre Dame football broadcast.

Still, fans of other schools have been known to say that, on any football Saturday, they root for their favorite team and for whichever team is playing against Notre Dame. For our part, Irish fans don't mind that our team is the one everyone else wants to beat. It just makes football weekend that much more exciting and our wins that much sweeter.

Fan or foe, anyone who has ever spent a football weekend on the Notre Dame campus understands that it is a special experience. First, the beauty of the campus itself is heightened in autumn as the trees change colors, the geese fly over in 'Vs', and the walkways and parking lots are crowded with visitors sporting Irish gear who are often also filled with a bit of Irish cheer.

Football weekends begin on Friday afternoon as classes wind down and students retire to their dorms and off campus houses, apartments and condominiums to get ready for at least a half a weekend away from classes and books. The Friday festivities kick off with a pep rally at the Joyce Athletic and Convocation Center— known on campus as "the JACC". Other fall sports often host opponents on their respective athletic fields, offering opportunities for Irish fans to warm up their lungs. For many, Football Friday means party time. Like any college town, South Bend has its share of bars and restaurants catering to the student crowd and weekend visitors. Houses, apartments and condominiums are also gathering spots for pre-game celebrations.

I've never been much of a partier, but my reasons for taking it easy were pragmatic. Mike, our conditioning coach, was all too willing to remind us that a night of partying would undo the gains in strength and conditioning we had worked so hard to attain all week long. Even without that reminder, big-time partying wasn't my style. But I didn't begrudge other people a good time. I liked going to parties to talk and laugh with friends, meet new people, and just relax. After a week of studying, working out, and practicing, I deserved a break.

Most of us would sleep in on Saturday morning before the game. With early morning workouts and classes most days of the week, I really relished getting up late on autumn Saturdays. But I couldn't sleep in too long. By mid- morning the text messages and phone calls would begin flying between teammates and friends as we began to plan where we'd meet to start tailgating. The softball team had its own tailgate party before most games and we wanted to be on hand early for all the food and fun. If softball recruits were on hand for their official visits, some of us would serve as their hosts. It was our responsibility to make sure the recruits rolled out of bed, had breakfast if they wanted it, and were at the tailgate in time to spend time with their parents and the coaches before the game. Non-hosts still wanted to be on-hand to spend time with the recruits and share in the good times between teammates.

Shortly before kickoff, we'd troop into the stadium and head for the student section where we'd stand along with all of the other students for the entire first half. During the game, cheering was almost non-stop. Every time the Irish scored, students would be hoisted over head and perform pushups, one for every point. Doing the pushups was a workout, but holding someone over your head while they did it was a real endurance test!

By halftime we'd be hoarse after calling out "We Are N D" and other cheers over and over again. We'd take a seat on the wooden bleachers, watch the band perform, talk with teammates, and text friends at other schools who were enjoying their own festivities on campuses across the country. I'd often text my cousins Wendy and Randy who were at Penn State and always willing to razz me about my choice of college. After standing for the entire second half cheering and doing lots of pushups to celebrate Irish scores, we'd join the postgame tailgate scene outside the stadium and make plans for the evening. It wasn't long, though, before we were looking ahead to class assignments and our softball training schedule. By Sunday morning, it was time to get back to work.

Fall Ball

NCAA rules govern off-season team practice and conditioning. Most softball programs try to get the maximum allowable practice and conditioning time in before the late fall cut-off prescribed by the NCAA. Coaches use this time to assess the talent on the team, identify positions on the field where they think specific players can make the greatest contribution, and decide what individual and team skills to work on over the winter and in preseason practices.

Fall practices at Notre Dame culminate in a couple of fall ball tournaments with other college teams. Although the fall games are little more than exhibition games, for the players, they are the pot of gold at the end of the rainbow...the reward for all the hard work on the practice field, in the batting cage, in the weight room, and on the indoor turf during conditioning sessions. For me and my freshman teammates, it was our turn to show we were ready to take the field and help our Irish team to victory.

Coach Gumpf had recruited me as an infielder and outfielder and I received practice time in both areas. But with plenty of returning athletes in the infield, I spent most of my time working in the outfield. That was fine with me. I had played lots of outfield in my travel ball career and enjoyed playing there. However, I soon learned that, as good as my arm had felt when I had arrived on campus in August, the huge amount of throwing the Irish coaches put us through during every practice was taking its toll. Instead of getting stronger, the more I threw, the weaker my shoulder and arm became. It wasn't long before I was feeling a sharp pain like someone was stabbing me in the shoulder and arm. The training staff applied plenty of ice after every practice and we began a stretching routine and some strengthening exercises, but the pain would not go away and the arm just would not gain strength.

Coach scheduled a consultation with an orthopedic surgeon who assessed my arm and shoulder. After discussing my history, including the months of physical therapy I had already been through, the doctor said he advised surgery to repair what he believed was a rotator cuff or labrum tear in my shoulder. He said we would not know the exact extent of the injury until he could view things during the arthroscopic surgery. I was devastated. Surgery would mean an end to my fall practice and conditioning and would eliminate my chance to play fall ball. It would also mean a lengthy rehabilitation process. It was unlikely I would practice all winter. It was not clear if I would be ready to play the next spring.

Coach said she wanted to shut down my participation in practice and schedule surgery as soon as possible. I pleaded with her to reconsider. I wanted a chance to play in the fall ball tournaments, and I thought if the games went well, maybe I wouldn't need surgery. I wanted to avoid a procedure that could sideline me for my entire freshman year. With only a couple of weeks remaining before the first doubleheader, she agreed to wait until after fall ball, but she said I would probably participate in the games sparingly. Still, I had invested too much in my dream of playing college softball to miss out on my first chance to take the field with my Irish teammates. I wanted to play ball.

Fall ball came and went quickly but I got to pull on the Irish uniform and sprint onto Ivy Field on the Notre Dame campus to officially start my college softball career. Standing along the base line with my teammates for the National Anthem and then hearing the home plate umpire yell, "play ball" was almost unreal. But the start of the action on the field quickly brought me down to earth. I might be finally living my dream, but it was still softball, after all. See it and hit it. Catch it and throw it. Seven innings per game. Twenty one outs per side. Nothing new about any of it. Except this was softball at a higher level than I'd ever experienced.

True to her word, Coach limited my playing time. But I got a taste of what it would be like to take the field as a member of the Irish softball team and that was enough to convince me to accept that I needed surgery to regain my shoulder strength. I was confident that the upcoming operation and months of rehabilitation couldn't keep me from getting back on the field and playing with my Irish teammates in the spring.

Surgery

Just before Thanksgiving, my parents picked me up at the dorm and drove me to the outpatient surgery center where I would go under the knife. Coach Gumpf arrived as the surgeon came out to the waiting area to describe the procedure he planned to perform. The surgery would be completed using an arthroscope, which is much less invasive than the old style of surgery where a large incision was made to give the surgeon access to the shoulder joint. With the "scope", a series of small incisions—three in my case—is made and the surgeon peers into the shoulder joint and performs surgery through a tubular instrument.

To help me understand what was going on with my shoulder, the surgeon had described how this critical softball body part functions. The shoulder is an unstable joint because of the range of motion required for it to function properly. To remain stable, the joint must be anchored by its muscles, tendons, and ligaments. Damage to these soft tissues due to injury or from overuse can cause pain, instability, weakness...serious shoulder problems if you are a softball player.

The first tissue I had to be concerned about was the labrum. A torn labrum would cause my arm to become unstable and move unacceptably in the joint, causing irritation and further injury as well as loss of control of the shoulder. The second thing I had to worry about in my shoulder was the rotator cuff, the structure of tendons that works with muscles to hold the ball of the main upper arm bone in the shoulder socket. If the rotator cuff is irritated, inflamed, and swollen, it can be squeezed by movement of the upper arm in the socket, causing considerable pain. If the rotator cuff is torn, it can catch as the joint moves, causing even sharper pain and forcing adjustments in throwing motion to prevent further tearing.

The surgeon said he believed my rotator cuff was torn and that there was a good chance that my labrum was also damaged. He said he would go in and repair the damage and, with proper rehabilitation, I should regain full strength and resume my softball career without further limitations. Although apprehensive at the thought of surgery, I was anxious to get it over with. Despite my initial reluctance to have surgery, I decided if this was the answer to putting my arm and shoulder problems behind me, then I was ready to go for it.

I woke up in a recovery room feeling no pain but already vaguely aware that my life after surgery would be very different and far more taxing than anything I had ever endured. As I slowly came out of the fog of anesthesia, I learned that the doctor had found more damage in my shoulder joint than he had anticipated. Both the rotator cuff and the labrum were torn and had to be repaired. There was also some fraying of the cuff and evidence of bursitis. Still, he said the necessary repairs had been completed successfully. Although I would have to work hard to rehabilitate the shoulder over the course of the next several months, he expected me to recover fully and be able to resume my career in the spring.

Recovery and Rehabilitation

After a couple of days in a hospital bed in the Notre Dame student health center, I needed to get back to class. My parents had returned home the previous day so Coach Ganeff picked me up and drove me the block and a half to my dorm. In three days I had gone from an active and well-conditioned 18-year-old to a cripple too weak to walk a half a mile.

After my surgery, my shoulder had been immobilized in a bulky sling. My right arm was fixed in the shape of an "L" with my upper arm descending vertically from my surgically repaired shoulder, with a right angle at the elbow directing my forearm horizontally across my chest. The forearm was supported tightly about three-inches in front of my body by a large foam pad. The sling came equipped with a Velcro "cup" inside of the palm of my hand. The cup held a soft rubber ball, which was always at the ready so I could squeeze it to rebuild strength in my confined limb.

Except for showers, during which I would carefully hold my forearm as though it was in an invisible sling, I had to wear the real sling constantly, even while I was sleeping. To make sleeping tolerable, I'd prop a pillow under my shoulder to support it while I lay on my back. The doctor had given me a prescription for Vicodin, a powerful pain medicine, but I didn't care for the queasy, dizzying effect of the medication, so as soon as I could tolerate the discomfort, I switched to ibuprofen, which helped dull the pain and also helped quell the inflammation in my damaged shoulder joint. Whenever I could find the time and the frozen water, I applied ice to the shoulder to further reduce the swelling and inflammation.

Trussed up in my sling, I had to work harder to do a lot of the small daily tasks that we all take for granted. I had to dress myself and brush my hair with one arm, figure out how to tie my shoes, and, when it was time for bed, get into my top bunk bed without help. I couldn't put my long hair up without help. And I could tell right away that getting up and getting to class was going to be a minor ordeal. Fortunately my roommate, Kelsey, helped me conquer the routines necessary to get out the door each morning and get ready for bed at night. I don't know what I would have done without her help.

The days were equally trying. I not only had to get to the dining hall to eat, and to all of my classes, study halls and group project meetings, I also still participated in team strength and conditioning sessions, even if I could only ride a stationary bike and do lower body weight lifting. In addition, I had daily sessions in the training room where the trainer manipulated my arm and put me through an excruciating series of exercises designed to build strength and mobility in my crippled arm. These daily sessions actually began the day after my surgery and continued for the remainder of my freshman year.

For the first few days I was not only physically crippled, but also had to fight through the drowsiness created by the pain medication. I was taking a full academic load in Notre Dame's already challenging First Year of Studies and now I had to work extra hard just to stay awake. Lucky for me, the pain in my shoulder kept me from falling asleep most of the day. Of course, it also meant I wasn't able to get much sleep at night either.

My routine started before dawn and lasted until late at night: I began the day with Kelsey's help getting dressed and snacked on a granola bar as I rushed to 6 a.m. workouts or 8 a.m. classes. I typically had a rehab session between classes in the morning and then squeezed in lunch before heading to more classes or freshman study sessions at DeBartolo Hall. After that there were team strength and conditioning sessions, more studying, dinner, and, if I was caught up on homework, a chance to hang out with teammates or other friends at Reckers or LaFortune, the nearest campus snack shops. Then it was back to the dorm to hoist my body into bed for what I hoped would be a few hours of uninterrupted sleep

Fortunately, I only had to get through two weeks of classes, study week and final exams before I could head home for the holidays and a more forgiving schedule. The old saying, "That which doesn't kill you makes you stronger", must be true because after the first couple of days, I began to take the sling, my lost mobility and even the lingering pain in stride. I focused on rehab, workouts, studying and exams and, before I knew it, the semester was over and I was headed home. There I was greeted by A.J., Mom and Dad, and my old friend Jolene who would take over supervision of my post-surgery rehab until I returned to campus in mid-January. It hadn't been the start I'd envisioned for my college career, but I wasn't discouraged. I'd been hurt before. I was committed to rehabbing my arm completely and coming back stronger than ever. After all, I still had my entire Irish career in front of me.

Winter Break

Getting home for the holidays gave me a chance to exhale deeply and take stock of my situation. A.J. who had graduated with me from East Kentwood High School, was continuing his baseball and academic career locally at Grand Rapids Community College. That meant I'd be able to spend time with him as well as other friends who were home from college for the holidays and buddies who were still in high school.

It was great to be with family and friends but my first order of business was to attack my rehabilitation with the same work ethic that had taken me from the sandlots of the KBL to Ivy Field at Notre Dame. The surgeon had told me that it would take four to six months of almost daily rehabilitation exercises to heal my shoulder and regain the strength necessary to resume my softball career. I immediately did the math. Four months from the date of my surgery meant I could potentially take the field in mid-March, barely a month into the coming season. There was still a chance for me to make some noise on the field as an Irish freshman.

But I knew my goal of helping the team win big in the spring would depend on 120 smaller wins, one for each day of my recovery from surgery. I also knew from my leg injury back in 14-and-under ball that you can't rush the healing process. All you can do is work as hard at rehabilitation as you can, resisting the urge to do more than you should.

The trainers in South Bend armed me with a complete rehab routine to share with Jolene. The stretching, manipulation and massage exercises were designed to carry me through the holidays so I wouldn't miss a beat in the weeks before I would return to campus in mid-January. Mom became my chauffer as we made the trek across town to Jolene's office several days each week for my rehab sessions.

My sessions with Jolene were the few times when my arm and shoulder were free of the sling that at all other times immobilized my right arm and shoulder. The shoulder was still pretty tender even when encased in the sling. But when the sling came off and Jolene started manipulating the shoulder, ouch! I'm not a crier, but at times I wanted to let out a howl as Jolene moved my arm and shoulder to restore my range of motion.

Jolene started as gently as she could, lifting my arm, and moving it slowly into positions that wouldn't faze a healthy shoulder. Although a casual bystander might not think Jolene was giving my shoulder a strenuous workout, just a few weeks after surgery, adhesions and scar tissue were beginning to form in the joint. The surgical repairs themselves were not fully healed. There was still plenty of inflammation, despite lots of ibuprofen and liberal application of ice packs throughout each day.

The first few weeks of rehabilitation were a really rude awakening. Like most young athletes, I had always felt I was bulletproof. I worked hard to be the best I could be, but there was always a small part of me that took my strength and athleticism for granted. Not anymore. I knew I was in uncharted territory as an athlete as soon as I endured my first stretching and manipulation session in the athletic training room the day after my surgery.

In high school, I had been among the school leaders in weight lifting in the girls' strength and conditioning program. On the prep basketball court, coaches had me in-bound the ball from the base line because I could throw a basketball with one hand over the defense and past half court to a streaking teammate, often for an easy score. I was the shortstop who could backhand a batted ball in the "hole" behind third base, and with all of my momentum headed to the foul line, leap and gun the ball on a line to first for the out. Now, after one semester of college, all of the shoulder and arm strength I had built up over the course of my athletic career had evaporated.

If my shoulder was starting back at square one as far as mobility and strength went, my expectations as an athlete were still where they had been before surgery. Yes, my shoulder was in sad shape. And, yes, I had a long way to go. But I still wanted to play softball for Notre Dame. I still wanted to reach my full potential as a student athlete. And, most of all, I wanted to win. If I had to first conquer a decimated shoulder and nagging, mind numbing pain to get back on the field, then so be it. "Bring it on, Mean Jolene!" I wasn't going to let a little pain and the slow pace of recovery stand between me and playing ball in the spring.

Jolene and I gave it everything we had during our four weeks together. Then I headed back to South Bend to resume rehabilitation under the care of the Irish athletic training staff. I still had a long way to go, but a week earlier, the surgeon had cleared me to stop using the sling. Now I could put my hair up, tie my shoes, and climb in and out of my top bunk more easily. I was ready to take my rehabilitation to the next level.

Pre-Season

Spring classes at Notre Dame don't start until mid-January. That meant a nice long winter break for students, but for softball athletes it meant, once we were back in school, we had only about four weeks before we'd start the series of southern and western tournaments that are an annual rite of spring for northern softball programs. How else to begin playing ball at roughly the same time as teams from warmer climates?

In college softball and baseball, the traditional perception was that teams from the South and West enjoy an almost insurmountable advantage over northern teams because of the favorable climate and resulting longer practice and playing seasons. Because they can draw from a local prep athlete recruiting base that's cultivated under the same favorable conditions, it just stands to reason that schools from the South and West should be dominant in sports that can't be played in snow, rain, or on muddy or flooded ground.

The West Coast was the historic stronghold of college softball, especially Orange County south of Los Angeles. But the competitive landscape in softball has changed dramatically in recent years. The advent of Title IX, the 1970's federal law that mandated equal opportunities for female athletes in high school and college sports—and the media exposure provided to elite U.S. softball athletes in Olympic competition—has meant greater nationwide participation in developmental softball leagues and more regional equality in college softball. Now teams in the Southeast Conference such as Tennessee, Alabama, and Georgia have become fixtures in the annual NCAA College Softball World Series.

Big Ten Conference teams including Michigan, Northwestern and Iowa in the upper Midwest—as well as PAC 10 teams from the rainy Northwest—have also made national tournament appearances, demonstrating that college softball is no longer the exclusive province of teams from Southern California or elsewhere in the sunny Southwest. In fact, the spring after I chose Notre Dame over Michigan, Coach Hutchins' Wolverines defeated traditional powerhouse UCLA to become the first school from east of the Mississippi River to win a national championship in softball. Within a couple of years, Northwestern would also make it to the championship series before falling to Arizona in the best-of-three finals.

I chose Notre Dame because I was sure Coach Gumpf was building an Irish program that could join those Big Ten schools on the ultimate stage at the College World Series. Notre Dame travels more frequently, and more widely, than many other northern softball programs. This means we have the chance to play more games before the snow melts in the North and we have the opportunity to become battle-tested against high quality teams from across the country before the start of the Big East Conference season in late March.

To get ready to dive into our series of road tournaments against the best teams in the West and South, we had to go all out in practice from mid-January until we hit the road in mid-February. If individual Irish pride wasn't enough motivation to achieve peak readiness and avoid humiliation at the hands of our sisters from the South and West, Coach Gumpf and her staff saw to it each of us was pushed to the limits of our capabilities.

Just because northern teams like ours were closing the gap with the traditional powers didn't mean the playing field would be perfectly level during our early spring road campaigns. When we arrived at warm weather tournament sites, the host teams and other local competitors had already been practicing and playing games outside for weeks. For those of us whose home campuses were still blanketed by snow—or at best, ankle deep in mud—our first outdoor action would often begin within hours of touchdown at the local airport. As Curtis used to say in the batting cage, we needed to be ready.

Of course, my recovery from surgery placed some limits on what I could do to get ready. While my teammates embarked on a rigorous practice and conditioning routine that included lots of time in the batting cage, fielding drills, base running and indoor scrimmages, I worked on the sidelines, running, retrieving loose balls, riding an exercise bike, and filling in as a base runner during infield defensive drills. I was also up at the crack of dawn for daily rehab sessions in the training room, followed up with periodic icing and stretching when I wasn't in class or studying throughout the day.

Soon the surgeon cleared me for light throwing under the supervision of the training staff. I was really pumped up! After weeks of painful and tedious rehabilitation exercises, I had finally turned a corner in my recovery. Instead of focusing on simply healing my wounded wing by regaining normal range of motion and enough strength to prevent further injury, I was actually going to begin training my arm to perform its softball job.

It wasn't like learning to throw all over again. I still had the footwork down and knew what my shoulder and arm needed to do. I just didn't have the strength I'd had before surgery. Regaining a strong accurate throw became an additional part of my daily rehabilitation routine. My progress was slow but steady. I knew I would not be ready to play when the team hit the road. But I hoped to be 100 percent and competing for playing time when the Big East Conference season began.

Balancing Books and Ball

Despite my inability to take the field, I'd be traveling with the team and getting used to a student-athlete's compressed in-season schedule. I soon learned why many spring sport athletes load up on classes in the fall, and then lighten their load in the spring. Taking a full schedule of classes in the spring requires maximum discipline and time management. When the season begins in February, our first games take place in the South and West. Typically that means leaving campus to travel to tournaments on Thursday afternoons and often getting back to campus very late Sunday evening or in the wee hours of Monday morning.

Notre Dame sets limits on how many classes a student athlete can miss so our spring class schedules were compressed around practices, other training sessions, and our late week departures for the airport to catch flights to weekend tournament sites. Student athletes at Notre Dame aren't exempted from the out-of-class academic demands placed on other students. Participation in group project assignments required some advance planning and negotiation so that we could do our part when we were on campus and others in the group could do the remaining work while we were away.

Monday was typically an in-season off day, with no practices, training or conditioning sessions. We worked hard on Mondays to get a head start on reading and other assignments that were due in the coming week. In my first spring season, I still had rehabilitation sessions on Mondays but otherwise, I could hit the books without other athletic commitments.

Tuesday, Wednesday and Thursday before our departure, we had practices and individual training to balance along with our classes, group meetings, and formal and informal study sessions. Athletes were required to attend study sessions and tutoring at De-

Bartolo Hall unless we maintained a high enough grade point average. Although I earned high grades, I still took advantage of the extra academic support Notre Dame offers its athletes. The study halls and tutoring helped me get more out of the limited time I had available for studying.

When we hit the road to play ball, we didn't leave our books and laptops behind. The bus rides to the Midway or O'Hare airports in Chicago provided an additional two hours of study to and from our flights. And the flights themselves gave us more time to catch up academically. It's not that we studied every free minute on the road. Let's face it, if you put 18 softball players on a bus or plane, it's only a matter of time before some type of entertaining nonsense breaks out. But we all were under the same pressure to perform in the classroom. It wasn't unusual for all 18 of us to have our faces buried in our books for an hour or more at a time.

In late March when the weather in the North was finally mild enough to allow us to practice and play outside, our study schedules became even more compressed. With the beginning of the Big East season, we typically played a double header against one conference opponent on Saturday, and a second double header against another league foe on Sunday. If the conference games were on the road, we'd leave Friday afternoon after classes, flying to one city for our Saturday games, then board a plane or bus to get to the site of the Sunday games. We'd fly home late Sunday. Home games eliminated the travel time and allowed us to sleep in our own beds, but still consumed a good portion of our weekends.

The real difference between our early spring schedule and our calendar once we started playing in the North was the number of mid-week games that made April and May anything but routine. Sometimes we'd board a bus at 2 in the afternoon on a weekday and travel to Chicago, Valparaiso, Kalamazoo or another campus site to play one or two games before returning to South Bend to resume academic life. More frequently other teams came to visit us at Ivy Field. For a 5 p.m. game, we'd have to be in the locker room by 3 p.m. By the time the game or games were over, we'd quickly have some dinner and be back to our homework or study sessions by 8:30 or 9 p.m. Although my injury as a freshman limited my pregame preparations, throughout the remainder of my Notre Dame career, I always tried to arrive at the locker room early when we had a midweek game so I could take a few cuts in the batting cage and clear my head for a few minutes before we started our warmups and other game preparation. Despite my personal weekday pregame routine, it was definitely easier to relax and focus 100 percent on softball when we played on weekends.

Heading South

When we hit the road in mid-February for our first spring tournament of the 2006 season, our destination was Las Vegas and the UNLV Desert Classic. I might not be physically ready to play, but I was starting my Irish career in the gaudy and glamorous city I'd previously only seen in the movies or on TV. For a kid from West Michigan, this was a long way from the sandlots of KBL!

In addition to the glitter and excitement of Las Vegas, I was expecting some old fashioned Southwestern sun and heat, but we arrived in the middle of an unusual cold snap. I'd played in the cold for years, so my disappointment was only momentary. I was more interested in seeing how the Irish stacked up against the competition, even if I would be doing so from a seat on the bench.

Our foes for the weekend would be teams from the PAC 10, Big West and the Mountain West conferences. Although those conferences tend to be strong in softball, except for UNLV and Cal State Fullerton, the other schools in the tournament were, like us, there to escape the cold and rain back home. Oregon State, ranked number 14 in preseason polls, Colorado State and BYU joined Notre Dame to round out the field.

There were eighteen of us on the Irish squad, four seniors, four juniors, three sophomores, and our 'cult' of seven freshmen. Three of my classmates had earned starting roles, including Alex Kotcheff in center field and Linda Kohan at third base. Brittney Bargar would be our number 2 pitcher and starter in game two. I hoped to join them on the field in a greater capacity in a few weeks but, for now, coach said she would use me in a limited pinch running role because the training staff had not cleared me to play in situations that could involve dive plays or other physical contact. Other than that, my contribution would be limited to helping during warm ups, cheering from the sidelines, keeping stats, and learning as much as I could about college ball from my spot in the dugout.

We ended up winning just two of five games that first weekend, but except for a 5-0 loss to Oregon State, we hit and scored runs and our pitching was strong. I did get an opportunity to run and actually scored what turned out to be the winning run against UNLV. It was great to contribute to a win, but it wasn't anywhere near enough to make me feel good about the weekend. I hate to lose and I knew my Irish teammates well enough by now to know they didn't like it any more than I did. The flight back to Chicago and the hour-long bus ride to campus were quieter than the outbound trip had been. It's not that we were pouting over the weekend's results. But losing would never be acceptable. We were serious, focused and determined to get ready for better results the next weekend.

The next Friday we were off to Florida and the Florida International University (FIU) Invitational. The weather was a bit warmer when we arrived in Miami than it had been in Las Vegas. It turned out, our pitching was also starting to get hot. We gave up only one run in the first three games before losing a close one to host FIU in the weekend finale, 4-5. It looked like we were starting to hit our stride as a team.

Meanwhile my rehabilitation was also progressing. I had barely made it on the field, but I was optimistic it wouldn't be long before I could play a bigger role. I sat down with Coach Gumpf to assess my progress. Over the winter, she had said there was a possibility I could redshirt my freshman year if I wasn't ready to contribute in 2006. Redshirting would allow me to preserve my year of eligibility instead of using it in a limited playing role. In order to redshirt, a college athlete can't see more than limited action. Redshirt status must be declared before the NCAA's spring deadline and before I participated in too many games. That was why coach wanted to talk.

I was strongly against redshirting because it would put an end to my hopes of playing in my freshman year. After fighting to get healthy through my senior year of high school and last summer of travel ball, then undergoing surgery and spending the winter and early spring rehabbing my wing, I wanted to play badly. Plus, staying in school an extra year after my classmates had all graduated didn't sound like much fun. Coach and I had been told by the training staff that I would be healthy enough to play soon, probably by the time the Big East season started. We both believed I would receive a complete medical clearance. Weighing this information with my strong desire not to redshirt, Coach reached her decision: "We won't have to redshirt you." I had passed another hurdle on my road back to playing ball.

We headed to Tulsa the next week to play a three-day weekend tournament at the University of Tulsa. We lost to number 8-ranked Nebraska in the first game and then stumbled to lose a close 2-1 contest against the host school. We rebounded with a couple of wins on Saturday but then stumbled again with a 2-1 loss on Sunday morning. It wasn't the best way to end the weekend and start our journey back to campus.

We weren't in high spirits as we took off for the flight home, but all thoughts of softball wins and losses were soon gone as a severe storm sent our plane on an extreme roller coaster ride over the Great Plains. We were holding onto the arm rests and our teammates' hands for dear life as the ordeal unfolded. Every passenger on the plane was terrified and some were crying. It seemed like forever, but we finally flew out of the turbulence. Landing in Chicago never felt so good! As our bus pulled away from the airport in Chicago and headed into the darkness toward South Bend, it occurred to me that a really bad plane ride can be a pretty effective way to get over losing a softball game.

A week later, we'd gotten over any lingering fear of flying and were on our way to California for the annual ten-day Irish spring break softball tour. We'd start our week on the West Coast with a double header at Cal Poly in San Luis Obispo, then head to the five-day Judi Garmin Classic at Cal State Fullerton, one of the biggest spring tournaments of the year.

We began the week by winning both ends of our doubleheader against Cal Poly. Then we bused to Beverly Hills and Alex's house in a neighborhood populated by movie stars, directors, producers and other members of the Hollywood elite. Alex's Dad was the director and executive producer of a popular TV series and the family home was gorgeous. We stayed for dinner and the hospitality of Alex's family before traveling across Los Angeles to our hotel in Orange County. We'd have Monday off before resuming practice Tuesday to prepare for our first tournament game on Wednesday.

Many of the girls on the team were from California and would be going home Sunday night for the off day. Other parents had flown to L.A. for the tournament and would be spending time with their daughters during the break. I had told my parents I wouldn't be playing so they should save their money and vacation time to use later in the season when I'd be on the field. I was relieved when Heather Booth, our senior pitching ace, invited me to stay at her house until our Monday night team rendezvous back at the hotel.

Coach was all business as we gathered at the practice field Tuesday. It was pretty clear that she had no intention of being embarrassed by an Irish meltdown against some of the toughest softball competition in the nation. We were scheduled to play five games, including contests against three top ten teams. We were also playing on Coach Gumpf's home turf. Her father coached Gordon's Panthers, one of the all-time leading travel ball teams in the country. In addition to Coach Gumpf, Lisa Fernandez and other stars of the game had gotten their starts playing ASA Gold travel ball for the Panthers. Coach was part of the Southern California softball network and every year she brought the Irish back to the fields where she grew up. No one likes to come back home and look bad. Coach Gumpf planned to have us ready to win.

Unfortunately, in our first game, we ran into a motivated Cal State Fullerton team determined to defend its home turf. We lost 2-1 in eight innings. The next day we redeemed ourselves with a 3-2 upset win against number 10-ranked Arizona State. Then we followed up with a 1-0 win over Florida State and it looked like we were on a roll. Our roll ended quickly as two consecutive 6-5 defeats at the hands of number 4 Texas and number 7 Alabama put a damper on things. We headed home just three runs short of an undefeated week. Coach didn't like the results any more than we did, but after coming so close against top competition, all of us could tell we were very close to being a special team.

Back North

The end of spring break also meant the end of our southern and western tour. With the snow barely melted and the frost hardly out of the ground, we headed from the Notre Dame campus about an hour north to Kalamazoo, Michigan, to play a doubleheader against the Western Michigan University Broncos. Our games against WMU were an annual Irish rite of spring. The trip to Kalamazoo was the closest my college team would get to my hometown of Grand Rapids. I had played a few travel ball tournaments in Kalamazoo in my younger years, so the trip seemed a little like a homecoming. My parents made the 45 minute drive down from home and watched with some friends from the area as we swept the Broncos 5-0 and 2-1.

Afterwards my parents followed the bus to a local hamburger franchise. The team was ordering its meal to go but as we trooped back to the bus with our sacks of burgers and fries, my teammates had the chance to meet Gus, our golden retriever. Gus made it clear he hadn't forgotten me, and true to his breed, he shared the love with every Irish teammate who paused to greet him. It was a fleeting but nice taste of home.

Three days later, we won an 11 inning contest against Bowling Green University and then it was time for our first Big East weekend. Connecticut and Providence would be coming to South Bend for doubleheaders Saturday and Sunday at Ivy Field. For seven freshmen, it would be our initial taste of conference competition and a chance to play in front of a weekend home crowd for the first time. We started the conference season with a bang, sweeping the Huskies on Saturday and the Friars on Sunday. Four games into the race for a conference championship and we were off to a great start.

By now I had participated in enough game action that all thoughts of redshirting were in the past. It was the Big East season and I expected to be fully cleared to play. But just before the conference season began, the training staff threw a curve at me. They told Coach Gumpf I could play, but that I could still not be used in situations where there was a chance I would have to dive into a base or for a ball in the field. Also forbidden was any activity where I might get into a collision on the base paths.

After more than six weeks of carefully keeping me out of harm's way, this new directive from the training staff wasn't what Coach Gumpf wanted to hear. "You're no good to me!" she said in frustration. I was just as upset. I had been aiming since November to be ready for action in time for Big East play and now those plans were on hold. I would continue in my role as a designated runner with my participation dictated by game situations and the safety of my shoulder.

The team had played enough games without me that I now understood this latest setback sealed my fate. I was not destined to assume a significant playing role the rest of the season. The starting lineup had been tweaked over the course of our southern and western tour and in the first couple of games back in the North. By now, even the primary pinch-hitting and substitute fielding roles were established. That left me at the far end of the bench. As disappointed as I was at the way my first Irish season was turning out, I was determined to be ready when the team needed me, no matter what the role. I even filled in as a bullpen catcher while continuing to work hard at my rehab and in team practices. I was prepared to do whatever I could to contribute to the team's success.

We played three non-conference games at Ivy Field the week after our initial Big East weekend and won two of three. With a double header on Tuesday night, then a single game the next night, it was one of those weeks that tested our ability to balance academics and athletics. It was a relief to hit the road on Friday for our second weekend of Big East play. We had a double header scheduled at Syracuse on Saturday, then two games at Pittsburgh on Sunday.

It was one of the more difficult weekends of travel we would face the entire season. We would fly into Syracuse, New York, on Friday night, then get up and play our double header in the fickle April weather of upstate New York. Then we'd board a bus and travel for hours in the dark to Pittsburgh where we'd be up early the next morning for breakfast, a short bus ride to the fields on Pittsburgh's urban campus, play our games, and then bus all the way home to South Bend.

Our success in conference play so far had us riding a wave of confidence when we arrived at the field at Syracuse. It was cold and windy and the grounds crew was actually using blowers to remove ice from the playing surface but we were accustomed to nasty spring weather after playing for a couple of weeks in the North. What we weren't ready for was a very stubborn Orange team that eked out a 2-1 victory in the first game. The home team then extended us into the 10th inning of the second game before timely hitting by Carissa Jaquish gave us the lead and the win. We'd be starting our bus ride to Pittsburgh a little later than planned, but leaving on a winning note sure beat the alternative.

Our split with Syracuse was unexpected, but an untimely injury to my classmate and our starting centerfielder, Alex Kotcheff, put a real damper on our spirits. Alex dove for a ball in the outfield and broke her hand. Her season was over. We all knew injuries were a part of the game. Although softball is a non-contact sport, there's an old cliché that says, there's nothing 'soft' about it. To play ball effectively, you have to go all out without regard to preserving your body even though only a slender ligament or brittle bone stands between you and the sidelines. Alex's injury was a reminder to all of us how fragile our athletic careers could be.

By the time we arrived in Pittsburgh, we were exhausted and ready to catch some sleep in our downtown hotel. Sunday morning dawned a bit ominously. During the night, one of our teammates had come down with a really nasty case of the flu. While the rest of us gathered for breakfast, the team trainer made her as comfortable as possible and confined her to bed in the hotel until our bus could swing by and pick her up after the day's games.

If any of us were worried about whether injury and illness were signs of impending bad fortune, those fears were quickly dispelled by our performance on the field. We played long ball with the Panthers' pitching staff, driving several balls out of the park in the first game on our way to a 7-0 win. We continued to batter the fences in the second game, taking the nightcap 14-4. Coming to bat with the bases loaded late in game two, Irish third baseman Megan Ruthrauff capped a three home run afternoon with a grand slam blast that served to put an exclamation mark on the day. I almost put an exclamation mark on the weekend for myself when Coach put me in to pinch hit—my first at bat of the season. I fell behind in the count but then connected solidly, lacing a line drive that unfortunately went right to the shortstop's glove. It felt great to hit it hard. Given more chances, I knew if I hit the ball hard, I'd eventually find a hole.

I was also really happy that my parents were on hand to see my first at bat in an Irish uniform. They had driven to Pittsburgh the night before so they could watch the doubleheader. Also on hand earlier in the day were my aunt and uncle and cousins who lived in the area. All in all, it was a great day to be Irish (unless, like our teammate, you were stuck in a hotel room and faced a long bus ride home with a fever, chills and other symptoms of the flu).

The Season Rolls On

The Big East had not been known as a strong softball conference in the past. Year in and year out, Notre Dame had always been the strongest team in the league, although Seton Hall and Connecticut had also won conference championships in the past. The complexion of the conference had changed in 2006, however, with the addition of three strong softball programs: DePaul, Louisville and South Florida. Now the road to a regular season conference championship, or the top spot in the conference tournament, would go through those three teams.

After a non-conference win early in the week against Ball State, we hosted DePaul for a Thursday night doubleheader. We swept the Blue Demons 5-0 and 3-1 as our pitching tandem of Heather and Brittney dominated the DePaul hitters and our hitters took care of business on the offensive end. The Big East might be a tougher conference but the Irish were proving we were up to the task.

After sweeping Villanova and Rutgers in a pair of double headers at Ivy Field a week and a half later, we were 13-1 in league play and in control of our own destiny. That all changed the next weekend when we hit the road for a double header at South Florida on Saturday followed by a scheduled Sunday twin bill in Louisville. The addition of Louisville and South Florida to the Big East added significant mileage to our travel resume for the season. With a Friday night flight to Tampa, a Saturday flight to Louisville, and then the return trip to South Bend on Sunday afternoon, we were going to be real road warriors this weekend. We would have to take on the Bulls and Cardinals without senior leader, Mallorie Lenn, our starting catcher and one of our leading hitters. She had been called home to California due to a family emergency.

Stephanie Brown, our almost unstoppable leadoff hitter led us to a 7-4 victory in the first game against South Florida's Bulls, but we stumbled in the second game, falling 7-3. It was an unwelcome setback as we continued our quest for the regular season conference crown. Still, we were 14-2 and in the driver's seat if we took care of business the rest of the season. Unfortunately our games on Sunday were delayed due to rain in Louisville. After waiting a few hours for the rain to pass, the games were cancelled for the day. Louisville was also battling for the conference championship, so both coaches agreed to try to play on Monday morning. That meant another night on the road and some quick emails to professors explaining why we'd be missing class on Monday and, in some cases, why we would be late turning in papers and other assignments.

Although the unexpected delay getting back to South Bend created a little more academic pressure for us, we'd get over it pretty quickly if we arrived home in sole position of first place. It didn't work out that way. The Cardinals swept us 2-1 and 10-3. To add insult to injury, we had to immediately board a bus and travel from one end of the State of Indiana to the other to get home. A couple of devastating losses made the long ride seem even longer.

A week later we finished the regular conference season at home winning three of four games in Saturday and Sunday doubleheaders against Seton Hall and St. Johns. We had finished third in the regular season race. It wasn't the regular season championship we had been aiming for, but we had qualified for the Big East Tournament, a last chance to bring home conference honors and also the surest way to earn a post season bid to the NCAA Regionals.

The conference tournament was held in South Bend at the Belleville Softball Complex on the southwest edge of town. Hard rain in the area on the day competition was scheduled to begin soon made those fields unplayable and the tournament was moved to Ivy Field on the Notre Dame campus. We squared off against Providence in the first game and defeated the Friars 4-1 behind strong pitching from Heather and equally strong hitting from Mallory Lenn, our starting catcher, who was having the best year of her career. The next day, Heather shut out Pittsburgh. The 5-0 win was propelled by some timely hitting by Sara Schoonaert, our senior shortstop. The upperclassmen were really stepping it up with our season pretty much on the line. Now we'd face our old nemesis Louisville in the championship game.

The tournament final lived up to all the hype as Heather was locked in a pitchers' duel with the Cardinals' powerful Australian hurler, Catherine Bishop. We came out on top, winning 1-0 as Mallorie and Stephanie Brown provided all the offense Heather needed to win the battle and avenge our earlier defeats in Louisville. With the final out, we rushed the field and celebrated wildly before lining up for presentation of the team and individual trophies. Looking back, my contributions to the championship weren't major, but it's a team game, it was a team victory and this was my team. Time to celebrate!

On to Regionals

We waited anxiously on selection Sunday to see where we'd be playing in the NCAA postseason tournament. Our success in the regular season had made it very likely we'd earn one of the 64 Regionals berths. But our win in the conference tournament sealed the deal. We were automatic qualifiers now. The question was, who would we have to beat to advance to the World Series?

The Regionals are the first stage in the Division I softball post season. Fields of four teams play in 16 double-elimination tournaments held on campuses coast-to-coast. The winners of the Regionals pair off in eight Super Regionals, where they compete to win twice in three games and earn one of eight spots in the NCAA Division I College Softball World Series. The trip to ASA Hall of Fame Stadium in Oklahoma City is the pinnacle of Division I college softball. The Irish had never earned a World Series berth, but it was what we all aspired to achieve when we signed on with Coach Gumpf.

When the berths were announced we learned we wouldn't have to travel far to start what we hoped would be an extended post-season run. The Northwestern Wildcats would play host to Southern Illinois, the University of California at Santa Barbara (UCSB), and the Irish on their campus in Evanston. Ranked number 11 nationally going into the post season, the Wildcats were the highest ranked team in the Regional and would face off first against Southern Illinois. As the second seed in the Regional, we would begin play against the UCSB Gauchos.

We came to Northwestern's Sharon Drysdale Field ready to play, dispatching UCSB 5-2 on Friday afternoon. Also on Friday, the host Wildcats beat the Saluki's of Southern Illinois to set up a showdown between the number 1 and 2 seeds. Unfortunately Northwestern lived up to its national ranking and thumped us 9-0 in a five inning Saturday morning game terminated by the run-rule. The Wildcats simply over powered us. It was a real wake up call.

There was no time for self pity. We had used up one of the two losses that could send us packing for home. We had to pull ourselves back together quickly to avoid an early exit from the tournament. The Saluki's sent the Gauchos back to Santa Barbara while we watched from the sidelines. Now we had to defeat Southern Illinois to get another shot at Northwestern. Starting her eighth consecutive game, Heather led us to a 5-4 win. We returned to our hotel to prepare for our Sunday morning rematch with the Wildcats. It would take two wins over undefeated Northwestern on Sunday to capture the Regional championship under the double elimination format.

We gave the Wildcats a battle Sunday but finally fell 7-4, putting an end to our season and to the Irish careers of Heather Booth, Mallorie Lenn, Megan Ruthrauff and Sara Schoonaert. We were all upset that our dreams of playing in Oklahoma City had come to an end for this year at least. But for the four seniors, there would be no softball tomorrow. I watched as they struggled with their emotions now that their days as students on that special campus in South Bend—and their four years as Irish teammates—had come to an end. It was my first glimpse of how quickly my own career would fly by. With only three at bats and a limited role as a pinch runner in my first season, I would have to cram almost a full career into the three years I had left.

A few days later Coach met with me in her office for my year-end meeting. She gave me my summer workout plan and said she was pleased I had decided to play an extra season of travel ball with *Finesse* to continue getting my game in shape for the next season. My birth date allowed me to qualify to play 18-and-under ball, even after a year of college. I have to admit, I had mixed feelings about playing ball that summer. I really wanted to play the game I loved, but I was a bit worn down by my first year of college softball, and all of the extracurricular rehabilitation I had been doing in addition to conditioning, practice, and the games. I had also hit the books hard, earning a spot on the Dean's list in the fall and spring.

Weary or not, I knew I had to knock the rust off of my game. The training staff encouraged me to throw as much as I could over the summer to build strength and Coach and I agreed that a summer of game action at the ASA Gold level would help me get ready to contribute during my sophomore campaign with the Irish. This was my chance to make up for lost time on the softball field.

Catching Up with Finesse

I'd made up my mind to rejoin Kevin and several of my former teammates for my travel ball curtain call. After nine months of Irish softball, I would hit the road for more than two months with *Finesse*. In addition to Kevin, the coaching staff would include Bill Martin, who had assisted Donny back when I first joined *Finesse* for 16-and-under ball. Also helping out on the sidelines was long-time *Finesse* coach Tommie Walker.

I had seen Tommie coach some very good *Finesse* teams back when I was still playing travel ball for the *Blaze* and *Force* and he had made a real impression with his unbridled enthusiasm and non-stop chatter. During my previous two years with *Finesse*, Tommie had been away from the summer game, taking time off to recharge his batteries. As soon as Tommie arrived on the scene, I could see that he ran a practice the way Donnie did: fast-paced, disciplined, and highly productive. Practices with Tommie were also a lot of fun as he alternately encouraged and razzed each of us from start to finish.

After packing up and moving home for the summer, I had a couple of weeks to get ready for travel ball. That meant practices with Kevin, Bill and Tommie, but first it meant a trip to see Curtis to see if I could get my swing on track. Although I had taken plenty of batting practice in the cage at Notre Dame, too much BP and not enough game action had my swing feeling tight and unnatural. My timing and mechanics were totally out of synch.

Curtis had a rule: his college girls hit free and as often as they wanted. I didn't want to wear out my welcome but if there was ever a time when I needed Curtis' help, this was it. There was a lot of eye rolling and whooping and hollering during my first session back between the wood beams at Morgan's Hitting Club. The surroundings in the second floor of the old warehouse were a far cry from the Eck hitting cages at Notre Dame, but it was just the place I needed to straighten out my swing. It didn't take long for Curtis to help me take apart my malfunctioning hack and turn it back into something more closely resembling a productive softball swing.

Within a couple of days with Curtis, I was feeling a lot more comfortable at the plate and launching line drives off the back of the cages. My friend Christina was also tuning up her swing with Curtis and we reconnected after my year away from the local softball scene. Christina had just finished up her senior year of high school and was going to play her final year of travel ball with *Finesse* before heading off to begin her college career at Central Michigan University. As we settled into our summer ball routine, Christina and I became fellow road warriors, sharing a weekly four-hour round trip commute together to practices in suburban Detroit.

Coach Greg had taught me at an early age that one of the keys to winning is relaxing and having fun while you compete on the field. Christina and I knew how to make each other laugh and I don't think I ever laughed as hard as I did on some of our midweek trips to practice. My Mom would play chauffer, allowing us to sprawl in the bucket seats of the minivan on both legs of the trip for four hours of largely uninterrupted goof off time. Mom sure got an earful as we watched movies, told jokes, and commented on some of the ridiculous behavior you see on and around a softball field and in "real" life as well.

Our team was split about evenly between previous teammates— including Christina, Ali, Roya, Kari, and Lauren—and newcomers who had left other teams to join us in another quest for a trip to the ASA Gold tournament. With a lot of newcomers, building team chemistry would be a challenge for Kevin and his assistants. I wasn't interested in participating in any team drama this summer. I was focused on playing winning softball. I needed to work on regaining my full strength and skills as a player, but I didn't want to treat the season as an extended practice. I wanted to win.

After a couple of weeks we played in our first weekend tournament in nearby Ann Arbor. The high school season had just ended for several of our players and the college players had not been available to participate in winter practices, so we were not real familiar with each other and Kevin was just deciding who would play where. We were pretty ragged in that first tournament and didn't make it to the championship.

After a few more weeks, we began playing better as a team. With Ali and Kari pitching, and some strong bats in the lineup, we had the talent to be successful. The defense rounded into shape more slowly but we were tightening it up with every practice and game. We were probably at our peak when we traveled to Indianapolis for an ASA Gold qualifying tournament that would immediately precede our trek to the big, weeklong tournament in Boulder, Colorado, over the Fourth of July.

My game was really beginning to round into shape. Kevin was experimenting with me at first base, the outfield and second base and my throw was just about back to normal. I felt great to warm up normally before games and then use my gun to do its job wherever I was playing. At the plate I was also starting to feel good again. I was driving the ball hard, moving runners around with bunts in key situations, stealing bases, and taking the extra base when the opportunity presented itself.

In Indianapolis, I took my hitting to a new level, smashing several hits into the gaps. I also laid down some bunts and moved runners when that was the high percentage play. On defense, I was tracking balls down in the outfield and at first base, and my throw was finally back where it was supposed to be. I had been feeling better and better in the tournaments leading up to Indy, but now I was almost all the way back physically and the difference was elevating my confidence as well as my game. We didn't win it all in Indy, but we went deep against good teams and I felt like I was at the center of the action. At last! Softball was a lot more fun than it had been in months. I couldn't wait to get to Colorado and play for a week against some of the best talent in the country.

We hit the road in a caravan toward Colorado. Several players were heading back to Michigan first before driving or flying out to Boulder. But my Dad, Mom and I were driving straight through to the Rocky Mountain State from Indiana. We weren't alone. Christina and her Dad, Kari and her parents and Ali and her Mom also set off on the long road through Illinois, Missouri and Kansas. I saw parts of the country I had never seen before. The last time we traveled to Colorado to play ball, we had taken the northern route through Iowa and Nebraska.

This time we passed through Terre Haute, Indiana, across the leafy southern tip of Illinois, through Saint Louis and into the heat of Missouri. The pavement shimmered under the summer sun as we worked our way toward Kansas City. We crossed into Kansas and stopped for a break in Topeka before heading out across the treeless plains, through Manhattan, Russell, Hays, Colby and other towns whose names I can't remember. I recall stopping for gas several times and we cruised the streets of one small town before finding a Dairy Queen for a burger and cone...dinner Great Plains style. But mostly, we drove on and on. Night fell as we worked our way through Burlington in southeastern Colorado. We called it a night at a truck stop hotel just off the freeway entrance ramp in Limon, too tired to make it to Denver, much less Boulder.

We were up at dawn to finish our journey. After filling our gas tanks and stomachs, we cruised through the sprawl of Denver emerging north of town and, before long, we were in Boulder and on the campus of the University of Colorado. We pulled into our hotel and piled out of our vans to await the arrival of our teammates. I was glad to be off the road and looking forward to getting onto the field. But there would be plenty of time for that. First several of us decided we had to get a closer look at an amusement park we'd passed in Denver. Tired of driving? Not us. We headed off to hit the roller coasters and other rides while our parents sat back on the porches of our hotel rooms, breathed the mountain air and enjoyed the view of the campus, nestled in the foothills of the Rockies.

Colorado

This was my second trip to Colorado for softball but the first time I had played in the Boulder tournament. The previous year we had played in Aurora on the southeast side of Denver. That tournament was a great experience, but I was looking forward to playing in Boulder this year to get a taste of a tournament my college coaches had said always offered strong competition. Both tournaments were held during the same week and just getting invited to play was a challenge. Many teams send entry fees in to both tournaments in hopes of landing one invitation. We were fortunate to land our second straight invitation to one of the tournaments.

We played a couple of games in suburban Longmont to get warmed up and then started play on the main fields in Boulder itself. The tournament started with pool play where we competed for seeding in double-elimination bracket play. This format ensured that every team in the tournament would get to play a minimum number of games before elimination. Once you got to the brackets, the more you won, the more games you would play.

We came out pitching and hitting strongly, earning a high seed in brackets. I continued to feel great in the field and at the plate. Kevin had decided he needed my glove at first base most of the time after using me in the outfield and at second base earlier in the year. That was fine with me. As much as I enjoyed playing the outfield, the position I was most likely to play in college, we needed a reliable glove at first and I'd played enough first by now to know my way around the right side of the infield. It just felt great to be healthy, to hit the ball hard and to play aggressively in the field.

To make things even better, we had plenty of time between games to explore the natural wonders of Rocky Mountain National Park, go for training runs through the beautiful campus of the University of Colorado and enjoy the sights and sounds of nearby

Denver. It wasn't long before four of us—Christina, Kari, Lauren and me—were hanging out together almost constantly. Kari and Christina had just graduated from high school and would be rooming together in their freshman season at Central Michigan University where they would play ball for the Chippewas. Lauren was a year younger and would eventually sign with Eastern Michigan University, my Dad's alma mater. I had played with Lauren and Kari on Donny's 16-and-under team, then with Kari and Christina on Kevin's team a year earlier.

We were like the "four amigos", taking advantage of every opportunity off the field to play hacky sack, go exploring, or just laugh and joke around. One afternoon we went touring with our parents in two vans in the nearby Rocky Mountain National Park. When we entered the park, our parents pulled the vans over in a parking area and we decided to change the seating arrangements. The parents all ended up in our van and the four of us took over Kari's family's vehicle.

We cruised up into the mountains to a trail head where we piled out of the cars and headed up into the woods to view a waterfall and other spectacular mountain scenery. We left the adults in our tracks as we sped up the steep trail, our non-stop chatter alerting any wildlife in the area that we were on our way. The view was well worth the climb and we sat back on the rocks alongside the roaring stream to wait for our parents who would come armed with cameras to capture this memory before we headed back down the path.

Exhilarated by the return hike we jumped in the vans and headed back to Boulder. It was still girls in one car, Moms and Dads in the other as we descended down the curving road out of the mountains. There was a rock wall on our left and a sheer drop into thin air on the right and Kari was "cooking" the brakes while Christina, Lauren and I did some serious in-board leaning to help the van hug the center line all the way down the mountain pass. Except for a few hairy moments when we encountered oncoming traffic on an outside curve, we survived the descent none the worse for wear, although our parents said the smell of overheated brake linings convinced them the van we were in would need a brake job when Kari's family returned to Michigan.

Back in Boulder, we started out strong in bracket play. In one game I took an outside pitch into right field for a line drive single. It was nothing special. I had been hitting the ball hard and getting my share of hits for weeks. It was only later that I learned Coach Gumpf was watching from the sidelines and liked the way I took the ball the other way.

Unfortunately we faltered a couple of games later, committing a series of mistakes that soon had us in the losers' bracket. Once we had that first loss, we had to keep winning to stay in the tournament to the end. But the mistakes seemed contagious. Just when it looked like we were going to knock off our next opponent and live to play again, we let the lead slip away. With the score tied, we decided to intentionally walk a girl who had earlier hit us hard so we could pitch to the next batter. Kevin had the corner infielders play in as our battery began the process of throwing four straight balls. The next thing I knew, a ball went screaming on a line past my head and over the outfield fence for a walk-off home run. One of those intentional balls had wandered into the strike zone and the alert batter had given it a ride. It was a moment of sheer terror for me as a first baseman. In all my years playing the hot corner at third base I had never experienced a close call like it.

Just like that, our vacation was over and it was time to start the long drive home. I had plenty of time to reflect on our week of softball in Boulder as we headed back east. The ending had been a real disappointment. Losing is bad enough, but to lose because we didn't play our best was very disheartening. Worst of all, the tough losses had fractured our already frail team chemistry. Fingers were pointed. Things were said. Some players threatened to quit. There was a very real possibility that the team would fall apart and our season would end right then and there.

As we drove back through Nebraska and Iowa, I could feel good about my hitting and fielding and about the great times I'd enjoyed with my buddies. But I couldn't feel good about the chances of our team staying together long enough to make it to the national tournament in Oklahoma City. Our season had reached a tipping point.

Keeping the Team
Together

Back in Michigan it felt good to be out of the car and sleeping in my own bed but we wouldn't have much time off. We were heading to our next tournament the following week and would have practice on Wednesday night. I wondered how many of the girls would make it to practice. It wasn't unusual to have a light turnout at the midweek sessions because of the driving distance and schedule conflicts. This week was different, though. Team unity was in tatters as we left Colorado for home so this practice would be a good indication of how many girls were committed to finishing the season.

Christina and I were "in". We climbed into Mom's van as usual Wednesday afternoon and headed for the practice field two hours away. When we arrived, we were glad to see a lot of the girls on hand to begin warm ups. There were a few no-shows, but we tried not to read too much into their absence. It was Wednesday afternoon, after all. The real test would come at the weekend's tournament. We needed our two pitchers and at least seven more girls to carry on with our season. Our fingers were crossed.

Fortunately, everyone showed up that weekend as we took the field in suburban Detroit. We even managed to have a pretty good weekend, winning the championship game in our division by beating a team that included some of my earlier *Finesse* teammates. It was a tight game—a scoreless tie into the last inning—until I singled, stole second, moved to third on an infield ground out and scored on a suicide squeeze play when our batter missed her sneaky bunt attempt but the pitch glanced off of the startled catcher's glove as I barreled into home. Kari had pitched every game of the tournament for us because Ali had come down with a stiff back and was unable to pitch. It was an impressive feat on her part and evidence that there was still some competitive fire left in our team despite the drama of the week before.

I can't say our team was completely healed, but there's nothing like a few wins to lighten the mood a bit. After the game, I was glad to see Nicole, one of my closest friends from my first *Finesse* team. We talked for a few minutes as we walked from the fields. She was one year into a successful career at Saginaw Valley State University and was looking forward to being joined by several other *Finesse* alums that fall. It reminded me of Donny's words to us during our recruiting year: there's a place for every girl with the talent and dedication to pursue a college softball career.

The next two-and-a-half weeks would be a busy run-up to the national tournament we were still hoping to play in. We were scheduled to play a weekend tournament on the campus of Ohio State University in Columbus, Ohio, before my parents were going to drop me in South Bend so I could work at the annual four-day Irish summer softball camp. My parents would pick me up on Thursday and we'd head to Orland Park outside Chicago to play in the big Sparks tournament. Then we would drive home for a few days of rest, a midweek practice and then on the road to Nationals. I was following the advice of the Notre Dame training staff and really throwing and playing a lot over the summer!

When we arrived in Columbus, it was about 100 degrees with a beastly bright sun beating down on the intramural fields on the OSU campus. We didn't know it yet, but we were going to be spending a lot of time out in that sun in the next few days. We did fine in pool play but stumbled early in bracket play, landing in the losers' bracket on Saturday afternoon. Dang! The only way out of the losers' bracket was to play from dawn 'til dusk on Sunday and win the championship…or lose earlier and go home in a bad mood. Looking back, losing our second game about noon on Sunday might have been a blessing. But instead we went on a tear, winning three games in a row to earn a shot at the championship against the team that had beaten us earlier. Our opponent enjoyed the benefits of remaining unbeaten, needing to win just one more game to emerge as the relatively well-rested top dog in the winners' bracket.

We were not only sun baked and tired, but our long day had been a war of attrition as teammates began to drop like flies. It wasn't the heat that was taking a toll. Instead, freak accidents were sidelining our players and decimating our starting line-up and our bench strength. First Roya, our Michigan-bound catcher and a big part of our offense and defense suffered a broken finger on a foul tip. She wasn't just out for the weekend, it would prove to be the end of her summer. Then Allysia, a utility player who would be attending Kent State, fouled a ball off her ankle. The swelling and pain made it impossible for her to continue. It would also prove to be a season-ending broken bone. Now we were down to ten players and we were missing our starting catcher. Our back-up at catcher was a starting middle infielder. We could patch the hole behind the plate but that would create another hole.

It was evening as we won our third game of the day and we learned that our next game would have to be moved to the OSU varsity field a short drive across the sprawling campus so we could play under the lights. Because our opponents had not lost in the double elimination tournament, we would have to beat them twice to win the championship. The first game didn't start until after 7 p.m. but in about two hours we had registered the first win. By now it was dark and the lights were on. Our parents were in the stands mentally calculating how long it would take to play the second game, then drive to our homes…or for my Mom and Dad, drive about three hours to South Bend, drop me off, and then drive two more hours to get home.

Kevin took a quick team poll. How many would like to concede the last game and start for home? As dead tired as we were, we all wanted to finish the job. We'd won four games so far that day. What was one more? It soon became apparent that our desire to play one more game was a case of the heart being willing when the body could no longer perform. About two innings into the championship game it was clear that we had hit the wall. The other team started lacing line drives and hard ground balls through the infield and took a lead that they would not surrender. It was after 11 p.m. when we trudged to our cars and vans and pulled away from the OSU campus.

After a pit stop just north of Columbus, we drove to Toledo, picked up the westbound Ohio Turnpike, rolling into Indiana where the ribbon of pavement became the Indiana Toll Road. My Dad drove while Mom dozed in the front passenger seat. I slept fitfully in the back. I was tired and dirty, but that was nothing new after years of travel softball. It was the throbbing in my surgically repaired right shoulder that had me worried. This was the first real pain I had experienced all summer. I hoped it was just tired after a weekend of abuse. Maybe it would feel better after a shower and a few hours of sleep.

No Rest for the Weary

We pulled into the Notre Dame campus after 2 a.m. Monday morning. After explaining to the guard at the gate that I was a camp counselor, we drove up the narrow road to one of the older dorms where we quietly unloaded my suitcase and equipment. I said goodbye to Mom and Dad and headed into the dorm to find the only two things that mattered at that moment: a shower and a bed.

Three-and-a-half hours after my head hit the pillow, I was up with the other counselors to go to an early morning workout before the campers woke up. Then, it was time to get started on the first of four dawn-'til-dusk days of camp activities. It was great to be back on campus and see my Irish teammates who were in South Bend attending summer school and also working at the camp. On the practice fields, I helped out with the various instruction and training drills and coached a team of girls in the daily competition.

The one drill I seemed to spend hours leading was a fielding drill that required me to throw pop flies endlessly into the air as the campers circled under them and gathered them in. By the end of the week, the dull ache in my shoulder had intensified. I was getting worried.

My Mom and Dad picked me up Thursday evening and we headed to the Chicago area for the Sparks tournament in Orland Park. Softball was beginning to feel like work. My shoulder needed a rest, but we had lost two players to injury the week before and the team was short-handed. Taking a week off wasn't an option. We had finally received our bid to go to the Gold Nationals and Kevin was trying to line up some pick-up players to give us some depth. But for the time being, we only had ten players.

Fortunately, Ali and Kari were pitching well and we were hitting well enough to win our games in pool play. Once we got into bracket play, we lost our first game. That meant we'd have to play two more games and win both just to get to play on Sunday. We won the first game as the weather turned windy, cold and rainy. There was something about the Sparks tournament that always seemed to bring out the bad weather.

The cold and damp wasn't doing my shoulder any good. In fact, there was a really weird new development. Now when I wound up to throw, the ball hit me in the back of the head before it left my hand. Try as I might, I could not get my upper arm and forearm to maintain the normal right angle during the throw. My arm was collapsing at the elbow and, as a result, the ball would not clear my head as I brought my forearm and hand forward. My head began to hurt almost as much as my shoulder.

Now I was really scared. I was also in denial. This can't be happening to me I said to myself. My arm must just be really tired. To make matters worse, as I tried with all my might to get rid of the ball without braining myself, I could no longer control the accuracy of my throw. Kevin was playing me at second and at first now, not so much because my arm wasn't up to making long outfield throws, but because we were running out of people to play the infield.

The weather cleared up as we made our way to the field where our next game would be played. Our hitters started out hitting the ball hard but we couldn't push a run across. The other team wasn't having any more success than we were and it was a scoreless tie when the skies darkened and the Orland Park storm sirens went off. That meant play was automatically called off. With darkness falling and the weather deteriorating, the game was suspended. We'd resume play early the next morning.

Up before dawn, we were on the field and ready to play as the sun began to rise above the trees. We were wide awake and ready to go, but apparently the umpire didn't like his early morning wake-up call. As hitters we were rudely introduced to a strike zone that was huge, giving the pitchers a big advantage. I managed to scorch a line drive into the left center gap in my first at bat but the centerfielder got a great jump and hauled the ball in on the run. It was our only solid hit of the morning. Meanwhile, our opponents managed to scrape across a run and, before the dew was even dry in the outfield, we were eliminated from the tournament and on our way home. My body needed some rest, but this was not the way I wanted the weekend to end. We would be heading to Nationals in less than a week and, with our patchwork lineup, we weren't exactly peaking as a team. I wasn't peaking physically either.

Heading to Oklahoma City

Girls who dream of someday playing college softball owe much of their inspiration to the NCAA Division I College Softball World Series, which is played each spring at Hall of Fame Stadium in the ASA complex in Oklahoma City. Every year the series is televised into living rooms across America, giving young players first-hand exposure to the game played at its highest level. Once in college, Oklahoma City, or OKC, is the goal all Division I players aspire to. It is our Mecca, the holy ground of softball. It's the place where NCAA National Championships are made.

This year the ASA Gold Nationals would be held in the same complex where Arizona had defeated Northwestern to win the NCAA title two months earlier. That same Northwestern team had put an end to my freshman season at Notre Dame by handing the Irish a 7-4 loss in Regional play. Although I am sure many players would be thrilled to have the chance to play in Hall of Fame Stadium, I had mixed feelings. Part of me didn't want to set foot onto that field until the Irish earned a World Series berth, leaving Northwestern and other strong teams in our wake. With three years of college ball in front of me, I was confident that goal was within our reach.

Mixed feelings or not, we'd earned a berth at Nationals and my team needed me. We stuffed the minivan with everything we'd need for a week on the road and headed out at dawn on the 15-hour drive from West Michigan to OKC. The good news was, my buddy Christina was going to ride along with us. Her parents would not be making the trip this year which meant we'd have plenty of time to laugh and carry on as we had on so many drives to practice.

We would be caravanning with Mikki and her mom. Mikki was a catcher Kevin had found to play in place of Roya,

The route to Oklahoma City started on familiar roads. We headed south and west along the coast of Lake Michigan into Indiana where we curved west and skirted the south Chicago suburbs until we reached Joliet. At that point, we turned south and began the long drive through the farmland of Illinois. Christina and I amused ourselves watching movies, discussing the upcoming tournament, and recalling good times from this and our previous season together. Christina was excited to be heading off to Central Michigan in the fall. We talked about what it was like to play college softball and the challenges of balancing academics and athletics while still striving to taste the social life that, for most students, is a big part of the college experience.

The temperature was in the mid nineties as we rolled onto the bridge across the Mississippi River at Saint Louis. Christina and I were dozing and hoping the minivan was eating up the miles while we weren't paying attention. But then we hit construction and gridlock. Instead of eating up the miles we were just gumming them. After about forty minutes, we finally broke out of the traffic jam and continued on our way, arriving at the hotel in Oklahoma City while there was still some daylight left. The van may have still had fuel in the tank, but after that drive, Dad, Mom, Christina and I were completely out of gas.

The next morning we were rested and ready to go. We headed out to a nearby field for some fielding and batting practice. It was early in the day but the sun was out and the temperature was already in the high 80's. Kevin laid out our pool play schedule. We'd start out playing a couple of games at a secondary set of fields, then head over to the ASA complex. After making plans to meet at the fields the next day, we headed back to the hotel to get cleaned up. We were going to spend the afternoon sightseeing but first my Mom, Dad and I drove across town to see Sarah Smith, one of my Irish teammates, compete in a triathlon. Sarah was a native of OKC and had just finished her sophomore season at Notre Dame. She was noted for her exceptional speed and athleticism.

We arrived at the finish line just after Sarah had finished her race. She greeted us warmly and it was great to catch up on what we'd been doing with our summers. As we stood melting under the Oklahoma sun talking to Sarah and her parents, I had to really admire my teammate's fitness and competitive drive. It takes a special kind of toughness to run, cycle and swim under sweltering conditions driven only by the love of competition and the feeling of exhilaration you get when you've pushed your body to the limit. Compared to her triathlon, our grueling team training and conditioning sessions in the Loftus Sports Center must have felt like a walk in the park to Sarah.

Nationals Again

We started out playing a strong California club in our first pool game and we came out swinging. We rocked their starting pitcher in the first couple of innings and I played a big part, with an RBI double that helped us build a lead we wouldn't give up. Our lineup was a patchwork affair, with Mikki doing a great job defensively at catcher and others playing in unfamiliar positions. We didn't have a big bat to replace Roya who had made the drive out with Ali to cheer from the sidelines and serve as an assistant coach. We also had no bench strength. But despite the handicaps, we eked out a win, erasing some of our doubts about whether we could compete against top competition.

We were not as successful in our second pool play contest, absorbing a loss that revealed the shortcomings of a team held together with bailing wire. Determined to keep our spirits as high as possible our parents put together a team outing and we traveled down to Oklahoma City's Bricktown district for dinner and to see the sights. We went to an Italian restaurant for great pasta, the ultimate comfort food, before strolling through the streets lined with restored brick buildings enjoying the company of teammates and the relative coolness of the evening.

During our walk we discovered that the local minor league baseball team was playing in the downtown stadium. The game was in the late innings, which meant we were able to enter for free. We settled into the grandstands to watch the rest of the game between two pro teams with players about the same age as we were. It seemed a bit odd when we thought about it. We still thought of ourselves as kids, yet now pro baseball players were our age. At least the game took our minds off of the challenges we'd face on the softball field the next day.

In the morning, we headed for the main complex for the start of bracket play. Every team would have the opportunity to play at least one game in Hall of Fame Stadium itself and our first bracket game would be our time in the limelight. The draw matched us against another team from the Midwest. Maybe this would give us a chance to pick up a win and jell as a team before we moved on to face a powerhouse from the West or the South.

If only it were so. We fell behind early due to the kind of fielding errors that had plagued us all season. The mistakes were becoming more frequent as we moved into unfamiliar positions and as teammates looked up expecting to see one teammate and saw someone else entirely. We tried to mount a rally but we couldn't seem to get the key hit at the right time.

Without Roya, we were missing a vital piece in our line-up. We had slappers and streak hitters, but we were short on hitters who could hit with consistency and match the right approach to game situations. Sometimes we just needed someone to make contact, hit the ball hard and put it in play, or move a runner with a sacrifice bunt. Unfortunately, we were even having trouble doing the little things right.

Then, to add injury to insult, our shortstop, Amanda, was hit by a pitch in the forearm. She went down in a heap. The arm was broken and her tournament and season were done. We'd play the rest of the way with a replacement shortstop and catcher, me subbing at second base and our pitchers playing first base when they weren't toeing the rubber. Hall of Fame Stadium might be every college player's Field of Dreams, but walking off the field after losing to a team we felt we should have beaten, we could feel our dream of playing deep into the double elimination tournament slipping away. One more loss and we'd be on our way home.

The next day we arrived at the ASA complex prepared to begin fighting our way through the losers' bracket. Our first opponent would be a team from Mississippi. We knew they would be as desperate as we were. It was now "loser goes home". Ever since the tournament in Columbus, my arm had been hurting more, my throw had grown weaker and it was increasingly inaccurate.

I was still hitting myself in the head when I brought my arm forward to release the ball. My handicap hadn't been very obvious at first base, but at second I'd be making longer throws and from a variety of distances, often hurried and off-balance. I tried to get as loose as possible during warm ups but I had to be careful not to let our opponents see that I had a problem. I also needed to limit my warm ups to save strength and avoid pain as much as possible. If throwing became too painful, I might hesitate involuntarily and that could hurt us during the heat of game action.

The game began slowly, but by the third inning we had a lead and were holding on defensively with Ali pitching a strong game. Then in the sixth the lead-off batter doubled up the middle. A steal of third and we were in danger of seeing our two-run lead cut in half or perhaps lost altogether. Kevin pulled the infield in to guard against a bunt and the next hitter poked a grounder to me at second, I came up with the ball and had to act decisively to get an out and also prevent the runner from third from scoring. I am supposed to check the runner back by convincingly faking a throw her way, then toss to first for the out.

As the runner at third moved aggressively toward home, I stepped toward home and pumped once to move her back toward the base. The runner baited me, moving a step closer to home. If she takes one more step toward the plate, I am supposed to run toward her front shoulder and force here to retreat, giving up the out at first to prevent the runner from scoring. But she hadn't taken that next step, so the play was to quickly throw to first to record the out and then give the first baseman a chance to peg the ball home if needed to thwart any scoring attempt. At that split second, I froze, doubting my ability to make the quick accurate throw to first that would have been a routine play for me earlier in the season. It was just enough to allow the runner to reach first safely and the lead runner to retreat to the base with a smile on her face. I had screwed up.

Now we had runners at first and third and no outs. It was looking like we were going to snatch defeat from the jaws of victory again, all because I had lost all confidence in my ability to throw.

After huddling to remind me of my responsibilities as second base-man, Kevin kept the infield pulled in to see if we could keep a run from scoring and get an out or two in the process. I resolved to just throw the ball next time. Why did the simplest things suddenly have to be so hard? The next hitter hit a screaming shot past Ali's left ear. Playing a few feet behind her, I stabbed as high as I could with my glove hand and snatched the ball out of the air, coming down ready to throw before the runners could begin to advance. We had our first out.

Ali worked the count on the next hitter before she hit a bouncing ball to my right. I pivoted and took a step to the right, gathering the ball in as the runner at first sprinted for second. A quick step forward and I made the tag, then, without hesitation, threw a rope that arrived in Kari's glove at first just ahead of the batter...double play, end of threat. After recording the final three outs in the seventh inning, we'd survived to play again.

In the morning, we had another elimination game. For us, it was still win or go home. I looked up in the stands and saw that Coach Gumpf and her assistant Kris Ganeff had arrived, taking a break from recruiting future Irish players to check in on me. They didn't see us at our best. We played hard, but for the first time since we arrived in Oklahoma City, we were up against a team that was just better than we were. We kept it respectable, but they had too much pitching and hitting for us. Our season was over.

There were no heroics for me at second base. I looked like the injured player I was, double clutching on a couple of tosses to first and just generally looking uncomfortable in the game I had played since I was seven-years-old. Afterwards, Coach said my arm looked weak. She suggested I rest it for the remainder of the summer and plan on seeing the doctor and starting physical therapy when I got back on campus in three weeks. It was a tough end to the sum-mer that had begun with so much promise. I'd gone from finally feeling healthy and ready to play at full capacity to being injured again. I was uncertain how bad I was hurt and if rest and therapy would be enough to bring me back in time to take the field for the Irish in the spring of 2007.

Second Year

When we arrived back on campus as sophomores, our group of seven classmates had been reduced by one. Alex Kotcheff had decided to transfer, leaving softball behind to pursue her academic degree on the West Coast. I couldn't imagine turning my back on the game I loved, but Alex was not the only girl I knew who had done just that. De, my close friend from high school, had also felt her passion for the game slip away. She had given up her softball scholarship at Eastern Michigan University after a nagging knee injury made playing almost unbearable. I knew of another girl who had given up her spot on the Michigan team. For some, the sport that had held such a strong allure in their younger years simply didn't have the same magic once they moved on to college.

One of my first stops when I arrived in South Bend for the fall semester was the office of our new team athletic trainer, Kathy Laguens. I had already spoken by phone with her about the problems I was having and she had arranged for me to see the surgeon who had operated on my shoulder the previous November. We met with the doctor in the training room and he examined my shoulder, manipulating it through its full range of motion. He listened as I described the collapse of my forearm and the ball hitting my head. I described my inability to control the flight of the ball when it left my hand. And, I described the intense pain that accompanied each throw.

The doctor concluded that, based on his examination, there was nothing seriously wrong with my shoulder. He seemed annoyed and said that "the surgery I gave you is fine". His prescription was that I resume physical therapy and strengthening exercises. In his view, there was no need for an MRI and no reason to consider further surgery.

With medical options off the table, Kathy and I embarked on a rigorous program of strengthening exercises, stretching, deep muscle massage and other manipulation, a program that was to become an almost daily part of my routine in the months ahead. With the start of classes came fall practices and conditioning sessions. Now the condition of my shoulder would become really apparent to my coaches and teammates. My throwing arm was quite literally, out of control. And it was a condition that grew worse as our practices became more intense.

Based on the doctor's assessment that nothing was seriously wrong, Coach said from the start she expected me to do every drill that the team did, including making every throw from the outfield. That meant dozens of throws during every practice. The penalty for an off-line or weak throw was the same as for any member of the team: the entire squad would have to run a quick lap around the field. Unfortunately, my arm quickly became so weak and sore that throwing accurately and with power was almost entirely outside my control.

After one particularly bad practice when I knew my teammates were growing frustrated with all of the running I was causing them, I sprinted over to Coach and voice shaking, said, "It's not fair that they should have to run because *my* shoulder is messed up." I became emotional as I pleaded my case and the tears started falling despite my best efforts to hold them back. I wasn't feeling sorry for myself, they were tears of frustration. I was frustrated at my inability to perform that most basic of softball skills...throw the ball. And I was frustrated that my inability to throw was creating a lot of extra work for my teammates. Coach let me say my piece, then cut me short. "It's not something to cry about. If you miss the target, the whole team is going to run." And that was that. I still wasn't sure I agreed with it, but I knew who was the boss.

Impossible Is Nothing

I was determined not to lose another year of my career to injury, regardless of the pain in my arm, the frustration with my throw, and the impatience of my coaches and teammates. My first priority was to find a way to bring my throw under control. Kathy put together a physical therapy routine designed to strengthen my shoulder and maintain flexibility. We worked around my class schedule to find the necessary 60 to 90 minutes each day to give my shoulder and arm the workout it needed. In addition to therapy, I was also icing the shoulder after every practice and workout, as well as after my therapy sessions. The ice helped reduce the inflammation and accompanying pain in the joint so I would be ready to subject my shoulder to further abuse during the next practice or workout session. Nothing could eliminate the pain entirely, but the ice gave me some temporary relief.

With the addition of hours of physical therapy every week, my daily schedule was packed almost from dawn until dusk. I was registered to enter the Mendoza College of Business and I had a full load of classes, each with a hefty workload outside the classroom. Then there were fall team practices and individual workouts. We also had our strength and conditioning sessions in the weight room and in the Loftus practice facility.

The therapy sessions meant an extra trip over from the classroom buildings or the dorm to the training rooms in the basement of the Joyce. With classes already scheduled around the hours the softball team would be training or practicing, Kathy had to work me in whenever I could find a free period in my day. I was grateful that she was often willing to adjust her own schedule and even give up her personal time to treat me.

As we continued our sessions together, it became clear that we were fighting an uphill battle to rehabilitate my shoulder. Our daily sessions were actually just enough to bring my shoulder and arm back from every grueling practice and get them ready for the next one. Although Kathy's official role was softball team trainer, she must have realized I needed someone to pump my spirits up as we put my shoulder through the painful therapy routine day after day.

Kathy's team responsibilities included attending our practices in case one of us needed medical attention. With eighteen of us to watch over, she wasn't there to watch me put my arm through its paces every day. But during my physical therapy sessions, Kathy would comment on small signs of progress she'd noted in my performance on the field. If I became discouraged, she would remind me that even though my shoulder wasn't 100 percent, I was still performing at a high level in other aspects of the game.

The rare softball or baseball player who can hit for power, hit for high average, run the bases, field the ball, and throw is known as a five-tool player. Kathy would remind me regularly that, even without my former strong throw, I was still a four-tool player who was capable of making an important contribution for the Irish. She said all we had to do was make sure my shoulder would hold up under the heavy practice workload and allow me to throw accurately and with reasonable strength when the season began. That would give me four and a half tools.

I was lucky to have Kathy on my case. She worked tirelessly on my shoulder and on keeping my spirits up. Also keeping me positive and focused on my recovery were AJ, who was back home playing baseball for Grand Rapids Community College, and my parents. They talked to me almost daily, providing a steady dose of encouragement and a willingness to listen to me as I described the ups and downs of practice and rehabilitation.

I had made it clear to my parents before I left for the South Bend campus that I intended to follow Donny's counsel and work independently with my coaches and others involved with the Notre Dame softball program. My parents respected my decision, although there were times when I knew they wanted to get involved to help me. I told them frequently that it was enough that they were always there to talk when I needed them. I knew they were always 100 percent behind me.

AJ was also totally supportive and positive. Like my parents, he made it clear he loved me and would help in any way possible. I really appreciated his perspective as a ball player. I could describe what I was experiencing and know he understood what I was talking about. He had some suggestions that I used to try to overcome my physical limitations. But, like my Mom and Dad, AJ made his most important contribution by just listening and offering encouragement.

As fall practices continued, I tried to focus on staying positive myself while working as hard as I could to regain my throw and improve all of my other skills. One day I was looking through some papers on my desk and I came across a poster my Dad had sent me earlier in the fall. It was part of an Adidas advertising campaign and featured a picture of Muhammad Ali, the great boxer, standing in the ring glistening with sweat, gloves clenched, roaring in triumphant intensity. The headline on the poster was, 'Impossible is Nothing'.

Although I was too young to have witnessed the boxer's remarkable career in the ring, I knew of Muhammad Ali's athletic accomplishments and that he had relinquished his heavyweight title to remain true to his principles. Then he came back, shaking off the rust from his forced layoff to regain the championship.

The poster seemed to capture in a single powerful image the fighting mindset I was striving to maintain as I worked to get back on the field for the Irish. I hung the poster in my room for inspiration. The headline on the poster became my personal mantra. I decided no matter how discouraging my shoulder injury was, I had to believe, Impossible is Nothing.

Fall ball came and went and Coach made it clear I wasn't going to participate on the field. After the fall games, we switched to our winter practice and training routines but my rehab sessions with Kathy continued without a break. Throwing drills were a little less intense after our fall games and the lighter load seemed to help my shoulder improve. There was still plenty of pain whenever

I threw, and Kathy's manipulation and massage treatments dominated me physically while she continued to pump me up mentally.

My teammates helped keep me loose as we participated in official and unofficial team social events. Just as important were the team's participation in community service activities in the South Bend area. Irish athletic teams all contribute their time to help the less fortunate in the community. I thoroughly enjoyed visiting local convalescent homes to talk with the residents and share activities with them. I also enjoyed our time spent working with young students in local schools. My teammates and I knew we were very lucky to have the chance to play softball and earn a degree at Notre Dame. It felt great to give something back to the community surrounding the university and, in whatever way we could, enrich the lives of people less fortunate than we were.

As Thanksgiving break passed, the fall academic semester was drawing to a close. With all of the rehab, my sport was occupying almost twice as much time as normal. Despite my preoccupation with regaining normal use of my shoulder, I was also working hard to get off to a strong start academically in the business school. After all, injury or not, softball would end with my graduation from college. I knew I had to keep my focus on academics while I fought to get my softball career back on track. When exams were done and I was back home for winter break, I received my grades for the semester. I had earned all A's and a perfect 4.00 grade point for the term. I guess the intensity of my fall schedule on the practice field and in the training room had carried over to the classroom!

Finding a Balance

Over winter break I followed Kathy's advice and gave my shoulder and arm some rest. While resting my wing, I used a hitting net set up in my parent's garage to work on my swing with AJ and my Dad almost every day. Our routine included tee work from multiple positions so I could groove my swing to make solid contact with inside and outside pitches and balls up and down in the strike zone. We also did rounds of soft toss so I could work on adjusting to a moving ball as it crossed the plate. With a couple of buckets of balls to work with, I got in a lot of swings during each session as the walls of the garage sheltered us from the winter wind and snow piling up outside.

Although I was resting my arm from the rigors of team practices and workouts, I did work on throwing breakdown drills with my Dad as part of the strengthening and stretching routine Kathy had given me before winter break. The sidewalk in front of our house was the best available outdoor practice ground because it was just outside the door, allowing us to fit in our throwing before and after Dad's workday. The sidewalk was also largely free of snow; my Dad kept it shoveled to eliminate a slip hazard for our neighbors. A spotlight on our garage provided some additional light, allowing us to practice in the partial darkness of morning and evening.

The only problem with our sidewalk practice ground was it was narrow and unforgiving of wild throws. Anything outside of our reach would land in a snow bank. When that happened, we'd try to dry the ball off on our clothes and keep throwing. Balls that became too wet were retired for the day and replaced with a new one from the bucket.

To start each breakdown drill, we'd stand about ten feet apart and I would prop my right elbow on my left hand to toss the ball with just a snap of the wrist. My Dad used the same technique to toss it back to me. With his 50th birthday well behind him, he said his arm needed the slow warm up as much as mine did. After about 25 wrist tosses, we'd back up another five or six feet and perform the same number of swimming throws.

For swimming throws, we'd stand facing each other with our feet shoulder width apart and our hands together at about chest level. In one fluid motion, I would rotate at the waist and pull my right hand up and back behind my ear, then immediately come forward to throw the ball to my Dad. My feet would remain firmly planted on the ground and my lower body would stay stationary throughout the drill. The movement of the throwing and glove hands in the drill resembled a swimming motion, hence the name of the drill. Although it seems a little awkward at first, once you loosen up and develop some rhythm, the compact motion flows naturally without any hesitations or hitches.

You can't over think your throw when doing the swim drill. That was the beauty of the drill as far as I was concerned. I had to constantly fight the tendency to become too mechanical in my motion as Kathy, A.J. and my Dad worked with me to break down my throw and try to rebuild it as a stronger and more accurate softball weapon.

When the swim drill had me thoroughly loosened up, we would start right angle throwing drills. Standing facing sideways or perpendicular to the direction I would be throwing the ball, I would raise my throwing arm so that my upper arm formed a right angle extending out from my body. My upper arm and forearm created another right angle at my elbow as I held the ball up in the air with the palm of my hand and the ball turned away from my target. The object of the drill was to bring the ball from its position above and behind my head to its normal release point in front of my body as my right foot came forward past a pivoting left foot, all in one smooth motion. Starting from a stationary position without a windup, the drill isolated the arm and shoulder movement so I could work on consistently delivering the ball from the same "slot" or path. It was also designed to simplify my throwing motion and eliminate any hitch during the throw. Finally, the drill allowed me to regain a feel for the proper release point and follow-through, both essential elements in a strong accurate throw.

We would continue the right angle drill until I felt like I was consistently hitting the correct arm slot, not hitting myself in the back of the head, releasing the ball at the right moment, and creating the desired velocity and accuracy. Then it was time to get down to some real throwing, integrating the proper footwork and hip action with my upper body mechanics. The results were often mixed. I could do all of the drills and look like I had the mechanics nailed down perfectly but when we put the throw together sometimes the shoulder and arm behaved unpredictably. I would make two or three decent throws, and then the next one would fly off like a wounded duck into the snow. After that I might hit a streak of several more acceptable throws before the next cripple would crop up.

The erratic throws were very frustrating. No matter how much progress I was making physically—and the combination of more rest and a focused workout routine was producing noticeable results—it was hard to trust my throw and execute it without over thinking it. No matter how much I worked, I always felt like I had to fight my body to execute a throw. It simply would not come naturally.

Still, by the time I headed back to school I had made a ton of progress. The sharp pain in my arm was still there, but I had decided I would have to live with that. Throwing didn't feel natural or instinctive, but I decided I would have to make that work. I felt my arm was more accurate and stronger than it had been when I left campus a month earlier. The wild throws occurred more rarely and, when they did, they were not as wild as they had once been. My confidence was at its highest level in six months. I was sure I had gained enough strength and trained my shoulder and arm enough to withstand the rigors of practice. And I was optimistic I could honor Coach's rules about performing every practice throw and still maintain my shoulder and arm in game shape.

Sophomore Season

I arrived back on campus ready to participate fully in our preseason practices and earn a spot in the Irish lineup. It felt like I had turned the corner on my journey back from injury. With a little over a month before we'd head south to begin our season, the team dove immediately into full practice mode. I was careful to warm up before each practice to make sure my arm and shoulder were ready to perform and Kathy and I were still meeting for our regular therapy sessions. My shoulder and arm were better than they had been when I left for winter break, but there was still work to do before I'd have a throw to rival the best on our team. We also wanted to protect against re-injury by continuing to strengthen my shoulder. We weren't going to take any chances now that I finally seemed to be on the mend.

Coach Gumpf's practice rules remained in place. I was expected to participate in every drill and make every throw. Unfortunately, it quickly became apparent that my shoulder and arm were again weakening under the daily wear and tear of outfield drills. As the joint grew weaker, my throw also became weaker. The constant pain had also intensified. In just a couple of weeks I was back where I had started before winter break. I tried to keep it hidden, but inside I was devastated. I had invested so much in getting well only to get nowhere. Kathy talked to Coach about the connection between overwork and my physical decline but the response was, if I couldn't participate in practice, I would not be able to play in our games. Faced with that choice, I had to continue to gut it out despite the physical pain I was experiencing and the mental anguish I was feeling over my renewed struggle to throw properly. My overall confidence as an athlete was severely shaken.

I could take some comfort in Kathy's reminder that I was still a four-skill elite player who was only an injury-weakened throw away from being the complete player who could make a big impact in the Irish lineup. We continued to work hard to try to get my arm ready to perform but by the time we headed south for our first tournament, Coach had made her final decision: I would be a liability in the field. That meant I would start my sophomore season where I had ended my freshman campaign...on the bench. It was hard to disagree with her decision, but I was deeply disappointed to find myself sitting on the bench again at the beginning of my second season of college ball.

We began our campaign at the Tiger Invitational hosted by Auburn University in Auburn, Alabama. As expected, I was in the dugout as we began the season on a high with a 3-2 win against the host Tigers. Later the same day, Alabama-Birmingham humbled us with an 8-0 pounding that brought us back down to earth. We rebounded the next morning with a 6-5 win over Tennessee Tech before losing to Tulsa 4-2, to even our record. Our goal for our final game was to leave Auburn with a winning record. Virginia Tech had other plans, however. The Hokies defeated us 2-0 Sunday morning, sending us packing with a sub .500 record after the first weekend of the season.

There had been some bright spots. Except for the Alabama-Birmingham game, Brittney Bargar and Kenya Fuemmeler, had performed well overall in their debut as our 2007 pitching rotation. However, we had been outscored 21 to 11 in the five games. It would take more production by Irish batters to convert strong pitching into wins. I had a pinch hit single in the Tulsa game and walked in a pinch hit appearance against Virginia Tech, but it was hard to feel good about my personal performance. It's a team game and we had not consistently succeeded at the plate.

The next weekend we flew to California for the Palm Springs Tournament in Cathedral City. Our first game would be against Oklahoma, then ranked number 9 in the country. Before the game, Coach said she was going to shake up the lineup to see if she could find the right combination to generate more offense. One of the changes was to assign me a starting position in the outfield. I knew I was definitely earning a spot because of my bat and despite Coach's misgivings about my arm.

I had been working hard with Kathy and in practice to make my throw as strong and accurate as possible. To hedge my bets, though, I was also determined to use my ability to break quickly on fly balls, take the right angle and, if the game situations would allow, gamble on diving to make a catch. If I could keep the ball off the ground, I could reduce the number of times my throw would be called on to keep a runner from taking an extra base. Diving could sometimes hurt, but throwing definitely hurt a lot more. Besides, I'd been diving for fly balls since my Dad and I started practicing in the backyard. It was a skill I refined with Greg Youtzy and Coach Greenman and I had done plenty of diving in my years with *Finesse*. My willingness to try to catch almost anything hit my way was a point of pride and it was the part of fielding I loved the most. Now I considered it a necessity that would allow me to avoid using my arm in game action except when absolutely necessary.

My first start didn't end victoriously. The Oklahoma Sooners defeated us 7 to 3. Batting seventh, I walked twice and had a bunt single but didn't figure in the scoring. I also held my own on defense catching a fly ball, cleanly fielding other balls hit my way and hustling the ball back into the infield with acceptable throws. It wasn't a heroic start, but I wasn't complaining. The only thing missing was the sweet taste of victory. Greg taught me to be greedy back in KBL. I didn't just want to play. I wanted to help my team win. Winning was more fun.

Our next game was also against a ranked team: number 17 California. We fell behind early but clawed our way back to make a game of it before falling 7 to 5. After getting on base in all three at bats against Oklahoma, my fortunes at the plate were reversed in my second game. Coach had moved me to number 2 in the lineup, but I couldn't repay her confidence with a hit or two. I was safe once on a fielder's choice on a grounder to short but my best hits were a line drive and fly ball, both hauled in by the center fielder. As the saying goes, if you keep hitting it hard, eventually the hits will drop in. But one start without a hit and I was already impatient for the next one.

The next day against UNLV we finally broke through for a 4-3 win in eight innings. Still batting second, I had a single in the first and scored a run later in the game. The hero of the game was our shortstop Katie Laing who singled home the winning run in the eighth. It felt great to put an end to our losing streak.

Kenya was on the mound later in the day against Cal State Fullerton and was locked in a pitchers' duel before we fell by a score of 2-0. After giving up only four hits and two runs, Kenya deserved better. Unfortunately, we only managed three hits and couldn't string them together to score a couple of runs. I had a single in three at bats and continued my string of put outs and clean fielding in left field. Kenya's performance was emblematic of the kind of contribution she would make all year long. She was playing her final season in an Irish uniform with a torn ACL in her right knee. Despite a bulky brace and constant pain, she took the ball every time coach handed it to her during her senior season and did all she could to put us in a position to win. Her 27 appearances and 3.14 earned run average were a testament to her personal grit and determination.

On Sunday morning we had one final game before boarding the bus for the airport and our long flight back to South Bend. After dropping three of four since arriving in the Golden State, a victory wasn't going to completely wash away the pain of losing, but it would help make our trip home more tolerable. Our foe was Mississippi and Brittney would be pitching. She pitched well and we hit enough to earn a 3 to 1 win. It was just what the doctor ordered. My classmate Linda drove in the deciding runs and I figured in the other run, using a sacrifice bunt to move our leadoff hitter, Stephanie Brown, to second. She eventually scored our first run.

Ending the weekend with a win helped boost our spirits on the trip home. We were determined to build on the win and perform better in the weeks ahead. For my part, I felt good about making a contribution after working so long to get ready. After facing the prospect of a second straight year on the bench, my season had taken an unexpected new direction. The opportunity to play had arrived and I wanted to make the most of it so Coach would have no reason to pull me from the lineup. Hard work had carried me this far, I wasn't about to slack off now.

Jacksonville

A week later we found ourselves in Jacksonville, Florida, in a tournament hosted by Jacksonville University. We started out hot, compiling a three game win streak that included a 7-2 win over Jacksonville bracketed by 4-1 and 6-3 wins over Virginia. Unfortunately, we stumbled against number 9 Michigan, 1-0 in the final game before our return flight to Indiana.

Coach continued to pencil me in the lineup as the left fielder batting in the number 2 slot in the lineup. I was getting on base and moving runners over. Hitting behind Stephanie, the Irish hitting leader, was an ideal situation because she was on base constantly and I had a lot of opportunities to move her over with a bunt or a hit. I was also making plays in the outfield to deprive our opponents of base runners. Two diving catches against Michigan were particularly memorable and helped us keep the game close.

Playing in Jacksonville was also special on a personal level. My old *Blaze* and *Force* travel ball buddy, Simone Bruemmer, was playing college ball for the host team while pursuing pre-med studies at Jacksonville. It was great to see her, if just for a moment. There wasn't much time to catch up with anyone, including Simone, my *Finesse* teammate Roya St. Clair, and the other Michigan Wolverines or their coaches. Playing softball for Notre Dame meant lots of opportunities to travel—we would log more than 14,000 miles as a team during my sophomore season, but that didn't always translate into chances to see the sights or catch up with any old friends who might be visiting the same city. We usually arrived in town late, and left town right after the last game. If we weren't warming up or playing a game, we were on the bus driving back to the hotel or to a restaurant for lunch or dinner. As our coaches told us, these were business trips, not holiday excursions. No complaints from us; we were competitive to the core. We had signed on for softball at Notre Dame to play hard and win. Glimpses of the local scenery and tourist attractions—and everything else for that matter—were just unimportant details.

In between games in Florida, I was still spending a lot of time icing and getting therapy on the fly from Kathy who always traveled with us. The shoulder was plenty sore, but playing regularly made the pain a lot more bearable for me. Kathy was keeping me loose enough that my throw was doing the job defensively. I hadn't hit my stride yet at the plate, but I was trying to do the little things right, with productive at bats that worked the count and put the ball in play. I had my share of hits, but I was also earning some walks and moving runners with the bunt. I had even been hit by a pitch, earning a base by taking one for the team. It wasn't pretty, but I felt like I was doing my job to help the team win. Except for that loss against Michigan, the wins were starting to come.

When we arrived back in South Bend, we hunkered down for our last week of classes and practice before spring break. While our classmates were completing final plans for vacations in exotic places, or to go back home to work or just relax for a week, we were getting ready for our annual one-week pilgrimage to the epicenter of travel and college softball—Orange County, California. We were slated to play an early week tournament in Long Beach, then head a few miles inland to play in the big Judy Garman Tournament at Cal State Fullerton.

A year earlier, spring break had been difficult for me. I had been a freshman with an injury that kept me off the field. I had told my parents not to spend the money to travel west for the week since I would not be playing. I didn't know at the time that the week was a reunion of sorts for the players who had families on the West Coast and in Arizona, and that other parents also made the trip to watch a full week of Irish softball and enjoy some time with their daughters. I felt a little like a fifth wheel as the other girls spent time with their families. Not this year. My Mom and Dad had decided to make the trip. They had accepted Brittney Bargar's parents' generous offer to stay with them for the week, which not only gave them some good company, it also provided them with help navigating the freeways of the Los Angeles area.

We started play in the Long Beach Invitational tournament with a 10-2 win against Eastern Kentucky. I went 2 for 5 with a double, a run scored and an RBI, to contribute to our 15 hit attack. Traveling to the West Coast to play a team from Kentucky wasn't typical of the competition we expected to face that week. The second game was more like it. We squared off against perennial powerhouse, 12th ranked UCLA. Considering our performance against top ranked teams so far in the season, most observers wouldn't have given us much of a chance playing a team like the Bruins on what might as well have been their home turf. As it turned out, we gave them a battle and had a 2—1 lead before falling by the deceptive score of 9—3 to close out the tournament

We had a one-day break before beginning our preparation for the start of the Garman tournament and Coach gave us a day off from practice and allowed the girls to stay with their parents overnight and the next day. For the girls whose families lived in the area, that meant a night sleeping in their own beds and, in some cases, playing host to teammates. Since my parents were already staying at Brit's house, I'd be bunking with them in Corona. Our plans for the next day included a trip to Disneyland with Brittney, a couple of other teammates, Brittney's mom and my Mom and Dad.

We had a lot of fun at the park on a perfect Southern California day. In our day-long quest to hit every thrill ride we could find, we rode the biggest roller coaster in the place and several other gut wrenching but thoroughly enjoyable rides. We headed back out to Corona for a relaxing dinner and some down time before my Dad drove us back to the hotel to beat Coach's curfew. It was time to get back to business.

We headed out to a local practice field the next morning to begin getting ready for our five games in the Garman tournament. We'd be playing three ranked teams including Arizona State, Louisiana Lafayette and Texas, plus a couple of other West Coast teams that couldn't be taken lightly. This was Coach's home turf, so the intensity of our practices went up a notch higher than normal, which was saying something considering how hard we worked every day. We knew underperforming in front of Coach's hometown fans wasn't an option.

Unfortunately, a rough practice field caused an accident that seriously crippled the team before we played the first game. During practice, a hard ground ball took a bad hop and smashed into Stephanie Brown's face, shattering her teeth, lacerating her lips and blackening her eyes. A career .356 hitter who could slap and hit the long ball, Brownie was our most potent offensive force. She had moved from center field to first base a few games earlier to accommodate additional outfielders as Coach tried to get more bats into the lineup.

No stranger to the infield, Brownie had a great glove, but there was no defense against a bad bounce. That ball was in her face before she could get her glove up. With our best hitter gone to the emergency room—Brownie would require stitches, a lot of pain medication and eventually plastic surgery—Coach had to fill a hole on defense and replace an irreplaceable bat on offense.

I was an early option to take over at first base because Coach had seen me play a lot at the position in travel ball. But my shoulder wouldn't allow me to execute the throws I needed to make in the infield. I had been training so hard to make full throws from the outfield, the shorter "dart" throws, off balance heaves, quick strikes and flips required at first base gave rise to a lot of hitches and hesitation. With that experiment completed I was sent back to left field, my days as an Irish infielder at an end. From a longer-term team perspective, it was just as well because Coach next turned to one of our three freshmen, Christine Lux, who eventually took command of the position and, by the time she graduated, was the leading home run hitter in Irish history.

Brownie's injury was just the start of our misfortune. We faced number 2 Arizona State in the first game of the tournament and were shut out 3-0. After knocking off Fresno State 4-2, we then lost to number 16 Louisiana Lafayette 4-2. I had a shot at a big hit with a runner on first in the last inning against the Ragin' Cajuns but my blast to right field was tracked down on the warning track, a couple of feet short of a game-tying home run. Number 8 Texas shut us out 3-0 the next morning. And to cap it all off, we let unranked Pacific score a run-shortened 8-0 win over us in the tournament finale. Even my two hits in that one couldn't ease the pain. Coach was not happy. We were not happy. It was a really long, unhappy flight home to South Bend.

Back in South Bend

We arrived back on campus after our week in California and were greeted by the usual cold, wet and nasty weather that marks the early spring season in the upper Midwest. I was used to it, having grown up in Michigan and playing high school ball starting in early April when the weather wasn't much better. Besides, I had been out throwing surrounded by snow drifts over winter break. How bad could this be? I don't think many of my teammates from California, Arizona and Florida were quite as accepting of the conditions as I was. But, Coach saw to it that we were all tough enough to ignore the outdoor conditions and get on with the business of playing ball. As a Southern California native herself, she would tell West Coast recruits, "in the Midwest you get the cold, in SoCal you get the traffic; one is as bad as the other".

The weather was the least of our worries as we looked ahead to the Big East Conference schedule before us. We had three immediate goals every season: win the Big East regular season and tournament championships and earn a berth in the NCAA Tournament. We could achieve the third goal by accomplishing the first two or just the second. But if we didn't win the Big East Tournament, it would take a high finish in the conference standings plus wins against some highly ranked opponents to gain an at-large berth in the NCAA Tournament. Conference champions from across the country would get automatic berths in the tournament and the really strong softball conferences like the PAC 10 and Big West—and more recently, the SEC, Big 12 and Big Ten—would send several teams based on their overall strength of schedule.

In the past, we had helped our cause by racking up key wins against ranked opponents in early season tournaments in the South and West. But this year we had stumbled against every ranked opponent we had faced. What's more, unranked opponents had beaten us as well. That meant a strong Big East showing was our only hope of landing a tournament berth. We entered the conference season understanding that winning the Big East Championship was more than our first goal, it was virtually a necessity.

The preseason poll of conference coaches had us finishing third in the conference behind two of the teams that had joined the Big East a couple of years earlier, Louisville and South Florida, and just ahead of the third, DePaul. The entry of those three teams into the Big East had instantly elevated the conference into arguably one of the strongest softball conferences east of the Mississippi. Now they represented the most formidable adversaries we would face in the coming campaign. But with the stakes so high and our margin of error so thin, we couldn't afford to overlook anyone on our conference schedule.

We opened the season playing with the necessary sense of urgency. After beating Indiana University-Purdue University at Indianapolis (IUPUI) in a pre-conference warm up, we reeled off consecutive double header sweeps of St. Johns and Seton Hall at home in the first weekend of conference play. My bat showed signs of heating up as I followed up a double and run scored against IUPUI with a walk, stolen base and two RBI against St. Johns. I was hit by a pitch and scored a run against Seton Hall while Heather Johnson had her coming out party as a freshman with a three hit performance against the Pirates. Meanwhile, our pitchers gave up just two runs the entire weekend. It was the start we needed.

We played Toledo and gained a midweek win before hosting Pittsburgh and Syracuse the next weekend. Playing like a team on a mission, we kept our conference record perfect with sweeps of both opponents. Again, Irish pitchers surrendered only two runs the entire weekend while getting a total of 25 runs of support from our hitters. Stephanie Brown and Gessica 'Huffy" Hufnagel showed what senior leadership was all about, as both had multi-hit performances against Pitt in the first double header. I was in the thick of the action with a four-for-six performance at the plate against Pittsburgh. I also earned two walks, had two stolen bases and scored three of the team's eight runs in the two-game set.

Against Syracuse, Brownie went an amazing seven-for-eight to lead the Irish attack. Also on the box score for our side was Christine Lux's first career home run. Again, I was in the thick of things with a double, two runs scored and three RBI on the day. The twin killing extended our winning streak to ten straight games.

Next up was a Thursday night showdown at DePaul, our first test against one of the Big East's elite teams. We were pumped up to ride the crest of our winning streak onto the Blue Demons' home field, but the doubleheader was abruptly postponed as weather conditions rendered the DePaul diamond unplayable. What a letdown!

On a high note, we learned that Brownie's performance the previous weekend had earned her Big East and NFCA Louisville Slugger Player of the Week honors. The NFCA (National Fastpitch Coaches Association) award was particularly impressive because it meant even coaches outside of the Big East had taken notice of our teammate's stellar performance. She had put her severe facial injuries behind her and was back to terrorizing opposing pitchers and defenses.

My Biggest Fan

Although my softball career at Notre Dame had been a roller coaster ride so far, there was one constant positive note: my Mom. She was on the sidelines to support me at every home game whether I was playing or not. I don't think Mom ever envisioned herself as a sports mom when she first considered having children. Even though she was raised on a farm in a large family and ran wild with her brothers as a tomboy during most of her younger years, she eventually outgrew that phase and was a successful career woman when she met my Dad. I had the usual assortment of party dresses, ribbons and bows, dolls and pink jammies during my preschool years. But I think enrolling me in dance classes when I was seven or eight years old was Mom's last ditch attempt to make a 'girlie girl' out of me. By then it was a lost cause. I was playing hoops and football with the boys at recess, competing in AYSO soccer games on Saturday mornings, and playing softball for Coach Youtzy in KBL.

My Dad actively supported all of my athletic endeavors. He used all of his charm to convince Mom that they should make the investment of time and money to launch my travel softball career. Once my career got started, though, she was all in. Mom drove me to a lot of practices and for years joined my Dad at all of my travel ball tournaments. By the time I began playing at Notre Dame, she was my biggest fan. In my four years playing for the Irish, Mom never missed a home game and she even made some solo road trips to see us play.

When the Irish were playing at home, Mom's blue minivan was a familiar site in the parking lot across the street from Ivy Field and later in the lot outside Melissa Cook Stadium. She put a lot of miles on that van, driving between Grand Rapids and South Bend to watch our midweek games. She would make the two hour drive to watch a single game or a double header, then wait outside the locker room for me to join her for dinner. A couple of hours later, we'd say goodbye at the dorm and she would set off on the return trip. It was usually after midnight before she arrived home.

When our schedule called for midweek games on back-to-back evenings, Mom would get up the next morning, take care of things around the house, and bake treats to bring to the team, then drive down for more games before returning home after midnight again. Mom was usually one of only a few parents in the stands. Most of the girls' families lived too far away to travel to every game. The exceptions in my four years on the team were Gessica Hufnagel's parents who lived in nearby Middlebury, Indiana, Christine Lux' family who lived in suburban Chicago, and Alexia Clay whose family lived in Rochester, Indiana. Occasionally parents from Florida, Arizona, California or the East Coast would extend a weekend trip into the middle of the following week to catch a few more games. But those were the exceptions.

Mom spent a lot of time with the other parents who did make it in for the games and she got to know other fans who were regulars. Ushers Bob, Tom, and Dave became good friends who greeted her warmly when she'd show up to watch us play. But softball wasn't all about socializing. Mom was an intense Irish fan who watched all the action on the field, cheered loudly for us, celebrated our wins and consoled us after losses. No matter the outcome, by the time we finished our post-game routine, she was always ready to greet me and my teammates warmly, with a smile or a hug, and one of her treats.

The treats became her trademark and endeared her to everyone on the team including the support staff, the coaches and their kids. There's just nothing like fresh baked goods to celebrate a win or begin the healing process after a loss. It all began in the first home game of my freshman year, when Mom showed up with treats for me to share with all of the girls. I don't think she planned to start a tradition. She just thought I'd enjoy having a treat and might want to share with my teammates. Once she started bringing the treats she never stopped.

At first I wasn't real comfortable with her generosity. As a freshman, I just wanted to fit in with the older girls and my classmates. The whole treat thing seemed a little juvenile to me. After all, we were young women in college now, not little soccer players who needed orange slices as a reward for playing hard. But after Mom showed up with muffins, cookies, or trail mix at a few games, my teammates started asking what Mrs. Northway, 'Janet', or 'Momma Northway' would be bringing to the next game. It was clear the treats were a big hit. There was no way I could discourage Mom from continuing to bake unless I wanted to risk the ire of my Irish teammates.

Before long, they were telling Mom what their favorites were and she would tailor the menu to make sure everyone's preferences were served. That meant bringing banana bread to some games and no-bake cookies to others. She brought muffins, cupcakes, trail mix, and even made packages for girls with special preferences. I found myself delivering the girls' special treat requests and dropping hints to guide Mom's baking decisions.

For four years, Mom's treats were part of the Notre Dame softball experience. But having her there to cheer us on was a lot more important to me than her baking talents. It was great to look up in the stands while we were warming up before the games and see her sitting there joking with the ushers or chatting with Alexia's or Christine's mom. It reminded me of home and family and it meant I'd have the chance to spend time later in the evening with my biggest fan before it was time to get back to my studies and for her to start the van and head for home.

Playing On

After the rainout of our DePaul doubleheader, a non-conference game against Valparaiso was also postponed due to weather. We were really ready to play when we finally took the field again after the almost two-week layoff. Our next action was in Providence, Rhode Island, where we were scheduled to play the Friars in a Saturday doubleheader. It was one of those "take care of business" twin bills where anything less than a sweep would seriously jeopardize our chances to win the Big East Championship. Wouldn't you know it, after winning handily, 10 to 1, in the first game of the set, we allowed Providence to remind us that, on any given day, any team can take you down. The Friars proved they were plenty good enough to beat us, taking a run-rule-shortened win by a score of 9 to 0 in five innings. Huffy did all she could with a home run, a double and five RBI's in a career day at the plate. I went 3 for 4 with walk and two runs scored on the day. Unfortunately, most of our production came in game one. Normally a good day at the plate would make me smile, but letting that second game get away was too painful to forget.

Sunday morning found us in Storrs, Connecticut, where we would take on the Huskies and try to get back on a winning track. Unfortunately, severe weather caused the games to be postponed indefinitely, our second Big East rainout in a little over two weeks. Although the double header with DePaul would be played at a later date, we'd only make the trek back to Connecticut if it was necessary to decide the conference race or determine if we'd qualify for the Big East Tournament. With our backs to the wall, we needed chances to win games, but we couldn't win games we didn't play. If, as the saying goes, ending a game in a tie was like kissing your brother, what was not getting to play the game at all?

Back in Indiana, we played four straight non-conference games, racking up much needed wins against Western Michigan in a double header sweep, and Ball State and Valparaiso in single games. Katie and Heather led our offensive attack against Western with four and six RBI, respectively. My classmate Linda and I had two hits and two RBI apiece to balance the team's output. Against Ball State, Brittney and Kenya pitched a combined no hitter as we defeated the Cardinals 3-0. The opposing pitcher was Elizabeth Milian, one of my teammates from Donny's 16-and-under *Finesse* team, who was in her first season of what would be a great four-year career as the Cardinals' ace hurler. The last non-conference contest was a make-up date against Valparaiso. We made the wait since our earlier rainout worthwhile by beating the Crusaders 5-0 behind Brittney's strong performance on the rubber.

All told, we scored 22 runs in the four games and our pitchers gave up only a single run, restoring some of our swagger and getting us in the right frame of mind going into what promised to be the most demanding weekend of the conference schedule. Louisville and South Florida were coming to town.

Showdown in the Big East

Louisville arrived on campus Saturday for the first of three critical doubleheaders that would determine who finished the regular season at the top of the conference standings. The Cardinals came into the weekend with one loss in the conference, the same as us. Now we had to pin a couple more defeats on them. Our success against the Cards and the other top ranked teams in the conference would also decide our fate in our quest to earn a berth in the NCAA Tournament.

In the first game we started slowly and let Louisville take an early lead. Despite a couple of Irish rallies we were unable to withstand the Cardinal offensive output. They beat us 8-2. In the second game, we couldn't mount a rally at all, falling 5-0. Half the weekend was over and we had really dug a hole for ourselves. We were licking our wounds, but there was no time to sulk. We would face South Florida the next day and we had to get a couple of wins. Our margin for error was slipping away.

The Bulls were also trying to salvage their conference fortunes and were as desperate as we were. Their desperation paid off in two 3-1 wins. We had seven hits in the first game and five in the second, but we just couldn't string them together to push more than two runs across on the day. Meanwhile the Bulls had a total of 19 hits in the two-game set, enough to take both games and leave us reeling. My box score line was three hits in six at bats and I even gunned down a runner at home to prevent an additional South Florida score in the second game. Personal accomplishments aside, it was a sour way to commemorate Senior Day, the official ceremony to celebrate the Irish careers of seniors Stephanie Brown, Gessica Hufnagel, Carissa Jaquish and Kenya Fuemmeler.

After four losses in a row to Big East foes, we needed to get back on track. We wouldn't have to wait long to redeem ourselves because the next weekend we'd travel to DePaul to make up the two games that had been rained out earlier in the month. First, though, we had to take on Big Ten power Northwestern in a non-conference matchup at Ivy Field. It was no contest. We were totally flat and lost 12-0 in five innings. We didn't hit and our pitching couldn't prevent the Wildcats from getting on base. We had now lost five in a row and the most recent loss was the most lopsided Irish defeat in eight years.

Another non-conference game the next day was cancelled due to rain, so we wouldn't have a chance to regain our equilibrium in game action before facing number 11-ranked DePaul on Sunday. Coach worked us hard in practice to see if we could get our bats going but we would have to wait for Sunday to know if the batting cage therapy had worked.

Located on the north side of Chicago, DePaul was about an hour and a half away by bus but light years away from Notre Dame in terms of softball playing conditions. The Blue Demon field was squeezed between a student dorm and the El tracks on a converted soccer field without an inch of space to spare outside its fences. All of the grandstands were located in right field, the part of the soccer pitch that wasn't used for softball. Although the Blue Demons were ranked behind us in the preseason, they had ascended to the number 11 spot in the national polls as a result of a successful campaign against a strong schedule of non-conference teams early in the Spring. They were well coached, had great pitching, and the home field advantage.

The first game against the Blue Demons was tight from the start. Brittney was sharp and held the DePaul bats in check until the fourth inning when they broke through for two runs with three singles and a sacrifice bunt. Christine hit her second home run of the season in the top of the fifth, but DePaul answered with a run in the bottom of the inning and the 3-1 lead held up for a Blue Demon win.

In the second game, we loaded the bases in the first inning but could not push a run across. DePaul scored one run in the second inning on a couple of singles and a fielding error. They tacked on another run in the fourth and two more in the sixth. Meanwhile DePaul pitching limited us to three hits for the second straight game. Just like that, we'd been swept again, running our losing streak to seven straight games. We scored only five runs during the streak and we had allowed all three of our strongest conference foes to gain the upper hand on us in the race for the regular season conference championship.

After failing to take care of business in our three biggest conference showdowns, our only hope now was to win the rest of our conference games and then make a run in the Big East Tournament. Underdogs had won the tournament before. We had to hope that was the history we were going to write. In addition to earning bragging rights in the Big East, and a championship ring from Notre Dame's Monogram Club, the tournament champion would be awarded an automatic berth in the NCAA Tournament. It looked like that was our only shot to salvage success in this suddenly very shaky looking season

A couple of days later, we made a follow-up trek to the Windy City to take on Loyola-Chicago. This time the ride home was happier as we won 5-0. It was a good way to end our losing streak and get ready for our last conference road trip of the season. We'd be heading to Rutgers and Villanova for a pair of double headers that now loomed large on the schedule. After losing six conference games in a row, we had to sweep the final twin bills to ensure our spot in the Big East Tournament.

After beating Rutgers 5-2 and 5-1 on Saturday, we defeated Villanova 5-2 and 4-2. Now that was more like it! My bat was hot on Saturday, and I was 2 for 3 with a run scored in the first game and 2 for 4 with an RBI in the second. I contributed on Sunday, too, with a hit, a stolen base and 3 runs scored. I was also hit by a pitch, making my day arguably the softball equivalent of hockey's "Gordie Howe Hat Trick". Instead of a goal, an assist and a fight, I figured a hit, a stolen base and a pitch to the ribs was about as close as an Irish softball player could get to one of Mr. Hockey's namesake performances!

With the final four wins, we finished fourth in the standings and earned a spot in the conference tourney. Since the tournament was going to be held at the Belleville Complex in South Bend, we wouldn't have to endure the humiliation of hosting but not playing in the post season. With DePaul, Louisville and South Florida all finishing ahead of us in the regular season, we knew we had to have a strong showing in the tournament to get into the NCAA Regionals. It was unlikely that the NCAA would take more than two or three teams from the conference. DePaul was probably a lock with its high national ranking. That meant a second team would probably have to win the conference tournament to gain an NCAA berth. It was possible a third team would also sneak in, but not a fourth. There were just too many other deserving teams across the country.

Conference Tournament

Although the Big East Tournament wasn't at Ivy Field on the Notre Dame campus, it was like a home stand for us, considering that we would be sleeping and practicing in familiar surroundings and many of our parents would be in town to watch us play. There was an air of desperation going into the tournament this year because we were by no means a lock to gain a berth in the NCAA Regionals. If we failed to qualify, it would break an eight-year streak of consecutive tournament appearances for Notre Dame Softball and a five-year string under Coach Gumpf, one for every year she had been at the helm of the Irish program. We didn't want to be known as the team that fell short of that important post season goal.

To prevent disaster, we needed to rack up some wins in the Big East Tournament. Three wins would give us the tournament championship and an automatic berth in the Regionals. Our first opponent in the eight-team tournament was Connecticut, the only conference foe we had not played in the regular season. We felt the rainout in Storrs had deprived us of a chance to notch a couple of important conference wins...victories that would have allowed us to claim a share of the third spot in the final regular season conference standings.

That was all in the past as we faced off against Connecticut in South Bend. Both teams needed a win to stay alive in the single elimination tournament. We started getting runners on base in the first few innings but couldn't push a run across. Meanwhile, Brittney was mowing down Husky hitters to prevent Connecticut from mounting any kind of a threat. The Huskies managed to load the bases with one out in the third, but Brittney got a strikeout and a ground out to end the inning without damage.

Irish bats came alive again in the third as the speedy Sarah Smith hit a hard ball to short and reached first on the ensuing error by the panicked Husky fielder. Huffy followed with a single that allowed Smitty to use her wheels to take third base. Katie Laing was up next and manufactured a little Irish luck with a grounder to short that took an errant bounce past the infielder's glove and into left field. Smitty scored and a bobble by the left fielder allowed Huffy to take third and Katie to slide safely into second. A line drive single by Heather Johnson drove both runners home and, just like that, we had a 3-0 lead.

I led off the fourth with a liner onto the outfield grass for a single and Carissa Jaquish slammed a liner of her own to center field. I got a good jump and rounded second without hesitation, sliding safely headfirst into third. My aggressiveness on the base paths paid a secondary dividend, drawing a throw from centerfield that allowed the equally aggressive Carissa to take second base on the play. We had two runners in scoring position with no outs and a chance to stretch the lead.

Brittney came in to bat for Smitty and hit a ground ball. I was off for home as soon as the ball hit the ground and beat the throw to the plate with a slide by, reaching back to catch the plate with my finger tips as I avoided the catcher's lunging tag. Carissa took third on the play and Brittney was safe on the fielder's choice. Coach reinserted Smitty as our runner on first under softball's substitution rule and she quickly made her presence felt again by stealing second base. Up next was Huffy who responded in the clutch with a single up the middle, driving in our fifth and sixth runs of the game.

Brittney retired the last 12 opposing hitters in the game to notch a two-hit shutout. We had eight hits with contributions up and down the lineup. Huffy had two hits and two RBI, while Smitty scored two runs, and Heather also had two RBI. It was a great way to start the tournament and the kind of success we had to have to not only contend for a Big East Championship, but also land a spot in the NCAA tournament.

While we had sent the Huskies home, we didn't have time to savor our win. We had a showdown the next day against DePaul. The number 12-ranked Blue Demons had humbled us twice eleven days earlier, and they were a perfect 20-0 in conference play on the season. We needed to knock them off here to make a statement in the conference tournament and to the NCAA tournament selection committee.

After a scoreless first inning, we got things going in the second as Heather Johnson walked to lead off the inning. Coach put Brittany Glynn in to pinch run and my classmate Linda Kohan laid down a nice sacrifice bunt to move Brittany to second. After a fly out, we had two outs and it was my turn at bat. Becca Heteniak, who would factor into our rivalry with DePaul a lot in my Notre Dame career, was on the mound and quickly got ahead of me in the count with a first pitch called strike. In my first at bat of the game, I didn't mind taking a pitch to get a feel for the pitcher's stuff. Now that I'd seen it, I was ready to be aggressive. Heteniak's next pitch was just off the outside corner, but it looked like a hittable borderline strike coming in. I triggered and went with it, driving a low line shot over first base and into right field just inside the foul line. Curtis would have been proud!

Brittany scored standing up and a slight bobble by the right fielder was all I needed to reach second on the play. Just like that, we had the upper hand against our Windy City nemeses. One run wasn't going to win a game against a tough opponent like DePaul, but for once we had an early lead in a game with the Blue Demons. Combined with masterful pitching by Brittney, it seemed to boost our confidence while it simultaneously took some of the air out of DePaul's sails.

In the third inning, we broke the game wide open, taking advantage of a DePaul fielding error to score five more times. Again, it was Smitty whose speed caused a shortstop to panic and fumble a sharply hit ground ball allowing Smitty to beat it out. Although she was erased at second base on a fielder's choice, it was only our first out of the inning and now we had the almost equally speedy Stephanie Brown on first. Then Huffy was hit by a pitch to put two aboard. After a ground out, Heather was walked to load the bases. That brought Linda to the plate and she responded with a blast to the wall in left field that drove in Brownie and Huffy. Christine then belted her third home run of the year chasing Heather and Linda across the plate ahead of her. Just like that, our one-run advantage was now a six run lead. All of our runs in the inning were scored with two outs and, due to the error on Smitty's ball, were unearned. That mistake had cost DePaul dearly.

We weren't finished yet. Carissa came up first in our half of the fourth inning and knocked one out of the park to extend our lead by one. Meanwhile, Brittney was doing her part to make that lead stand up. She retired the first 17 DePaul batters in a row and didn't give up a run until DePaul managed a couple of scores in the sixth. We got one of those runs back in the seventh as Huffy singled, Katie Laing moved her over with a sacrifice bunt and Heather slammed an RBI double into the gap. We finished up with a dominating 8-2 win over our arch rivals, earning a berth in the championship game and giving the NCAA selection committee something to think about leading up to selection Sunday.

We were jubilant that night after delivering a peak performance against the league's top team. When asked by a reporter after the game what she felt was a key to our upset win, Coach didn't hesitate in stating that my two-out single to drive in the first run of the game gave us great momentum and confidence in our ability to get the victory. As happy as we were to send DePaul packing, we were also ready to take on Louisville the next day in the tournament championship. We had a lot to prove against the Cardinals, too.

Louisville came out strong in the first inning of the championship matchup, gaining a two-run lead after one Cardinal hitter was hit by a pitch and a second hit a home run. Meanwhile, Louisville pitcher Kristen Wadwell retired the first 13 Irish hitters in a row. Still, we were hitting the ball hard and the Cardinal coaching staff decided they needed to make a pitching change even though Wadwell was pitching a no-hitter up until that point. I came to the plate with two down in the fifth and, first-pitch-swinging, drove a single to center for our first hit. I was left stranded as the inning finished without an Irish score but it was a first sign of life for the Irish.

We broke through to tie the game in the sixth. Smitty got us started with a single to left and Brownie followed up with a single the opposite way. Huffy laid down a sacrifice bunt that was mis-played into an error and Smitty scored on the play. Now we had runners on first and third with no outs. A pop-up to first resulted in a double play but Heather came through in the clutch again with a single to left field that scored Brownie. We had tied it up!

It was still tied as the Cardinals came to the plate in the bot-tom of the sixth. A lead off infield single followed by a sacrifice bunt gave Louisville a runner in scoring position with no outs. A passed ball moved the runner to third base and then a single to left drove in the go-ahead run. We escaped the inning without fur-ther damage, but we were down by one with only three outs left to tie it up or take the lead.

The Cardinals brought in a new pitcher to try to get the final three outs. Christine had other plans, though, blasting a leadoff double on a first-pitch swing to give us an immediate chance to tie the game. I came to the plate with one job to do, move Christine to third base. Coach signaled for the sacrifice bunt and a dropped one down in fair territory along the third base line. I was out at first by a step but Christine was now standing on third. We had two outs left to bring her home. Unfortunately, the Cardinal pitcher struck out our final two hitters giving Louisville the championship and an automatic berth in the NCAA Regionals.

It was a disappointing loss. We had played Louisville tough and almost come away with the win. But in the end, our inability to get a key hit at the right time had done us in. There would be no Big East championship ring for us this year. Now we had just one more hope to extend our season. Our fate rested entirely in the hands of the NCAA selection committee. DePaul and Louis-ville were both locks to make the tournament. The Blue Demons had played a tough schedule and were ranked 12th going into the Big East Tournament. The Cardinals had just earned an automatic berth by taking home the conference championship trophy.

Would the selection committee take another team from the Big East? If they did, would it be us or South Florida? The Bulls had finished second in the regular season conference standings to our fourth place finish. But, they had stumbled early in the conference tournament and had not played as tough a schedule as we had. We were on pins and needles as we gathered at Assistant Coach Lizzy Lemire's house on Sunday afternoon. We sat around and enjoyed the team cookout Lizzy had orchestrated until it was time for the selection show on ESPN News. As the brackets were announced we mentally calculated how many at-large selections remained as the announcers worked deeper through the tournament field. We were down to the final bracket and were holding our breath as the Evanston, Illinois, Regional was announced. We let out a huge shout as Notre Dame appeared in the bracket alongside number 6 Northwestern, number 25 Illinois State and Wright State. We'd made it!

Back in Evanston

For the second consecutive year, we headed to Evanston, Illinois, to participate in the NCAA Regional at Northwestern University. The host team was the overwhelming favorite in the four-team regional. Our first-hand experience with the Wildcats—a 12-0 loss in late April—gave us a healthy respect for Northwestern. But before we could worry about beating the Wildcats, we had to play a tough Illinois State team in our first game. As it turned out, my old teammate from the *Blaze*, Kaprice Williams, was a member of the Illinois State squad. Kaprice was still the most imposing athlete on the field, but the Redbirds looked tough from the top to the bottom of their lineup.

The game started with each team squandering opportunities to score in the first. Katie Laing doubled for our side but we left her stranded. Illinois State had a single, a stolen base and a walk in their half of the inning, but Brittney got two strikeouts and a ground out to escape the inning. In the second, we again left runners on base. Christine walked with one out and I managed an infield hit to give us two aboard. Christine was out at third on a ground ball fielder's choice and the next Irish batter grounded out to shortstop to end the inning.

Illinois State threatened to score in their half of the second, after Kaprice and a teammate both reached base with two outs. But we got lucky when the next batter sent a hard ground ball toward right field. It looked like a sure single and potentially an RBI but the Redbird base runner on first ran into the batted ball on her way to second for the third out.

The game remained scoreless through the third inning. In the fourth, Heather led off with a single. Brittany Glynn entered the game as a pinch runner and moved over to second base on a sacrifice bunt by Linda. Christine then lofted a fly ball that was misplayed by the centerfielder, allowing Brittany to score from second. Carissa hit a hard line drive down the left field line, but the Redbird third baseman stuck out her glove and flagged the ball down for the third out. Illinois State tied it in the bottom of the fourth after the leadoff hitter was hit by a pitch. Two groundouts later, she was on third. Kaprice came through in the clutch, with an infield single to drive home the tying run.

The game was like a heavyweight boxing match. Each side kept punching away hoping to wear down the other and gain the upper hand. We were held scoreless in the top of the fifth but in the bottom of the frame, the leadoff hitter for the Redbirds reached first on an error, moved over to second on a sacrifice bunt, and then scored on a double to give Illinois State the lead for the first time in the game.

We came out battling in the sixth to try to even the score and regain the advantage. Heather singled with one out in the inning to get things started. A ground out sent her to second and Christine came up with two outs and lashed a single to centerfield, allowing Heather to round third and rumble for home. A perfect strike from the centerfielder gunned her down at the plate to end the inning. We went down 1-2-3 in the seventh and found ourselves on the wrong end of a final 2-1 score and in the loser's side of the tournament after just one game.

Northwestern defeated Wright State in the second game of the day, setting up a win-or-go home game between the Irish and the Raiders early Saturday afternoon. We were up to the challenge against Wright State, pinning a 3-0 elimination loss on the Raiders and extending our tournament by another game. Neither team could mount a scoring threat in the first two innings of the game. After escaping without harm from a Wright State rally in the third, we mounted a rally of our own in the fourth. Katie singled to lead off and moved to second on a sacrifice bunt by Heather. A balk was called on the Raider pitcher to move Katie to third and she came home on an error by the Wright State shortstop.

We almost scored again in the fifth when Carissa doubled to lead off. She was held at second after the next batter lined out to third base. Brownie was safe on an error on her grounder to shortstop. Then she and Carissa moved up a base on a wild pitch giving us two runners in scoring position. Huffy lofted a fly ball to the centerfielder and Carissa tagged up and sprinted home as the ball was caught. For the second time in the tournament, a perfect strike by an outfielder gunned down an Irish runner at the plate, ending our rally.

We finally gave Brittney some breathing room with a two run rally in the sixth. Katie and Heather both reached base on bunt singles and each took an extra base on errant throws, setting up an RBI opportunity for Linda who came through with a single that scored both runners. After Christine's sacrifice bunt moved Linda to second, I singled through the left side to move her to third. A pop out to first base resulted in a double play to cap the scoring. Kenya came in to relieve Brittney in the seventh and she retired three Raider hitters on strikeouts to complete the shutout win.

As expected, Northwestern continued its winning ways by defeating Illinois State, setting up a rematch between the Irish and the Redbirds Saturday evening. We were eager to get another shot at the team that had narrowly defeated us the day before. We had to win to earn a shot at Northwestern and perhaps derail the Wildcats' roll toward the Super Regionals.

Our second game against Illinois State was as evenly matched as our first encounter had been. We put runners on base in the first inning with one out. Huffy singled up the middle, Katie was safe on a fielder's choice, and Heather also singled before a strike out ended our threat. Illinois State had better luck in their half of the inning, with two singles, an error and a wild pitch resulting in a run.

In the second, we began scratching and clawing to tie the score. Christine was hit by a pitch to get us started. I dug myself out of a two-strike count with a single to right center. Carissa followed up with a sacrifice bunt that moved Christine to third and me to second. A groundball to shortstop brought Christine home to tie the score. I moved over to third but was left stranded by a ground out.

Brittney retired the side in order in the bottom of the second, but the Illinois State pitcher was equally efficient in the top of the third inning. In the bottom of the third, Brittney hit the leadoff batter. The next batter managed a bunt single. After a ground out moved the runners over and a walk loaded the bases, a sacrifice fly to centerfield resulted in an RBI giving the Redbirds a one-run lead again.

In the top of the fourth, I doubled to right with two outs, but made it no farther as the Illinois State pitcher recorded a strike out to end the inning. After a scoreless fifth inning, we used a walk and a hit batter to put two runners aboard in the sixth but we couldn't bring them home. Kaprice came up in the bottom of the sixth and showed my teammates the awesome power that she'd displayed back when we played 14-and-under ball together for the *Blaze*. Kaprice launched a blast to left field that easily cleared the left field fence, putting the Redbirds ahead by two, 3—1. We failed to muster a base runner in the seventh and, just like that, our season was over. We'd only managed four hits in the game compared to six for Illinois State. Even a strong pitching performance by Brittney couldn't compensate for our cold bats.

Reflecting on Our Season

The season hadn't ended in victory. On the road to an NCAA national championship, only one team ends the year with a win. In 2007, that team was Arizona. Northwestern went on to win our Regional and then won the Super Regional to earn a spot in the College World Series. But even the mighty Wildcats ended their season with a loss, finishing third in Oklahoma City on the heels of their second place finish the year before.

Although we hadn't earned the chance to play for a national title—and that was our goal every year—we did accomplish a lot considering how our season began. Among all Irish performances, none was more impressive than Stephanie Brown's. Brownie earned first team All Big East honors and was named ESPN the Magazine Second Team All American...a huge accomplishment. She recovered from her horrific facial injuries early in the season to finish the season with a .406 batting average, an on base percentage of .464, 67 hits and 40 runs scored. She was a dominant force for us in the leadoff spot in our lineup.

Joining Brownie with All Big East honors were Katie and Brittney on the second team. My jaw dropped at the Big East banquet when they called my name as a member of the third team. My .362 batting average in conference play and .289 average overall got the attention of the conference coaches. Personally, I was just as proud of my perfect 1.000 fielding percentage. By working non-stop to maintain as much strength and flexibility as possible, I'd managed to prevent my shoulder from being a liability in the field. I even had a couple of assists along the way to show I could still sling it when I needed to.

I also thought my overall aggressiveness in the field, at the plate and on the base paths helped make the Irish a grittier team and harder to beat. Diving to get an out, taking the extra base, putting the bat on the ball when we needed to move a runner into scoring position—they were all small things that could pay huge dividends in tight games. Perhaps seeing me sacrifice my body to make plays inspired others to reach back and demand more of themselves. I wasn't the only one on the team doing whatever it took to help the team win, but I felt I was doing my part to elevate the team's desire and effort to the highest level.

Coming off my first full season of action in an Irish uniform, I was pumped up and ready to build on my initial success to play an even bigger role in our team's success in 2008. In my year-end meeting, Coach offered what I considered the ultimate compliment and vote of confidence. "I couldn't keep you off the field," she said, reflecting on my season. But then she commented that there was a lot more talent coming in with the next recruiting class. "If your arm isn't better next year, you won't play." That made it crystal clear. I knew where I stood and what I had to do to be ready for my junior season.

Sophomore Summer

The beginning of summer didn't come without some sadness. A few weeks earlier, the second member of our original seven player "cult" had decided to leave Notre Dame. Erin Glasco, a talented catcher, had decided to transfer to Texas A&M. Playing behind the plate or as our designated player, Erin had hit some of the most memorable home runs of the season including a line shot off of the Ivy Field scoreboard in deep centerfield. She had also been my roommate in the Spring semester and I'd spent a lot of extra time working in the batting cages with Erin and her Dad. We were both committed to do whatever it took to perform our best in every at bat. Erin went on to have a great career at A&M as a player and later as an assistant coach.

A second development was even more heartbreaking. While we were in Evanston at Regionals, my parents received a phone call from our neighbors who were taking care of Gus, our family dog. They said Gus had suddenly lost the ability to stand up and was having trouble breathing. By the time we arrived home the next day, Gus was in pretty bad shape. Our neighbors had taken him to the vet while we were gone, but there wasn't much the doctor could do without further tests. We called him and explained that Gus was getting worse and he referred us to an emergency veterinary clinic where the doctors on staff diagnosed Gus with myasthenia gravis, a genetic condition that not only would not allow him to stand, it also had permanently damaged his esophagus and prevented him from properly swallowing and digesting his food. Undigested food had apparently entered Gus' lungs, giving him pneumonia. They recommended taking Gus to the Michigan State University veterinary school and clinic where experts could treat his disease and its side effects. We left Gus in East Lansing with heavy hearts. We didn't know if he was going to live for another day or long enough for us to ever see him again.

After a week of treatment, though, it looked like Gus might recover. The vet explained to us that, although his condition was incurable, with proper care, Gus could lead a long and normal life. We only had Gus home for a few days, though, before his pneumonia returned. A day later we had to make the difficult decision to put him down. At only six years old, Gus should have been in a Golden Retriever's prime of life. Our neighbors were as heartbroken as we were. Our house and yard seemed really empty without Gus there to greet us each day.

Losing Gus was a tough way to start the summer but I had work to do to get ready for my junior year at Notre Dame. It was hard to believe that my college career was half over. It seemed like just yesterday that I was working with Donny to get recruited. I knew that the second half of my career would go just as quickly as the first half so I wanted to make the most of it. After all, I had already missed playing most of my freshman year. In effect, my just-completed sophomore season was my rookie campaign. Now I wanted to keep my momentum going. Coach's message in my year-end meeting gave me plenty of motivation to keep working on my hitting, fielding and throwing, not to mention the strength and conditioning drills Mike had compiled in our inch-thick summer workout plan.

In the spring, keeping my shoulder and arm in game shape had taken all of Kathy's and my focus. As I compensated for my shoulder stiffness and pain, I would add strain on my throwing arm, so the whole arm was sore and frequently felt 'dead'. Kathy arranged a consultation with the surgeon who had performed my surgery and he prescribed a stretching routine over the course of several weeks. When that didn't help, he put me on a strengthening routine. After performing the workout regimen through the end of the season, I was still unable to throw without pain or with normal strength and accuracy.

Before I left South Bend for the summer, Kathy and I asked the Doctor if he would prescribe an MRI of my shoulder and see if the imaging test would help him identify a physical cause for my problems. I had already missed one season, and had played my second season in pain and at less than full strength. The doctor said he still didn't think there was anything wrong with my arm and that an MRI was unnecessary. Instead he gave me a cortisone shot in the shoulder joint to see if that would reduce the inflammation, stiffness and pain. He said I should not throw for most of the summer to let the shoulder rest and heal.

As a result, my summer began without a staple of my offseason workouts—throwing practice. I'd have to wait for clearance to begin light throwing late in the summer and then continue to progressively throw harder when I returned to campus for fall practices. In the meantime, A.J. and I worked through Mike's offseason strength and conditioning program with our full energy. We had access to the high school weight room and the outdoor track to take care of the strength and conditioning work. If I couldn't throw, I could at least make sure I was in peak condition, avoiding any exercises the doctor said would be bad for my arm.

Dad, A.J. and I quickly settled into a practice routine. When Dad got home from work, we'd take advantage of the long West Michigan evenings to work out. We'd start with hitting. I normally did some tee work into the net in my garage at home during the day, so on the field after dinner, we'd start out with some soft toss. Dad would sit on a bucket a few feet up the first base line and toss balls to the plate where I'd connect and drive them to the outfield. A.J. would track down the balls and, when we'd used up 30 or 40 balls, he'd help Dad and I refill the buckets so we could do a second round of soft toss.

We'd keep going with soft toss until I felt like my timing was good and my swing was producing a consistent barrage of line drives and long fly balls. The high school coaches had left one of the hitting screens out for softball players who wanted to take some batting practice during the summer. We'd set up the screen about 20 feet in front of the plate so my Dad could pitch front toss to me. The short distance from my Dad's release point and the batters' box made up for the fact that he wasn't going to be pitching as fast or with as much movement as a college pitcher.

He threw with enough velocity and accuracy that I had to re-act quickly to his pitches. Job one was to swing only at strikes. Job two was to hit the pitch where it was thrown...inside pitches to left field and outside pitches to right. I'd try to pepper the screen in front of my Dad with a line drive if the pitch was down the middle. Dad was pretty good about ducking behind the screen before a batted ball could hit him, but once in a while I'd hit a hard, low comebacker that would make him dance a little bit.

Once I was satisfied with the quality of my swings—typically after five or six buckets of balls—we'd put the screen away, and get ready for some fielding drills. I wasn't allowed to throw because of the cortisone shot I'd received before leaving campus in the spring. But I could work on catching fly balls and grounders. Dad would position himself at home plate and I'd go to left field where he would hit fly balls, pop ups, ground balls and line drives in my direction. He tended to spray the ball around, which meant I had plenty of opportunities to work on getting a quick jump, taking a good angle and tracking down balls to both sides as well as in front of me and over my head.

Once I'd fielded each ball, I rolled them underhanded into the infield where A.J. gathered them up so we could refill the buck-ets and keep going. I was taking no chances with my shoulder. If the doctor and Kathy said no throwing, I wasn't going to ignore them. I really hoped that the cortisone shot would clear up any lin-gering inflammation in my shoulder and allow me to once again throw hard and accurately without the sharp pain I had endured throughout my sophomore season.

Several weeks into the summer, A.J. and I cooked up a scheme to fill the empty place in my parent's home and in our hearts with a new puppy. Dad was on board, but my Mom required a little more convincing. She was thinking about the practical matter of who would take care of a dog when we were back in school and my Dad was at work. To bolster our argument, A.J. and I decided we would fund our puppy purchase by holding a garage sale. We gathered up just about everything we could imagine never using again and ran our sale for three consecutive days. When floor traffic was slow in my parents' garage, I'd get out the classified ads from the daily paper and call breeders with Golden Retriever puppies for sale. After three days, we had several hundred dollars in our pocket and leads on a few promising litters.

Then our plans took a twist. My brother Andy said he had a friend who was a breeder and had a litter of Golden pups that we should check out. After our experience with Gus, we had talked to the vet about what to look for in our next dog. He said to find a reputable breeder with dogs that had a history of good health and long lives. My brother's friend not only had the mother dog and litter, but also had the 13-year-old grandma dog that was still reasonably spry and healthy. We felt that was about as good an assurance of healthy bloodlines as we were likely to find.

The pups had been born in early July and would be ready to leave their mother in late August. After paying a visit to the breeder, we decided we had found our pup. Even Mom couldn't resist those little guys. We'd have to wait a few weeks, but that was fine. The puppy would be ready to come home before I left for South Bend to start my junior year of studies and softball.

A.J. Chases His Dream

I worked hard but smart for the rest of the summer and A.J. and Dad were there with me for all the workouts. Since Dad was working all day, I really depended on A.J. I did most of my strength and conditioning workouts during the day, taking advantage of our high school's weight room and track. There would be conditioning tests when I returned to campus and I planned to exceed Mike's and Coach's goals for me, arriving on campus in peak condition. I hoped my teammates would take conditioning as seriously as I did, because there'd be extra sprints and other team penalties if any of us arrived out of shape.

A.J. was my training partner and almost constant companion. We had been dating since our senior year of high school and had been close from the start. He was smart, funny and, most of all, he was a warm, caring person with a calm way about him that helped me relax to get through the rough patches in my softball life. He was also a committed athlete, which meant we had a lot in common when it came to training and practicing. Both of us worked hard every day to hone our skills and get better.

It's not like we were so harmonious that we were boring. We both were very competitive, stubborn and strong-willed, and we would razz each other a lot, pushing the right buttons to really rile each other up. In the end though, we were a good match. We offered encouragement, pushed each other, listened, talked, and shared our hearts. I felt really lucky to have found A.J. and was pretty sure he felt the same.

A.J. had played shortstop and pitched for our high school baseball team and had just finished his second year as an outfielder in junior college baseball. This summer he was training to get ready for his third season of college ball. He was going to follow his dream of playing ball for a university down South where the seasons were longer and the quality of ball was often higher than in the North. This was a big deal for A.J. An illness had hurt his recruiting process in high school so he'd decided to play for a couple of years near home before chasing his dream to play at a four-year school.

The wait had paid off. He was recruited and signed an offer letter to play for Limestone College in Gaffney, South Carolina. A.J. was really excited to take the next step in his college career and to have the chance to play ball in the South. I was really happy for him. I'd had the chance to live my dream at Notre Dame. A.J. absolutely deserved the chance to live his.

Still, this was the first time we were going to be living more than a couple of hours apart. During the recruiting process and ever since he signed his letter, we'd shoved that unpleasant detail into the backs of our minds. I was living my dream and now A.J. was going to live his. Life couldn't be better. We both pursued our training with added excitement. But as July turned to August and the beginning of fall classes drew closer, we both began to think about the separation that lay ahead. The reality of how much we were going to miss each other began to sink in.

It wasn't as though our parallel athletic careers had allowed us to see much of each other in the previous two years. During my first years of college, I didn't see A.J. except for an occasional football weekend, a party in South Bend, or when I made the drive home for a weekend. With our sports commitments, neither one of us could get away to visit the other frequently. Mostly we saw each other on holidays and over winter break, but we talked every day by phone, staying close even though we were two hours apart.

We had learned to live without seeing each other at all during our spring sports seasons. My Irish team played ball every weekend and often during the week. Many weekends we were on airplanes or busses. A.J.'s schedule was similar. In the first two years, I think I made it home for one weekend each spring. We typically had Easter weekend off and I'd drive home to spend the weekend with my family and A.J.

After two school years of college and living apart, I tried to convince myself that the coming year shouldn't be any different. But it had dawned on both of us how important those few visits the past two years had been to us. The planning that led up to them was fun as well. Now the end of the summer was upon us and we realized the next time we'd see each other would be Thanksgiving break. That seemed like an eternity away.

As much as we were going to miss each other, there was no way I wanted A.J. to reconsider his plans. If you give up your dreams, you face a lifetime of regrets. We believed that, if our love was strong, it would withstand the challenges of a long-distance relationship. Meanwhile, we both had goals to pursue on the playing field. If we were each going to be satisfied when our playing careers were over, we needed to know in our hearts that we had worked as hard as possible to be our best and had played to our full potential. If that meant living 700 miles apart, so be it. As they say in poker, we were *all in*.

I made plans to accompany A.J. and his family on the long drive to South Carolina to drop him off at school. We had one last detail to take care of before the trip: pick out our new puppy. When we arrived at the breeding kennel, there were only two puppies left. They were both really cute, but one was a chunky little bruiser who fit the name we had pre-selected for the newest member of our family. We had decided to name our puppy after Ivan "Pudge" Rodriguez, one of the all-time greats in Major League Baseball and, at the time, the leader of the resurgent Detroit Tigers. Who names their dog Pudge? If you lived in our family of softball and baseball players and fans, it was a question you didn't really have to ask.

A few days later, we loaded up A.J.'s parents' van and headed off for South Carolina. We stopped in Nashville to visit friends along the way and tried to make the trip a kind of vacation adventure. But our impending goodbye was never very far from our minds. Finally we reached Gaffney and the Limestone campus. We moved A.J. into the apartment he would be sharing with a couple of teammates and toured the town and campus for a day before the dreaded moment arrived. It was time to say goodbye. A.J. and I hugged and kissed, prolonging things as long as we could, but there was no delaying it any longer. I climbed into the van and A.J.'s parents and I started our long drive home. My heart was really heavy. I tried to be sociable with A.J.'s parents and they did their best to lift my spirits, even though I know they were also sad that A.J. would be living so far from home for the first time.

A week later, it was time to leave for school myself. For the third time in my college career, we packed up my Mom's minivan and hauled my clothes, softball equipment, and assorted other belongings down to South Bend for move-in day at my dormitory. I was glad to be back on campus. Although getting to know Pudge in the past few days had been fun, being home without A.J. wasn't the same. I wanted to get back to school and get back to work in the classroom and on the field. There was no point in sitting around and moping and it was time to take my game to the next level.

I was also looking forward to meeting my new roommate for the year. With Erin's departure the previous spring, I'd been left without a plan for a roommate in my junior year. Then, Coach announced that we would have a transfer player joining us in the fall. Alexia Clay had played her freshman year at the University of Tennessee, making it all the way to the World Series where she hit a pinch hit home run. She had decided a softball career at Tennessee would not allow her to pursue her academic goal of attending medical school, which led her to transfer to Notre Dame.

Alexia was a catcher and was from nearby Rochester, Indiana. She had played her travel ball with the *Indiana Magic*, the opponent that had figured so prominently in my own travel softball career. It turned out her Dad was the coach of the Magic and still managed the team even though Alexia's travel ball career was over. As we began to move my stuff into the dorm room, Alexia and her parents arrived. After a round of introductions, we went about the work of moving two girls into one dorm room. It's amazing that almost four carloads of stuff will fit in a room that small.

With everything moved in, my parents walked me over to the bookstore so I could pick up the bundle of books and other classroom materials reserved under my name. After lugging the books back to the dorm, we hauled my bat bag and equipment over to the locker room and I moved it into my locker. Before long, it looked like I had never been away. Now it was time to say good-bye to Mom, Dad and Pudge. The little guy had waited patiently while we unpacked the van and moved into my room. Now it was his turn to be the center of attention again. With me and A.J. off to school, he'd have my parents all to himself.

Junior Year

With two autumns at Notre Dame behind me, it didn't take long to settle into my academic and softball routine. The fall started with our strength and conditioning testing. Then we began our fall practice and training schedule. After my cortisone shot in the spring, and the doctor's and Kathy's instructions to limit throwing activity for most of the summer, I arrived back on campus with a rested shoulder. But I was just beginning the process of rehabilitation to gain strength and build accuracy so I was behind my teammates in getting ready for fall ball.

I knew the competition for playing time this year would be intense. In addition to Smitty who would be a senior, and my classmate, Stephanie Mola, there were a number of younger girls vying for a spot in the outfield. The freshmen and sophomores were great athletes and their ranks include several talented outfielders. Although I felt I had proven as a sophomore that I could help the team with my performance, this year's freshmen and sophomores had a couple of advantages over me: Their throwing shoulders were healthy and the coaches knew their futures were ahead of them.

Still, I was determined to show Coach I could get my throwing arm ready to start the season in the starting lineup. The first order of business was to get ready to play fall ball. I wanted to finally get to play in the field as well as hit against our fall opponents. This year Michigan, Nebraska, Western Michigan and the University of Illinois at Chicago (UIC) would be coming to Ivy Field for the Worth Classic fall tournament in late September. The competition would be top flight and I wanted to be in the thick of it.

Coach wanted to take it slow with my shoulder to make sure we were strengthening it properly to withstand the throwing workload I would face in practice and in games. Since it was fall, she wasn't worried about full participation in practice. During outfield drills I was allowed to underhand the ball back in after fielding it to reduce strain on my shoulder until it was stronger.

Kathy and I had begun our daily stretching and strengthening routines immediately when I returned to campus from summer break. We needed to keep the swelling and pain under control and continue to build strength and mobility. The process was slow and still painful but I was determined to fight through it. I was hitting well in practice and, if I could bring my throw along far enough, I was sure Coach wouldn't keep a strong bat out of the lineup.

After several weeks of practice and therapy, it became clear that the cortisone and a summer of rest hadn't healed me. The condition of my shoulder and arm was right back where we had left off in the spring. Now we were all really discouraged. Kathy arranged for me to see the orthopedic surgeon again. The doctor had evaluated my shoulder during my sophomore year and said a second surgery was unnecessary. Now, a year later, it seemed like another evaluation was in order. This time the doctor not only said there was nothing wrong with my shoulder, he said the problem was probably all in my head. I was certain that was not true. But to make matters worse, he shared that opinion with the coaching staff and they seemed to take his word for it.

I was frustrated, angry and hurt. I knew that I was doing everything I could to rehabilitate my shoulder. I wanted nothing more than to be healthy enough to earn a spot in the line-up. How could the doctor and my coaches believe I was inventing the pain and inability to throw properly that stood between me and having the career I had dreamed of for years? In their defense, I know my situation was frustrating to the coaches. They had a lot invested in me as an athlete, both financially and in terms of time and effort. The doctor was the expert they depended on to make sure players were healthy and physically ready to play. They trusted him to provide an accurate picture of the situation and for the proper advice on how to handle an injury and a player's recovery. Still, I hoped they knew me well enough to know I wasn't a head case...that I really was physically hurt.

My parents were worried about me and we talked about what to do next. I could ask for another doctor's opinion. But that would mean telling Notre Dame's doctor and the softball coaching staff that I didn't trust their judgment. I was worried I might further jeopardize my place on the team by rocking the boat. What if another doctor said I needed surgery and it cost me another year on the field? What if the other doctor did the surgery and botched it, making my situation even worse? Where would I stand with my coaches and Notre Dame then?

That left only one option: continue to rely on the judgment of the team doctor, even if we knew my pain and loss of arm strength and control were not all in my head. In hindsight, I guess we may have taken too much to heart Coach's cautionary comments at our freshman dinner about parent interference with her team. But Donny had also counseled me to check my parent's involvement at the door when I arrived on campus. Perhaps we should have spoken up more loudly, but that would have meant changing the rules of engagement I had agreed to when I accepted Coach's offer to play at Notre Dame.

Pushing aside my disappointment, I became even more determined to overcome my physical problems by working harder, spending more time with ice bags strapped to my shoulder, enduring more stretching and manipulation, and just generally doing whatever it took to beat this problem and keep my dream alive.

As the fall tournament approached, I wasn't surprised when Coach said she would use me as a designated player and give younger players the chance to play in the outfield. They were physically healthier than I was and she wanted to give them playing time. I could understand the reasoning behind her decision. But I was still disappointed that I wasn't at full strength and ready to participate fully in the field for the third autumn in a row.

Defense had always been an important part of my game as a softball player. I loved making plays in the outfield. There was nothing sweeter than running into the gaps to snag line drives, sprinting and diving to catch balls in front of me, going back deep to the warning track to snag long balls before they could carom off the fence or leave the park. Charging a ground ball, gathering it on the run and drilling a throw to the right base to nab a base runner for an out—or to prevent a runner from taking an extra base—was also special. Even the routine plays were simple pleasures that gave me a thrill.

Playing in the field not only gave me a lot of personal satisfaction, it helped me as a hitter as well. After sprinting in from the outfield to grab my batting helmet, gloves and bat, I strode to the plate relaxed and full of confidence that the opposing pitcher couldn't stop me from getting on base. It was a far cry from the feeling I had when pinch hitting or serving as the designated player. Having time on my hands to plan each at bat or to dwell on the previous at bat just didn't suit my aggressive personality. I needed to be fully involved in the game action to absorb the rhythm of the game, channel my aggressiveness, and feed off my involvement in the field when I was at the plate.

Although my role as a fielder would be limited in this year's fall ball action, I redoubled my efforts to show Coach I could be an effective weapon for the Irish. As a team we split our games in the Worth Invitational, losing 7-2 to Michigan and 3-0 to Nebraska, but beating Western Michigan 6-5 and UIC 14-4. The next weekend, we played at Loyola of Chicago to close our fall ball season and we beat the Ramblers 6-1. I was on a hitting tear all fall, playing as the designated player and as a pinch hitter. Although no official statistics were published, Lizzy told me later that I ended up hitting over .800 and contributed several RBI. I was especially gratified that I had managed hits against the toughest pitching, including the Michigan and Nebraska hurlers, and that a number of my hits had come in clutch situations with runners in scoring position. I felt I had made a strong case to keep my spot in the lineup when we took the field in the spring.

With fall ball behind me, it was back to rehab with Kathy. For the third year in a row, physical rehabilitation was a daily part of my life. By now I had become an expert in balancing classes, outside reading and study sessions, group projects for my business classes...plus our normal team strength and conditioning sessions and one-on-one coach's workouts. I was also taking my turn as a bullpen catcher for our pitchers, a duty I shared with most of my teammates. Add an hour or more in the training room most days of the week, and my schedule was jam packed. I had spent so much time on rehab so far in my college career, my Dad joked that I had a double major in accounting and physical therapy.

Busy as we were, my teammates and I had more on our minds than softball and academics. After the fall season ended, it would be barely a month before we would leave on our team trip to Italy. It was an event each of us had been thinking about since we arrived on campus and one of the highlights of our softball careers. NCAA rules only permitted the Notre Dame Softball team to take an overseas trip every four years, but that was often enough that every athlete could participate once in her four years on campus.

The trips were Coach's way of allowing her players to participate more fully in the Notre Dame experience. Most Notre Dame students have an opportunity to study abroad at some point during their college careers. Our softball schedule would not allow most of us to take advantage of that opportunity, so Coach made an overseas trip a part of every Irish softball player's career. We did our part to make the trip possible. Our softball camps and clinics were fundraisers and we sold raffle tickets and other items to raise the money for the trip. Now fall break was upon us and we were finally going to leave on our Italian adventure.

Italy

I'd never been overseas before we boarded the transatlantic flight to London but I was really looking forward to the adventure. It was a long flight, but our enthusiasm was high as we waited in anticipation for our arrival in London. Although it was just a stopping point on our way to Rome, the short time we spent exploring the airport gave us an early glimpse of the exotic land we'd be touring over the next week. It was like no airport we'd ever seen, with fine shops and restaurants lining the corridors. We had to remind ourselves that this was just a brief stop on the way to Italy, and not the destination itself.

Finally we boarded the plane for Rome and settled in for the two-hour flight. Some of us napped to try to recover from the first leg of our journey, but others were too excited to sleep. When we finally arrive in Rome, we gathered our luggage, boarded our bus and headed for the hotel that would be our home for the next couple of days. When Sadie, Katie and I opened the door and stepped inside our room we were astonished at how small it was. That was alright, sleep was the last thing on anyone's mind. In fact, we were back in the lobby a few minutes later to leave on our first sightseeing excursion in the Eternal City.

We boarded a bus and headed out through the narrow, historic streets of Rome to visit the Spanish Steps. We also sampled some of the shopping and had our first authentic Italian pizza and gelato—as the saying goes, "when in Rome, do as the Romans do"! Jet lag was beginning to catch up with us, so we called it an early evening and headed back to the hotel for some sleep, but not before learning about the full day of sightseeing we'd embark on the next day.

After breakfast, we headed downtown to sample more of the historic architecture of Rome. We saw the Coliseum, the Trevi

Fountain, the Pantheon, Piazza Novona, Piazza di Fiori and other sights. It was incredible. Also intriguing were the street vendors who sold just about anything a tourist could ever desire. I selected a few smaller items in a couple of the shops, but decided to save most of my money for the glassware factory that Lizzy said we'd be visiting in Venice. As we were heading back to our hotel for dinner, we watched at the bus stop as the coach we thought we were supposed to board zoomed by without pausing to pick us up. We waited around for another bus but it was Sunday and the buses were marked differently than we were expecting. After seven more buses went by, we finally boarded a coach that seemed headed in a favorable direction when suddenly, the vehicle started smoking. The driver screeched to a halt and quickly ushered us off onto the sidewalk. We were bus-less again.

We began walking to see if we could avoid the expense of a taxi and stumble on the right bus to get us back to our suburban hotel. Although it was night time, there were enough of us that we weren't scared or worried. Strange city or not, Rome was a beautiful place. In our wandering, we happened upon the Vatican and Saint Peter's Square and Basilica. The buildings and square were brilliantly illuminated and absolutely stunning. Getting lost had provided us with the unforgettable opportunity to walk through the square and marvel at the historic architecture, which was spectacular as it glowed in the night. We eventually found another bus stop, but, after waiting for buses that never came, we gave up and piled into a taxi for the ride to the hotel.

On our third day in Rome, we were up early to tour the Vatican again, this time the way our tour guides had planned. They escorted us through Saint Peter's Square and Basilica, and provided us with historical background on all the sights, including the great works of art and architecture created by Michelangelo and other masters. It was as awe-inspiring in the daylight as it had been the night before.

Our time in Rome was not entirely consumed with formal tours lead by official guides. In addition to our nighttime visit to Saint Peter's, several of us took a liking to gelato, the Italian frozen delicacy. It turned out here was a gelato shop near our hotel. During our frequent visits to the shop, we discovered that it was a meeting place frequented by the young men of the neighborhood. Before long we were making friends, hanging out, talking and joking around. I'm sure they didn't see a team of female American athletes in their neighborhood very often. Then again, it wasn't every day that we were in Rome meeting a lot of Italian guys. Abbracciare la diversità (Embrace diversity)!

Next on the itinerary was Florence where we toured churches and other historic buildings and enjoyed the view of the scenic hills of Tuscany. Along the way we viewed works of art by Michelangelo and Donatello before gathering for another terrific Italian feast. Next to art and architecture, great food was becoming the predominant theme of our Italian adventure.

Venice was our destination the next morning. Upon arrival, we checked into the hotel then split into a couple of groups for some sightseeing. The city was a lot less congested than Rome or Florence and the signature canals and gondolas were like nothing we'd ever seen before. I took a gondola ride with several teammates and Assistant Coach Kris Ganeff's dad, Neil McCleary, who had joined us on the trip. With the romance of Venice all around us and a gondolier guiding our passage, it was postcard perfect experience. Poor Neil. It wasn't long before my teammates and I had decided he was my "date" on our romantic cruise through the canals. We had become good friends earlier in my career when we both helped out at the Irish summer softball camps (and shared expert opinions on how to make the perfect peanut butter and jelly sandwich for campers), so making Neil uncomfortable for an entire gondola ride seemed perfectly natural. I think he eventually forgave us.

We finally made it to the glass factory and Lizzy was right, it was worth waiting for. I bought some unique blue glass figures for my parents and a vase for myself. I'm not a collector of that sort of thing, but the glassware was too beautiful to pass up. That night in the hotel, I spent a lot of time creating cocoons out of the clothing in my suitcase to protect those treasures for the rest of our Italian journey and the trip home.

The final stop on our Italian adventure was the town of Forli near San Marino. We would spend our last night in Italy in a local hotel before waking up to play an exhibition game against a team comprised of players from Italy's professional softball league and members of the Italian national team. That made this the ultimate softball road trip! After a week of touring, eating, and more touring, we weren't exactly in peak condition for competition. But Coach did her best to whip us into shape with a practice the afternoon before the game.

We exchanged gifts with the Italian team and then got down to business when the umpire yelled, "Giocare a palla!" or 'Play ball!" in Italian. We came out a little slow but ended up with a 10-0 win. After the game, we said goodbye to our hosts and boarded the bus for Rome and our flight back home. It had been the adventure of our young lifetimes, a memorable week shared with great friends. In the air over the Atlantic, I promised myself I'd return to visit Italy again someday, but I knew it would be hard to match the camaraderie and fun we'd shared traveling overseas as Irish softball teammates.

Back on Campus

Upon our return from Italy, we settled back into our fall athletic and academic routine. After making the Dean's list my first two years at Notre Dame, and earning Notre Dame Student Athlete Academic Honors, I was continuing to do well in the classroom. I had firmed up my decision to major in accounting and I tapped into Notre Dame's career counseling program to begin assembling a resume and develop the interview skills I would need to be ready for the upcoming on-campus career days. The events would include recruiting visits by the leading accounting firms and I wanted to be on my game.

The goal was to secure an internship with an attractive firm that would allow me to gain valuable work experience during the summer between my junior and senior years. Students who performed well during their internships would often receive job offers, allowing them to begin their careers with the same company as soon as they graduated. While there could be many internships available in larger cities such as New York, Chicago and Washington, D.C., there wouldn't be as many in available in Grand Rapids, where I hoped to live and work after my college career was over.

Career goals aside, there were very practical reasons to try to land an internship in Grand Rapids. Gaining my work experience close to home would save me the expense of paying rent and buying groceries during my summer on the job. If I worked in Grand Rapids, I could live at home, enjoy Mom's cooking, and save the money I earned all summer to repay student loans. I would also be able to practice in the evenings and on weekends with A.J. and Dad. At the first career day, I met with representatives from three prestigious firms that said they would be hiring interns in Grand Rapids. Over the course of the next few months, I interviewed with and received offers from all three. I eventually accepted an internship as an auditor with PricewaterhouseCoopers (PWC), an international leader in business accounting. I was really excited to have the chance to work with the team I met during my interview visit. I liked being part of a close team, and they had impressed me with the way they seemed to enjoy working together.

While my hard work in the classroom and on the career trail was paying off, I was still struggling athletically. Despite all of my and Kathy's efforts, I could not regain throwing strength and accuracy. In fact, the grind of practice throwing just seemed to wear my shoulder down. The pain in the shoulder had also become more intense. I was worried that I was doing more damage the more I threw.

Near the end of the fall academic term Coach met with me to discuss her plans for the coming season. When we returned to campus in January, there would only be a month of practice time before the season began. Coach had to have her lineup pretty well set now so we could spend that month working on honing our defensive play to razor sharp perfection. Even though my throw had not gotten better and the act of throwing was painful, I was prepared to play and felt my four intact tools—I could still hit for average and power, run the bases well, and catch balls that might otherwise drop in for hits—were strong enough to help the Irish on the field, even if the fifth tool was subpar.

Coach quickly gave me a dose of reality. She told me I would not be a starting outfielder for the Irish the coming season. "Your arm isn't ready," she said bluntly. I knew from our conversation at the end of the previous season that what I had accomplished as a sophomore with the same arm didn't matter. There were too many other gifted outfielders on the team this year to risk using me and have other teams exploit my arm to take extra bases and score runs.

The odds were stacked against me, but I wasn't going to take Coach's decision lying down, even if I understood why she had made it. I was discouraged, but I wasn't giving up. I would change her mind by continuing to hit and showing in practice I could perform in the outfield without hurting the team.

Changing Sides

I had continued to hit strongly all fall in practice and during our fall ball games, so I was sure Coach would have to weigh my offensive productivity in her final decision. But transforming my throw from a liability into a non-factor in her decision would be harder. Kathy and I had tried everything to get my shoulder and arm into game shape. I didn't have a clue what to try next.

The weekend before my last couple of exams, A.J. made the drive down from Grand Rapids to see me. He had just arrived home after wrapping up his first semester at Limestone and he didn't want to wait another week to see me. While he was in town, I asked him to help me work on my throw in the Eck softball and baseball practice facility. There were no team workouts during exams and I wanted his help and guidance. A.J. knew me better than anyone else. I shared all my personal ups and downs with him in our daily phone calls and he knew when I needed to be encouraged and when I was ready for advice. As my offseason training partner, A.J. also knew what I was dealing with physically. He knew the training drills we had tried in the past and what had produced results. I hoped if we worked together he would detect something that would help me straighten out my throw.

We began playing catch and, before long, I became extremely frustrated with my inability to just throw the ball and hit his glove. Playing catch was the first softball skill I had learned as a little girl. It is the most fundamental skill in the game. Since the beginning of my injury problems, I had never gotten over the fact that I could no longer make my shoulder and arm perform this basic task with strength, accuracy and consistency. If anything, it seemed the harder I worked, the worse my throw got. On the heels of learning that my substandard throw had probably cost me my chance to play in the field in the upcoming season, my frustration became almost unbearable. I am not usually a crier, but at that moment I was overwhelmed with emotion. I couldn't hold back the tears.

After months apart, I'm sure the last thing A.J. wanted was to see me in total despair over this latest softball setback. At that moment he inadvertently did the one thing that could turn things around: he jokingly asked, "Have you tried throwing with your left arm?" I knew he was joking but I was so frustrated that I thought, "What the heck, I'll try it." Almost no one can switch from right- to left-hand throwing and expect to be successful at any level of the game. To do so as a Division I college softball player is unheard of.

My injury had been such a longstanding impediment to my softball career that I had considered just about every option available to help me get back on the field. While the idea of throwing left handed seemed ridiculous to me, I was desperate. Here on the threshold of my junior season of college softball, I was running out of chances to play the game I loved. I took my fielding glove off of my left hand and slid it awkwardly onto the right. It was time to try something really crazy to see if I could restore sanity and order to my softball world.

Still not entirely serious—really just to give me a break from my frustrating right handed throwing drills—I tried a few left-handed throws. It didn't feel nearly as awkward as I had thought it would. In fact, besides the lack of strength in my left shoulder, the throwing motion felt much better than from the right side. Perhaps it was only because my right-handed delivery had become so strained and awkward. A.J. gave me a reality check when he switched his throw from the right to the left side to see if he could match my left-handed throws. It wasn't even close. His throws from the left side were awful. Apparently I had the rare ability to throw reasonably well as a southpaw even though I was a natural right hander. I began to think perhaps throwing left handed was a serious alternative way to regain a spot in the Irish outfield.

A.J. and I decided to work through the warm up routine we had been using to try to retrain my injured right shoulder and arm. We wanted to see if the same drills would help imprint the proper mechanics as I tried to build a throw from scratch using my left side. When A.J. left to drive home, I was no longer a frustrated wreck. We'd played enough catch to convince me I could become a left hander. Instead of beating my head against a wall trying to make my right arm cooperate, I could now work on something that showed a lot more promise. It was a radical move, but it was a last desperate attempt to salvage my career as an outfielder and achieve my goal of contributing to Irish success on the field.

My performance as a southpaw wasn't perfect right out of the gate, but it showed more potential than my increasingly erratic right handed throws. Plus, I could throw left handed without the sharp pain I experienced from the right side. As time went on, my left arm would ache after hard throwing, but it was the kind of ache you get when you work an unused muscle, not the pain that says, "Stop, you're hurting me!"

Before I left town to go home, my classmate Stephanie Mola, a natural lefthander, lent me one of her old Irish fielding gloves so I would have a mitt to use in my quest to become an "unnatural" southpaw. I called my Dad and Mom and gave them a heads up that I was working on something new. I wanted to alert them that I had made a big decision and gauge their reaction. It wasn't that I wanted their approval, but I valued their judgment. I knew I had a lot of work to do to transform myself from a right hander to a left hander. It wasn't a decision I had made lightly. I valued Mom's and Dad's opinion.

They listened to my reasoning and recognized that I had considered my options carefully. Mom and Dad also knew I was in the best position to make the decision. When I finished describing what I was up to, I paused to listen. I was relieved to hear them say they were 100% behind me and would do whatever they could to help. If I had harbored any doubts when I dialed their number, my parents' confidence in my instincts immediately laid them to rest.

I didn't know it, but my Dad immediately went to the mall and had a special Irish green tee shirt made for me that listed things in life that begin with the word left: "Left Lane", "Left Turn", "Left

Wing", "Left Hand". The final line on the shirt said in large gold letters: "Love an Irish Lefty Today". When I opened the gift box on Christmas morning, the words on the shirt told me that my parents really did have total confidence in me. It meant a lot to me that, no matter what happened, A.J. and my parents supported me completely.

Winter Break

When I arrived home for winter break a week later, I had a plan. I would use every available minute during my time away from campus to try to refine my left-handed throw. Then, if I was happy with my progress, I would call Coach and arrange a meeting and a throwing showcase several days before classes were scheduled to resume. I didn't want to blindside her by showing up at our first team practice of the New Year throwing with the wrong arm. I needed to give her a preview of my new look and get her blessing before letting the cat completely out of the bag in front of the entire team.

Throwing with the other arm is pretty much like learning to throw all over again. Except now I wasn't a three- or four-year-old imprinting muscle memory on the blank slate of a young and impressionable body. I was a 20-year-old and my body's movement patterns were pretty much already set. Establishing new softball moves with the high levels of coordination necessary to perform at the Division I level would be a daunting task.

A.J. and I worked out daily at the high school and a local baseball and softball training facility, running through the full litany of throwing drills I had used to try to retrain my right arm, but now using them to learn to throw left handed. I made progress every day and it soon became clear that I had a knack for throwing from the opposite side. It wasn't particularly stylish, but I quickly found I could work through wrist flips, swimming throws, right angle drills and light tosses with reasonable coordination. My throws were accurate and, when I snapped my wrist, relatively strong. I had to really focus on the wrist snap. I had a tendency to push the ball, shot put style, when I tried to wind up and throw harder.

The real challenge in learning to throw from the left side was the footwork. After a lifetime of leading with my left side and striding through with the right side, turning around and trying to master the opposite footwork didn't come easy. The secret to generating a powerful throw is to clear the front side out of the way as the back leg drives through toward the target. As an outfielder, I would eventually have to incorporate a crow hop to give my throw even more velocity. But first things first: I had to get my hips, legs and feet to move properly before I could work on more advanced choreography.

A.J. worked with me tirelessly during the day and my Dad worked with me in the evening and on weekends. Little by little, I could feel myself improving. A.J. called on a relative for some additional assistance. Larry Ike was a former college baseball pitching star at Michigan State who gave pitching lessons at the training center where A.J. and I practiced. He knew the mechanics of the overhand throw from a pitching perspective and he was intrigued with the challenge I had taken on. I'd show up while Larry was giving pitching lessons and he'd watch me throw out of the corner of his eye. Occasionally he'd pause in his lessons to give me a pointer or correct an improper mechanic. With Larry's help my efforts to refine my new throwing motion were far more productive than they would have been if I tried to figure everything out for myself.

In addition to learning to throw left handed, I also had to re-learn to catch using the opposite hand. Catching everything that came my way had always been one of the strengths of my game. Now I had to sacrifice the perfectly good left hand glove work that was one of the four intact tools in my arsenal and teach my right hand to catch the ball just as well. Any loss of fielding skill was simply unacceptable to me...I wasn't changing throwing arms to make myself mediocre in other phases of the game.

We took advantage of the field house at the high school and any other indoor facilities we could find to work on fielding grounders and fly balls. Getting to the ball wasn't a problem but getting the glove in the proper position to catch the ball and then gather my feet to make a quick throw took some work. I picked up catching balls backhanded across my body pretty quickly. Balls hit in the air to my right were a little more difficult; for some reason, I sometimes tended to short arm them. I found that the instincts I'd developed in years of playing catch and in fielding practice were no longer enough to ensure that I would get the glove on the ball. I had to concentrate hard on every catch, watching the ball all the way in and then consciously instructing my glove hand to grasp the ball the instant it hit the mitt.

When A.J., Dad and I weren't turning me into a southpaw, we were in the batting cages working on a skill that would remain unaffected by my throwing transformation. I was still swinging the bat from the right side. We'd do T-work, soft toss and front toss in the indoor cages at the training center, spending 90 minutes or more per session to keep my swing sharp. A.J. would work a tee in one cage while I worked a second tee in a cage nearby. We'd help each other with the toss drills. When a pitching machine was available, we'd feed balls for each other. On weekends, Dad would help out as well.

We worked all holiday long until it was time for A.J. to head back to South Carolina. Saying goodbye again wasn't easy. I wouldn't see A.J. again until our seasons ended in June. But, it was time for both of us to get back to chasing our dreams. Because A.J.'s winter break started and ended a week earlier than mine, I would remain at home training for another week after he returned to school. That gave me the window I needed to arrange a trip to South Bend with Dad to preview my new throw for Coach, Lizzy and Kris. First I had to break the news to Coach over the phone. While she didn't call me crazy, her skepticism was apparent as she said we needed to meet so she could see what I was talking about.

We drove down to South Bend the next week and met Coach and Lizzy at the Loftis indoor training facility. Under their watchful eyes, I warmed up a little bit with Dad, then Lizzy took over and we began to throw back and forth, gradually lengthening the distance between us. Before we finished up, Coach timed how quickly I could get rid of the ball and deliver it to Lizzy's waiting glove. Then Lizzy, a former Irish outfield great, was timed. It was no contest.

Coach said my new throw showed promise, but I would have to be able to match Lizzy's release time and velocity to be ready to take the field. She was setting the bar pretty high, considering that few Irish outfielder's past or present, could match Lizzy's arm. But, I wasn't about to argue the point. Coach decided who received playing time or "PT". I intended to earn my PT just like everybody else...by performing in practice and then on the field. Lizzy and I outlined a practice plan for the spring to include the extra throwing drills required to bring my throw up to speed and agreed to get started as soon as I returned to campus for the Spring term. Dad and I drove home happy that Coach was going to let me continue to reinvent my throw and confident that I would soon add a Division I arm to my other four softball tools. I was sure I would regain my status as a five tool player yet!

Getting Ready

A week later we arrived back on campus to begin our one-month preparation for the start of a new season. Like my freshman and sophomore years, we went at it full-tilt, with strength and conditioning workouts, team practices and individual workouts. Of course, we were also entering the spring academic term, which meant planning out when we'd work on group projects for our classes, how we'd fit reading, written papers, studying for quizzes and tests and other class assignments into our busy schedules. For me, there was also daily physical therapy with Kathy, my one-woman pit crew.

Now that I was throwing left-handed, I faced different challenges. I didn't need to work on my injured right shoulder because it was no longer bearing the burden of daily throwing drills. Now I needed Kathy's help to turn my left arm into a throwing weapon. After 20 years of using my right arm for almost everything, my left arm had to get up to speed fast. First and foremost I needed to strengthen it, stretch it and condition it so the new work load I was applying would not result in injury. The arm was pretty sore most of the time as I continued to build my throw from the ground up. I was working on getting the proper hip and lower body mechanics established to relieve some of the strain on my arm. But until I could crow hop and clear my right side out of the way, I was overworking my arm to compensate for my inadequate leg action.

Lizzy volunteered to help me out as I worked on my throw. I needed a throwing partner to allow me to get the number of repetitions necessary to make progress and I needed someone who could observe my mechanics and coach me to improve. Lizzy already had her normal skill training responsibilities; she didn't need to take my throw on as an extra project. But she said if I was willing to take this extraordinary step to reinvent myself as a softball player, she would do what she could to help me. Throughout the winter and into the spring, Lizzy made time during my individual workouts to work on my throw. I really appreciated that she cared enough to help me try to resurrect my career as an Irish outfielder.

During our team practices and individual workouts with the coaches, we spent a lot of time in the cages working on improving our performances on the offensive side of the ball. The previous season had been a real wakeup call for the team as we consistently failed to support our pitchers with the offensive output needed to put our opponents away. Lizzy in particular was focused on coaching us on our hitting mechanics and our approach at the plate. I returned from winter break and picked up where I had left off in fall ball. I was really seeing the ball well and making solid contact in the cage.

My stock in trade as a hitter had always been the line drive, powered by a strong top or right hand that attacks the ball like a hammer. I never adopted the uppercut swing that so many of my high school and summer travel ball teammates used to try to jack long balls out of the park. For many hitters, that approach seemed to produce more strikeouts and pop ups than home runs. Besides, there are many game situations where the team doesn't need a home run. A single, or even a ground ball, can move or score a runner, whereas a pop-up or a strikeout is the last thing the team needs. Donny always said in clutch situations, our job as hitters was to "make a mistake on top of the ball".

As our preseason preparations continued, I was really hitting the ball well. At one point after a hitting session in the Eck cages, Lizzy stopped me and said admiringly, "Beth, you just hit 21 straight line drives!" My left-handed throw might still be a work in progress, but my right-handed batting swing was looking good.

I have never been overly superstitious, but I also know that it can be dangerous to peak too early as a hitter. Like baseball, hockey and other sports where eye-hand coordination is so important, softball hitting can be streaky. Even great and consistent hitters like Stephanie Brown tend to go on runs where it seems like they can't miss the ball. Then, their bats cool off for a few games. In my own career, I had experienced the same phenomenon enough to know that they only thing certain about a hot bat is that it will eventually cool off.

So far this preseason, I was hitting the ball great, but Lizzy's job was to help us build swings that would not be as susceptible to breakdowns during the grind of the spring season. If we built a solid mechanical foundation, we should be able perform more consistently and avoid developing small mechanical flaws that could lead to mid-season funks. Since my early days with Curtis, I had worked hard at swing mechanics. Curtis used to tell me that he expected me to get to know my swing so well, I would be able to make adjustments in mid-season and even in the middle of a game. He said that swing knowledge would allow me to get back on track quickly at the first sign of a breakdown in mechanics.

As the season opener drew near, our practices intensified including our work in the cage. I was focused on refining my swing to trigger back more deeply. Then the unforeseen happened. My timing was no longer on. I wasn't getting the bat head into the hitting zone in time to drive through the ball. After a few sessions in the cage it was clear I was late on just about every pitch. Instead of line drives headed for the gap, I was hitting a lot of ground balls, pop ups and fouls. Okay, I thought, I must need to bear down and concentrate harder. But even with more focus, the problem didn't improve. Lizzy and I could see there was now a hitch in my swing, a slight hesitation as I started to bring the bat forward. That hesitation was ruining my timing and, just like that, my swing was no longer looking so powerful.

Working Still Harder

As the start of the season drew near, I was really working hard to make a statement to Coach. I wanted to show her that my left-handed throw was strong and accurate enough to allow me to perform effectively on defense. I felt my ability to take a direct angle to the ball, my speed, and my glove work reduced the importance of a strong throw. I knew I had to overcome Coach's skepticism about my arm and her reluctance to allow opponents to test my throw. There were other outfielders with healthy arms to choose from. Why play a fielder whose throw still looked awkward and weak? Even though my throw was getting stronger, it was still weaker than my teammates' guns.

Still, I wasn't going to sit down easily. I had played my entire sophomore year with a weak arm and in a great deal of pain. Over the course of that season, I felt I had proven I could overcome my handicap and perform at a high level in the field and at the plate. I wanted the chance to do it again this season. My left-handed throw was rounding into shape remarkably. It didn't look pretty, that much was clear. But I was able to deliver the ball from point A to point B accurately and with reasonable velocity. In the outfield, I was confident I could get the ball into the cutoff man without delay on anything that hit the ground in front of me. Balls to the fence would test the strength of my throw because I couldn't match the distance my teammates could hurl it. But I was confident that I was going to continue to get stronger and gain distance and velocity as the season progressed.

Unfortunately, as fast as my left-handed throw was progressing, it was still a work in progress as we put the finishing touches on our preseason preparation. With the completion of our final practice sessions it was clear that I was not going to be selected to play in the field. In hindsight, it was probably unrealistic to assume that I could make the switch from righthander to lefthander in mid-December and by mid-February earn a starting position on a Division I college softball team. But I was disappointed all the same. I still believed in my ability to earn a spot in the Irish outfield. I wasn't giving up on that part of my dream just yet.

With my arm still a major handicap in Coach's eyes, I knew the key to playing lay in my ability to hit. I threw myself into training to get rid of the dreaded hitch and return to the form that had made me a .800 hitter in fall ball and a line drive machine in the batting cages all winter long. Getting rid of my swing flaw wasn't easy. The harder I tried, the worse it seemed to get.

Anyone who has ever swung a bat will tell you that effort in the batter's box doesn't often translate into results. The more you press, the tighter you grip the bat and the more tension you introduce into your forearms, wrists and hands. All that tension is the enemy of quick reflexes, a fluid swing and the release of the wrists and hands that whips the bat through the hitting zone with lethal velocity. Tension can also lead to extra movement in the head and lower body that ruins the path of bat to ball. Of course, by tying up your swing, tension wreaks havoc on a hitter's timing.

Once, you begin to struggle, the first instinct is to try even harder to overcome whatever it is that has taken your swing hostage. Before you know it your swing mechanics are in a downward spiral, dragging your confidence down with them. This was one time when my aggressive, impossible is nothing mindset hurt me more than it helped. The attitude that sustained me as I worked to transform my throw—and had helped me achieve success as a sophomore—was working against me as I tried to correct my swing flaw. Of course, none of that was obvious to me at the time. I was fighting to prove to Coach that I still deserved a spot on the field and at the plate. I wasn't about to let a stutter in my swing or lack of effort stop me.

Time Out

My third year as a member of the Irish softball team was taking me for a rollercoaster ride that rivaled the rough airline flight my teammates and had experienced two years earlier after taking off from Tulsa. From the high of hitting the cover off of the ball in fall ball to the low of hearing Coach tell me I wasn't going to play, my emotions were being whipsawed back and forth. Deciding to change throwing arms was both a relief and a source of frustration. I was no longer fighting against an arm that just would not function properly, but no matter how hard I worked, learning to throw lefthanded could not be hurried. On top of that, my swing had been taken hostage by a mysterious hitch.

Meanwhile, here I was halfway through my third year at Notre Dame and my two-hour lifeline to A.J. had been extended significantly. He was hundreds of miles away in South Carolina preparing for the start of his own season at Limestone College. We still talked by phone every day, but we were a long way apart without hope of seeing each other at Easter or at any time before our seasons ended in late May or early June. Ironically, we both hoped our next rendezvous would be delayed as long as possible because that would mean our teams had gone deep in our respective NCAA tournaments.

Fortunately, I was in the company of teammates and friends who formed a great support system that helped me keep my equilibrium as this unpredictable year rolled on. Kathy was great to talk to during my hours in the training room. She was in a committed relationship with a special guy who lived in her home state of Florida, so, in addition to our many hours of work together on my bum right shoulder and on my left arm, we also had long-distance relationships in common.

I also spent a lot of my down time hanging out with senior teammates Katie Laing and Sara Smith, plus our team manager Amanda Caravalho, who was also a senior. Katie lived off campus and, once our studying was done, her condo became a place where we could hang out, talk, watch a little television, or just chill. The softball team was a great topic of conversation; there always seemed to be something humorous going on. We also had our futures to discuss. As seniors, Katie, Sarah and Amanda were looking ahead to graduation and their post-graduate plans.

Although I had another year before graduation, I would be interning with PWC during the coming summer, the first step in my post-graduate career plans. It seemed like my college career was speeding to its conclusion, too. But Katie's condo wasn't a place for deep and serious discussions of our plans for the future, the softball team, or personal woes like my injury and struggle to get back on the playing field. It was a place to just hang out and enjoy a few laughs and the company of good friends.

Season Opener

Our 2008 season began on the road in Tempe, Arizona, at the Kajikawa Classic hosted by Arizona State University. As usual, we'd be playing some southern teams, but we'd also meet Western Kentucky and Utah whose campuses were farther north. My parents decided to make the trip down for a long weekend and I was hoping to get on the field to make their trip worthwhile. I warned them that I'd just be pinch hitting or playing as the designated player, but they said they were excited to see me play even if my game time would be limited.

For my part, I was hoping to rediscover my timing at the plate so I could start hot and convince Coach she needed me on the field. Our first game was Friday morning against Utah. We came out swinging and knocked off the previously undefeated Utes, 6 -2. A couple of our freshmen, Sadie Pitzenberger and Brianna Jorgensborg led the offense. Sadie had three hits and three stolen bases and Brianna knocked in three with a double in her first collegiate at bat. I started the game on the bench but was called on to pinch hit with runners on first and second in the third. I hit the ball hard to short and was safe on an error while my teammates were also safe at second and third. Unfortunately, we were left stranded there as the Utah pitcher worked her way out of the jam.

We were scheduled to play perennial Pac-10 and national powerhouse Arizona later that afternoon but rain showers blew in and the game was cancelled. The next day the weather was better, although a bit chilly by Arizona standards. We weren't complaining, though. Compared to South Bend, it was plenty warm enough. We were scheduled to play two games, with Western Kentucky up first. The Hilltoppers had come almost as far as we had from their campus in Bowling Green, Kentucky. I checked the roster before the game and learned that Shannon Smith, who had been my teammate on the 14-and-under *Blaze*, was on the Western Kentucky squad, proving once again that it's a small softball world.

The game was a seesaw battle as Western Kentucky took an early lead only to lose it in the fifth when Sadie Pitzenberger doubled home two runs and a third run scored on a Christine Lux sacrifice fly. We couldn't hold the lead, though, as the Hilltoppers managed a grand slam home run in their half of the inning to take a 5-3 lead. Down to our last three outs, we got another double from Sadie and then a two-run blast from Heather Johnson tied it up. Our opponents drove a dagger in our hearts, though, scoring the winning run on an Irish throwing error in the bottom of the seventh. I had one pinch hit opportunity in the sixth but popped up to second base. I wasn't happy with my at bat. I was pressing and didn't get a good swing at the ball. My Dad said later it looked like I was gripping the bat way too hard. At that point I wasn't looking for pointers from anyone, even if he did fly all the way from Grand Rapids to see me play. I was frustrated that I hadn't converted my chance into a hit. Dad understood.

We were disappointed to let the game slip away, but we didn't have time to dwell on it. We had to get ready to play number 3 ranked Texas A&M next. Our game with the Aggies started out as a pitching duel between Brittney and her A&M counterpart, Amanda Scarborough. Brittany struck out nine Aggies and pitched a strong game, but Texas A&M managed to push four runs across while Scarborough held us to two hits. Katie Laing drove in our lone run. My former roommate, Erin Glasco, was now catching for the Aggies and had the satisfaction of walking off the field as a member of the winning squad. That was great for Erin but not so great for her former teammates.

As in previous years, we found ourselves with more losses than wins as our first weekend of competition drew to a close. Our final game on Sunday morning would be against California from the Pac-10. The Golden Bears weren't ranked this year, but they were typically a tough opponent, had more games under their belt coming into the weekend, and definitely were not to be taken lightly. We moved over to Arizona State's home stadium for the Cal game, which meant we had a bigger crowd in attendance and a bigger stage to play on. We were anxious to deliver a better performance than in our previous two games, not only to please our parents and the rest of the fans in the stands, but to make the planned after-party at Katie's parents' home in Tempe a lot more fun.

Katie took matters into her own hands with a solo homer early in the game and a double that drove in the winning run as we registered a come-back victory behind four innings of stellar relief pitching from Brittney. I was called on to pinch hit in the fourth with two on and two outs and scorched a line drive right at the first baseman. That was the end of my weekend's tournament action. I had gone hitless, but the last at bat had felt good and gave me hope that I'd shake the doldrums soon. After a great dinner at the Laing's house and some downtime on the patio around their pool, we boarded the bus and headed for the airport and our flight to South Bend. Another season was underway.

Our Spring Tour Continues

The next stop of the spring was Gainesville, Florida, where we played in a weekend tournament hosted by the University of Florida Gators. We managed two 1-0 victories against North Florida but dropped two games to the host Gators, as I continued to struggle as a pinch hitter. It was becoming clear to me that I had too much nervous energy to sit on the bench and then jump into the action for one at bat. My performance at the plate had always fed off of my defensive effort in the field. With no outlet for my competitive drive for most of the game, I had too much time to think about that one at bat, both before I went to the plate and after my at bat had come and gone. The more I struggled at the plate, the more I was driven to make my left-handed throw the equal of the throws of my teammates. I knew if I played in the field, my approach at the plate would improve and the hits would come.

We headed to the West Coast for our annual spring break trip the next week, playing three games at the Worth Invitational in Fullerton, California, and a single game at the University of California Riverside, before competing in five games in the Long Beach Invitational at Long Beach State University. Mom had flown out to stay with Brittney's parents and watch me play for the week, which gave me the chance to share some downtime with her and recharge my batteries a bit during the week. Unfortunately, Dad had to stay home to go to work. It was another reminder that, beyond Irish softball and my college experience, the real world was waiting. As frustrating as my junior season had been so far, I was still well aware that this was a special time in my life.

We won the first two games of the Worth tournament, beating Pacific 11-3 and UC Davis 6-5 before losing the third game to Cal State Fullerton, 1-0. My bat finally woke up as I singled and drove in a run in a pinch hit appearance against Pacific. Against UC Davis, I had a pair of singles and scored two runs while playing as the designated player.

Two days later, we traveled to the outskirts of greater Los Angeles to play UC Riverside. We beat the Highlanders 8-2. Katie, Linda Kohan and freshman Katie Fleury had multiple hits to power us to the win, but I did my part as the DP and hitting number 2 in the lineup. I had an infield single, a sacrifice bunt that led to a score, and I was hit by a pitch and scored a run. It wasn't quite pretty enough to be considered another Gordie Howe hat trick, but amidst my recent woes at the plate, I'd take it.

After a couple of days off, we bussed back over to the coast for the five game set at Long Beach. Our first game was against the mighty UCLA Bruins, a perennial softball power and ranked number 2 team in the country. After allowing the Bruins to take an early lead we came back to tie it 2-2 in the sixth, only to lose it in the seventh on a fielding error, our third of the game. Freshman Jody Valdivia pitched well enough to get the win, but we didn't give her the run or fielding support she deserved as we fell 3-2.

Next up was host Long Beach State. Brittney started out strong with four no-hit innings before giving up the game's only run. Wouldn't you know it, after playing the number 2 team in the country almost even, our bats came out totally cold against the 49ers. Christine Lux managed three hits for our side and I had two hits and a stolen base, but it wasn't enough to prevent us from suffering our second loss of the day, this time by a 1-0 score.

We came back with a big win to start the next day, defeating number 24 Virginia Tech, 2-1 as Brittney outdueled the Hokie's Angela Tincher and got all the runs she needed courtesy of a two-run double by Christine. Then we avenged our defeat earlier in the week by beating Cal State Fullerton, 1-0. Jody hurled the shutout while Sadie and Katie Fleury teamed up for our lone run in the sixth with a double and a single, respectively. Our freshmen were coming on strong!

The next morning, we ended our spring break road trip by defeating Cal State Northridge, 3-1, on the strength of a Sadie Pitzenberger two-run double in the fifth. I contributed to the rally that produced our insurance run with a two-out single in the sixth. I then stole second base, which allowed me to score on Ashley Ellis' single. As we headed back to Indiana, we had to come to terms with the loss of our third baseman. Heather Johnson had torn her ACL in the final game of the trip. We all knew injuries were part of the game, but seeing a teammate go down was never easy.

After returning to classes for a week, we headed off to our final southern tournament, the two-day Lowcountry Invitational in Charleston, South Carolina. We split two games against Towson, winning 7-0, but then losing 6-2 a day later. We also played Charleston Southern twice, sweeping the tournament host, 16-2 and 10-2. I had a perfect three-for-three game in the first contest with the Buccaneers, including a double and two runs scored in the lopsided contest. The next day in the recap against our tournament hosts, I was one-for-two with an RBI and a run scored. I was starting to perform at the plate, but I still wasn't feeling comfortable pinch hitting or playing as the DP.

Back in the North

We returned to South Bend to begin mid-March play in the upper Midwest. We were scheduled to start with a double header against Western Michigan on Wednesday, but weather and field conditions forced our meeting with the Broncos to be pushed back until Friday, with only one game scheduled on the make-up date. Despite the delay, we beat the Broncos 2-0. We managed five hits with Katie and Linda producing RBIs and Brittney hurling a shutout. I had a miserable day at the plate with a couple of ground outs and a pop out. I was especially frustrated because Western's team included five players who had played travel ball with me at one time or another. Molly Lange, Sarah and Meaghan Thomas, Lexi Jager and Amanda McBride all were Broncos now, and living their own softball dreams.

My parents were in the stands after making the relatively short drive down to Kalamazoo from our home in Grand Rapids, probably adding to the pressure I placed on myself. In keeping with my pattern so far in the spring, I was working too hard to perform at the plate instead of relaxing and letting my skill and training take over to get the job done. If I didn't change my approach, this could be a really long and unproductive season for me personally. I tried to remind myself that I needed to stay in the moment and just do what the team needed in each individual game situation. But I'm a goal-oriented planner and perfectionist, a mindset that was great for managing academics and applying the discipline necessary to be successful as a college athlete. It wasn't the kind of thinking that would help me to relax, stay loose and shrug off the inevitable failures that are part of competition on the field.

When we faced off against Indiana University Purdue University Indianapolis (IUPUI) the Thursday after we defeated the Broncos, Coach started freshman Erin Marrone in the DP spot in the line-up and I stayed on the bench, not even getting a chance to pinch hit as my Irish teammates feasted on Jaguar pitching to take an 8-0 win. Sadie Pitzenberger, Sarah Smith and Christine Lux each had two hits and Katie Laing drove in two runs with a triple. While I shared in the team's satisfaction at gaining a big win in our last game before conference play, and I really respected Erin's skills as a player, I was too competitive to feel good about sitting on the bench.

I knew everyone on the team was good enough to start, it was up to me to make a strong case that I deserved it more. The problem was, I was doing everything I could think of to turn the season around, but nothing seemed to work. The decisions I had made in December and January to become a lefty thrower and change my swing had transformed softball from a labor of love to just plain hard work. By now I was learning that working harder and harder doesn't always translate into better results.

Conference Play

We started our conference season with a Sunday doubleheader at arch-rival DePaul, which was ranked number 17 in the nation coming into the game. For some reason, we always seemed to bring out the best in the Blue Demons, but on this day we played them even. We lost a tight one in the opener, 2-1, but took the second contest 2-0. Our pitchers both threw strong games. They were matched by DePaul's hurlers who held our hitters at bay most of the afternoon. Sadie had two of the team's five hits in the nightcap to lead us to the win.

After winning a midweek nonconference game against Toledo at Ivy Field, we hit the road for our first full weekend of Big East play. We started with a Saturday double header at St. Johns where we swept the Red Storm 5-0 and 8-4. The second game went 12 innings before we pulled out the win. On Sunday, Katie Laing led an Irish hitting barrage as we finished off Seton Hall in similar style, with a 12-1 win in the opener before taking the second game 6-2. The four wins gave us a five win, one loss record in conference play and the right kind of momentum in what we hoped was the road to a Big East championship. I played sparingly but managed to double and score a run against Seton Hall. I also drove in a run later in the same game.

The sweep seemed a lot less sweet as we considered the high cost of the wins. Our catcher and leadoff hitter Sadie Pitzenberger went down with a knee injury during the doubleheader and was lost for the season. Like Heather before her, losing Sadie deprived us of a strong bat and an important part of our defense. Erin Marrone was eventually pressed into service as our catcher and did a great job the rest of the season, even though she hadn't played the position in years. With Erin now in the regular line-up, I began to see more consistent playing time as the DP. Now more than ever, the team needed me to find my hitting stroke. It was up to me to gain the mindset necessary to be successful at bat without playing in the field.

We swept Eastern Michigan in a midweek doubleheader before hosting Villanova and Rutgers in back to back doubleheaders the following weekend. It was the inaugural weekend of our new softball facility, Melissa Cook Stadium. The story behind the stadium is sad but also inspiring and, at the time, it really put my struggles as an athlete into proper perspective.

Much of the funding for the project was donated by Linda and Paul Demo, the parents of Melissa Cook, a former Irish player who had lost her life in a Chicago construction accident. The Demos decided that the settlement they received after their daughter's death could be used to create a lasting legacy and enrich the lives of others. They generously contributed a substantial gift to Notre Dame to build a new state-of-the-sport softball stadium. Less visibly, but just as important, they also created the Melissa Cook Memorial Foundation to provide scholarship assistance to deserving students in Northwest Indiana.

We were thrilled with the new playing surface, locker room, team lounge, dugout and batting cages. The expanded grandstands provided more seating for Irish fans, increasing our home field advantage. But the Demo's generosity, strength and courage in the aftermath of a great personal tragedy gave us something far more important: an example of how each of us can face adversity in life and rise above it to help others. The Demo's made the small challenges we faced as students and athletes seem trivial in comparison.

The weekend of the stadium dedication included a Friday night dinner in the JACC that included a speech by Father Theodore Hesburgh, one of the most inspirational leaders in Notre Dame history, and a ceremony honoring Linda and Paul Demo. The next morning, we gathered under a tent near the new stadium for a special dedication ceremony before the first game. I had come down with a heavy cold earlier in the week and was not even sure I'd be able to play when I arrived at the field that morning.

Just standing up with my teammates during the ceremony was a real ordeal. I wasn't at all disappointed that the rainy and raw conditions became so bad, the ceremonial first pitch and our scheduled doubleheader against Rutgers were postponed. The Scarlet Knights left town to play a doubleheader in Chicago against DePaul on Sunday and I headed to bed, hoping I would feel better the next day.

Sunday's weather still wasn't ideal, but it was good enough to play Villanova, which had bussed over from Chicago for our scheduled Sunday twin bill. I was feeling a bit better and reported to the field ready to serve as a pinch hitter or any other role Coach needed me to play. We were excited to christen our field and post our first win in Melissa Cook Stadium but the combination of the overnight rain delay and the grand opening of our new stadium seemed to throw us off our stride. We split with the Wildcats, dropping the first game 4-1 before righting the ship and winning the second contest 10-5. I had a double and two RBI in a pinch hitting role in the second game of the twin bill. I guess I must have felt so bad, I let my instincts take over in my one trip to the plate.

With our doubleheader against Villanova completed, we learned that Rutgers had agreed to return to South Bend from Chicago to make up our postponed twin bill on Monday before flying back to the East Coast. Both coaches felt it was too early in the season to cancel games that would be difficult to reschedule later on. We were determined to gain a sweep after suffering a split the previous day. But instead we simply reversed the pattern set on Sunday by winning the first game 1-0 and then dropping the nightcap 5-4. Brittney threw a one-hitter in the first game as Linda drove home Smitty in the third inning to provide the margin of victory. Christine and I both scored runs in the second game but our offense couldn't overcome a four-run rally by the Scarlet Knights in the sixth that secured the win for the visitors.

We headed back to our studies carrying the humbling reminder that it's never a good idea to look past an opponent (or two) in anticipation of bigger games down the road. We had let an opportunity to log some important conference wins slip through our fingers. And we had also erased any thought that our new stadium came with a built-in reservoir of Irish luck. Our field might be new, but the game was the same as it had always been: we still had to make our own luck, out-preparing and out-competing our opponents to gain wins one at a time.

The Season Rolls On

We played two midweek games against Big Ten opponents the next week with mixed results. First number 13 Northwestern hosted us in Evanston, beating us 5-0. Coming on the heels of our losses to the Wildcats the previous two years, it was clear Coach Drohan's team still had our number. The next day we hosted Wisconsin and sent the Badgers packing with a loss. We had four home runs in the 11-5 win and my bat showed up to help, logging two hits including an RBI double in a stint as the Irish DP. I also scored a run. Although I was still inconsistent, having a chance to hit with greater frequency in the DP spot seemed to settle me down a bit.

We were ready for a highly competitive Big East weekend as we headed off to Louisville and South Florida on Friday afternoon. We came out swinging against the Cardinals in Louisville on Saturday, sweeping them on their home field 3-1 and 12- 4. The first game was tight and went eight innings before we broke the tie on a two-run homer by Linda. The second game wasn't nearly as close as our offense exploded. Linda and Ashley Ellis had four RBI apiece while Christine had three to pace our attack.

On Sunday we squared off against South Florida for two more critical games. We needed to continue to knock of the stronger teams in the conference to make up for our splits against Villanova and Rutgers the previous week. Unfortunately, South Florida had other plans. They took the first game 5-2 and then beat us in the second game 8-4. We were relatively punchless in the first game but hit decently in the second game with Smitty hitting safely three times. Katie Fleury, Erin Marrone and I each had two hits. Our hitting wasn't enough to overcome the Bulls' offense, though. That gave us five losses in conference play and the league season was only ten games old. If our season was going to end with a Big East championship, we were going to have to do it the hard way and overtake the league leaders from our current position back in the pack.

Back home in South Bend, we had our usual Monday off before making the short trip to Purdue for a doubleheader against our third Big Ten opponent of the season. We lost the opener 1-0 but came back to avoid a sweep, 3-1. Linda, Katie Laing and Katie Fleury drove in our three runs in the second game with timely knocks. I smashed my fifth double of the year in the first game but was left stranded. Christine had two doubles of her own in the second game but was left on base both times. The way our season was going, we needed to be more efficient in converting our scoring chances. Fortunately, Jody was able to limit the Boilermakers to a single run in the second game so we didn't have to regret wasting those doubles in game two. Brittney's performance in game one was equally strong, but our hitting wasn't.

Thursday we hosted Loyola of Chicago for a non-conference double header and squeaked out a 4-3 win in eight innings. The second game ended in a 2-2 tie as both coaches agreed to call it a night after seven innings when lighting flashed over the stadium. Even though we had the winning run on first with no outs, none of us were thrilled at the prospect of running around in metal spikes and swinging metal bats with lighting in the air.

The weekend brought two more conference doubleheaders. Providence came to town on Saturday and we got off to a fast start, downing the Friars 10-1 in a run-rule shortened five inning game. Ashley Ellis had a grand slam blast, while Katie Fleury, Smitty and Linda had two hits apiece. I had a two-RBI double in the third inning to add to our hitting barrage. In true Jekyll and Hyde fashion, we then proceeded to drop the next game 5-3. Smitty and Brianna Jorgensborg each collected two hits but it wasn't enough to gain us the win. Sarah Smith's stat line for the game was an impressive 4-5 with a walk and a sacrifice. It's no wonder she received Big East Player of the Week honors a few days later.

Sunday was Senior Day, the day Katie Laing and Sarah Smith would play their last home conference games. It was another reminder of how fast our college softball experience was flashing by.

Katie and Smitty were about to join the growing list of past Irish teammates and friends who wouldn't be there to share my senior season. Although senior day could have been a distraction, we took care of business against Connecticut, sweeping the Huskies 8-5 and 3-2 as Brittney pitched both halves of the double hitter to give us a couple of badly needed wins. Our seniors led us to victory, as Katie was flawless in 12 assists at shortstop, contributed a hit and scored two runs. Smitty was four for seven at the plate with a double, an RBI and two runs scored. Underclassmen Brianna and Christine slammed home runs and my classmate Linda had a two-run double to provide additional run support.

In the second game Smitty had an RBI double in the first inning and I scored on a Katie Fleury single after reaching on a fielder's choice play. Christine followed with a home run in the third to provide Brittney with all the runs she would need to earn the win. I singled with runners on first and second and two down but the centerfielder gunned our lead runner down at home to end the inning. The Huskies' leadoff hitter homered in the seventh to tighten the score, but Brittney retired the next three batters, giving us the sweep.

The following Tuesday, we made the short drive over to Valparaiso for a single game and recorded a 6-0 win. I went three for three at the plate with a double, an RBI and a run scored. In a season of few personal highlights, it was my strongest showing so far. The game capped a ten-game stretch in late April during which I hit .367 with hits in eight of the games and three multi-hit performances. Joining me in having a great day at the plate against the Crusaders were Brianna with two hits and two RBI, Linda with an RBI double, and Katie Fleury who tallied a hit and an RBI.

Although we knew we were unlikely to catch South Florida or DePaul for the regular season conference championship, as the next weekend approached, we knew we had to sweep our last two conference opponents—Pittsburgh and Syracuse—to finish in the top three in the regular season standings. We traveled to Pittsburgh for the Saturday twin bill and opened with a 1-0 win as Brittney pitched a gem. Christine's solo home run provided the only run support she needed. The win gave Brittney a school record 28 wins for the season. We stumbled in the second game, though, allowing the Panthers to escape with a 4-2 win. Pitt jumped out to a one run lead in the first game but I doubled in the third and was driven home by Katie Fleury's single to tie it up. Katie slammed a solo home run in the top of the sixth to give us a brief lead, but three runs on three hits in the bottom of the sixth put the Panthers ahead to stay.

Syracuse was up next, and we again opened with a shutout win. This time we gave Brittney eight runs to work with, but she didn't need all of them. She held the Orange hitless in seven innings to record the fourth no hitter of her career. Katie Laing had a grand slam to tally half of our runs while several others Irish hitters figured in the remaining scoring. Proving once again that we just couldn't handle prosperity, we dropped the nightcap 8-7. We scored four runs in the fourth as eight Irish batters came to the plate. I singled and scored a run as part of the rally, Erin singled to drive in a run, Katie Fleury tripled home a run and then scored on a single by Smitty. Throw in a walk to Katie Laing and a sacrifice fly by Brianna and it added up to a very productive inning of offense. Christine's home run in the fifth and a two RBI single by Smitty accounted for the rest of our scoring. Unfortunately, Syracuse scored three runs in the fifth and five in the seventh to take the come-from-behind win.

The weekend split gave us a final conference record of 14-8, behind South Florida, DePaul and Connecticut. We were in the Big East Tournament, but it was not the kind of regular season performance we had aimed for a month and a half earlier. Still, several Irish players were recognized for All Big East honors. Brittney and Smitty were named to the first team, Ashley Ellis and Brianna Jorgensborg were named to the second team, and Katie Fleury, Linda Kohan and Christine Lux earned third team recognition. Now it was time to see if we could capture lighting in a bottle at the Big East Tournament in Louisville, then land a spot in the NCAA Regionals.

Tournament Action

The Big East Tournament moved from South Bend to Louisville in 2008, which, for us, meant a long road trip south instead of a short drive across town. We bused the full length of Indiana to the Cardinals' softball stadium along Interstate 65 just south of downtown Louisville. Our first game would be Thursday night against the home team and we were eager to get started. Our desire to play was dampened by a long rain delay that threw all of the opening games off schedule. We spent several hours waiting for the earlier games to end before ours could begin.

Our game with the Cardinals started as a pitching duel with both teams held scoreless through the first two innings. Then Louisville scored twice in the top of the third, combining a double, a single, a stolen base and a fielders' choice with a fielding error by our side. We came back in our half of the inning as Erin Marrone doubled and Katie Fleury followed with an RBI single.

With the lead cut in half, Brittney retired the Cardinals in order in the top of the fourth. Linda led off in the bottom of the frame and worked the Cardinal pitcher to a full count before walking. After a strike out, Katie Laing singled to left. A ground out later, I came to the plate with runners at second and third and two outs. The first pitch was belt high on the inside half of the plate and I crushed it, sending it on a line toward the left center gap but not high or wide enough to elude the grasp of the Cardinal shortstop who reached out and snared it for the third out.

Brittney and our defense continued to keep the Cards under control. Katie Laing would amass a total of seven assists before the game was over, setting a new Irish career record of 471 and a single season record of 147. Louisville managed to scrape together another run in the top of the sixth with a leadoff walk, an infield single, a fly ball to center and a ground out, extending the lead to

3-1. For our part, we still couldn't seem to buy a break. Smitty hit a hard line drive to lead off the bottom of the sixth but the shot was directed right at the third baseman for the out. In the bottom of the seventh, I came to the plate and again went first pitch hunting, driving a shot into right center that the right fielder flagged down on the run. Another out followed and we were eliminated from the tournament after just one game.

We were in shock. As the third seed in the tournament, we had known we would have a battle on our hands to win the championship. But Louisville was the fourth seed. Their odds were longer than ours. Brittney pitched well but it all came down to hitting, or the lack of it. We only had three hits total and we left four runners on base. I left two of those runners stranded when my smash in the fourth didn't get the extra foot of elevation necessary to reach the gap and drive two runners home. Sometimes hitting it hard isn't enough…it helps if the ball has eyes for a gap in the defense.

Now we were really at the mercy of the NCAA selection committee. We had a fourth place finish in the Big East regular season and a few quality wins against strong opponents in our favor. We also had a high RPI ranking, a tool the NCAA uses to assess the strength of team's schedule. But we couldn't be sure if all of that would be enough to gain the Irish a berth in a Regional.

Two days later we had our answer. We'd be playing in the Ann Arbor Regional hosted by Coach Hutchin's Michigan Wolverines who were ranked number 6 in the nation. That was a huge relief. We knew playing the Maize and Blue on their home turf would be no picnic, but life was good…we were in the tournament and we weren't headed to Northwestern again. After two years of Evanston, we were ready for a change of scenery.

We started tournament action Friday night before a big crowd at Michigan's newly constructed Wilpon Stadium, taking a 9-1 win over Kent State in a game that was shortened to six innings by the run rule. Brittney pitched a no hitter and recorded her 30th win of the season. We unleashed our offense in the third powered by three home runs. Katie Fleury, Linda and Christine all hit it over the fence. Katie added a single and triple and scored three runs while Linda had a single and four RBI on the day.

Our win against the Golden Flashes earned us a shot at the Wolverines at noon Saturday. Once again Brittney was on the mound and she held Michigan at bay until the fourth when the Wolverines flexed their muscles and posted four runs in the frame on a three-run home run and an RBI triple. They posted four more runs on four hits in the fifth and, after holding us scoreless in the bottom half of the inning, walked off the field with an 8-0 run rule win.

That put us in the loser's half of the bracket. Now we had to beat the winner of the game between Kent State and Wright State that immediately followed ours. The Golden Flashes eliminated Wright State and we joined them on the field to compete for the opportunity to advance to Sunday play and a rematch with Michigan. A solo home run in the bottom of the first gave Kent State an early lead but we came back the next inning on a single by Christine that turned into a two-base knock after a Golden Flash error. Katie Laing laid down a sacrifice bunt to move the runner to third and I hit into a fielder's choice that led to a second error, which allowed Christine to score.

Kent State mounted a two run rally in the third on two singles, and a double. We countered in the fourth when Linda and Christine singled to lead things off. After a ground out, I singled to drive home Christine Farrell who was pinch running for Linda. I stole second, drawing a throwing error that allowed Stephanie Mola, pinch running for Christine, to cross the plate. I continued to be aggressive on the base paths, stealing third a couple of pitches later. Unfortunately, the Kent State pitcher struck out two in a row to leave me stranded sixty feet from pay dirt.

A solo home run in the bottom of the fourth allowed the Golden Flashes to regain the lead. We were fortunate to limit the damage to one run as a dropped fly ball and an infield error allowed a second runner to get all the way to third before Brittney extinguished the rally.

Like prizefighters who refused to go down for the count, we struck back in the top of the fifth. Katie Fleury drew a leadoff walk and Smitty followed with a single to give us two aboard with no outs. A single by Linda brought Katie home and Smitty scored on a ground out to give us a one run lead. Kent State wasn't done fighting, though. Their leadoff hitter doubled in the bottom of the fifth and advanced as far as third base, but we escaped harm when she was erased by a fortuitous line drive double play that ended the inning.

I led off in the top of the sixth and tried to use my wheels to beat out a bunt single. I was out by a half a step and the next two Irish batters struck out, setting the stage for more fireworks by the Golden Flashes. The leadoff hitter doubled and, after a pop out to our second baseman, the third batter walked. Brittney got the next hitter on a fly ball to right field and it looked like we would escape the inning. Unfortunately, an RBI single tied the score. Then, a wild pitch later, we trailed by a run.

We still had some fight left of our own. Brianna Jorgensborg led off the seventh with a single to third base and Katie Fleury put down the sacrifice bunt needed to move Bri over to second and into scoring position. With two outs Linda came through with a single down the left field line to knot the score again. The Golden Flashes went down quietly in the bottom half of the frame to set the stage for extra innings.

Shannon Kelly came on to pinch hit in the top of the eighth with two outs and smashed a double to give us a chance to rally, but a fly out to center field left her stranded there. The way momentum in the game had swung back and forth, we knew our failure to score had left the door open for Kent State to steal the win and send us home.

In the bottom of the eighth, Brittney began to show the effects of eleven straight starts. After retiring the first batter on a ground out, she hit the second batter with an inside pitch. A wild pitch allowed the runner to reach second and a ground out moved her over to third. There were two outs but the runner on third meant we had no margin for either a hit or an error. Kent State's next batter provided the former, singling to bring home the winning run. For the second time this post season, we were shocked to find ourselves the victims of a loss at the hands of a lower seed. We filed out of Wilpon Stadium in stunned silence. We wouldn't get a chance to unseat the number one seeded Wolverines on Sunday.

We went back to the hotel and immediately packed and boarded the bus for South Bend so that our three seniors—Katie, Smitty and Amanda—could participate in graduation ceremonies with their classmates the following day. It was their only silver lining in an otherwise disappointing day. I was going to miss my buddies next year. A girl couldn't have three better friends.

I was also going to miss the friend and sports medicine pro who had devoted the better part of two years doing her best to keep me healthy enough to play. Kathy had announced to the team that she had received an attractive job offer at Georgia Tech in Atlanta and would be leaving as soon as her team training responsibilities concluded at the end of the season. I would miss her skill as a trainer but, even more, I would miss her calm reassurance and nonstop encouragement. She brightened the darkest of my long hours of rehabilitation and kept me looking ahead to better days.

Notre Dame wouldn't be the same without Kathy, Katie, Smitty and Amanda. Now I'd be going forward to play my last year of Irish softball without them. I could clearly see my future on the horizon. Like my friends before me, I was eventually going run out of college softball games to play. And "eventually" was just a year away.

Summer Business

I arrived home disappointed with the way our season had ended and even more disappointed in my performance at the plate and my inability to contribute in the outfield. I felt I could have done more with my bat and my glove to help the team win. By my standards, the season had been a bust.

But I knew the past was history, useful only if it contained lessons that could help me perform better in the future. I gave a lot of thought to what had happened during the year and what I could take from it and build on to improve. I didn't have all the answers but I was determined to find them before my senior season began. I set my sights on earning a spot in the outfield in my senior season. I knew the odds were now steeply stacked against me. I not only had to take my left handed throw to a new level, I had to compete for playing time with the three recruiting classes behind me. All of those teammates had more future ahead of them than I did.

Others might have felt I was a long way from ever seeing the field, but I didn't agree. Throwing wasn't the only test of outfield play. I knew I could catch balls others might miss. If a ball landed for a hit, I was equally sure I could track it down more quickly and hit the cutoff or the proper base in time to prevent runners from taking an extra sack. If I could continue to close the gap in strength between my arm and those of our other outfielders maybe Coach would place more weight on those intangibles when choosing her outfielders for the coming season.

Working on my softball skills was going to be almost a full time job this summer. But it wouldn't be my only job. I would also be taking a huge first step in my post-softball career. I was scheduled to start my internship with PWC almost immediately after the season ended. For the first week I would train in the firm's Detroit office along with interns from Southeast Michigan and Toledo.

Then I would begin working full time as a member of an audit team serving clients in West Michigan.

I spent the last days before work getting a suitable business wardrobe together with my Mom's help. I'd been in my Irish soft-ball fashion mode—team training shorts and tee shirts or team warm ups—for almost as long as I could remember, but now I had to dress for success as a young career woman. Mom had a gleam of excitement in her eyes as she brought home several business out-fits for me to try on. After waiting for years, she was finally getting the chance to dress me up again. I have to admit, I looked pretty sharp! I had a hard time deciding which outfits to keep and which to send back to the store rack. With my wardrobe all set, it was time to go to work.

After my initial training stint in Detroit, I settled into the rou-tine of office work and audit engagements on the road. I was up at 6:30 a.m. and out the door by 7:00 most days. If I was working in the firm's downtown office or at a local client location, I was usu-ally home by 6:00 p.m. My Dad would get home by 6:30 and we'd meet A.J. and head to the high school fields for hitting, throwing and outfield drills.

The experience of my junior season had made me even more determined to regain my form at the plate and improve my throw-ing enough to make me a real option for playing time in the out-field. When I thought about it, my junior year had been my worst year on a softball field ever. I was upset that I had not played to my full capabilities and that the more I struggled, the more I let it affect me. I had pressed too hard, trying to force improvement instead of trusting my abilities and letting my years of experience and natural skills take over.

I wondered if Coach had written me off for next season. Not only did we have several outfielders returning from the previous year's team, she had recruited a large class of new talent to come in as freshmen. Several newcomers were likely to compete for im-mediate playing time. Coach had made it clear that I would likely be relegated to a limited role as a pinch hitter and pinch runner, but I was sure I could still play the game and I wanted to play badly. I was still willing to do whatever it took to get back in the lineup.

Our nightly workouts included familiar routines from the past. We resumed my hitting drills from the summer before. We'd start with several buckets of soft toss, with my dad doing the tossing from the bucket just up the first base line from the batter's box. Then we'd get the screen out and begin front toss. I was focused on finding a way to eliminate the hitch that had ruined my timing the season before.

By now, I could actually feel my right shoulder catch slightly when I triggered. I caught myself hesitating in order to adjust the start of my swing path, trying to free my shoulder before I continued the hitting stroke. It wasn't something obvious or I would have detected it earlier. But as time went on, the tissue in my shoulder must have been aggravated by wear and tear. The catching had become more noticeable and it explained a lot. My hitch had appeared the previous winter when I started working on a deeper trigger and it was more pronounced during the season as I tensed up and tried to drive the ball harder.

As a right-handed hitter, I was supposed to deliver power with a strong top or right hand. But in my effort to generate more power with my top hand, I was working my damaged shoulder harder. The result was the hitch that prevented me from executing the swing I had been taught by Curtis and that Lizzy had worked with me to refine. Practicing with my Dad and A.J., I concentrated on making adjustments in my approach to hitting the ball. I experimented by altering my trigger movement and my right side action, focusing on shortening my trigger and weakening my right hand as I used my left hand more dominantly to pull the bat through the hitting zone. Slowly but surely my swing improved. I began to make solid contact consistently again.

I knew I was probably giving up some power by changing my trigger and letting my left-side become a more dominant force in my swing. This new swing ran counter to all I had been taught about hitting in the past. But I couldn't argue with the results. My new cut put my bat into the hitting zone on time and in position to drive the ball. I was even popping a few balls over the fence in practice, a pretty good feat considering my Dad's front tosses weren't providing much of the power. Even he had to admit, it was all me. I spent the rest of the summer committing my new mechanics to both mental and muscle memory.

After completing hitting practice, we would put the screen away and I would warm up my shoulder and arm. I had made great strides as a lefty, but with my senior year almost here, it was now or never. Playing defense was still my first love as a softball player. I was going to give it my best shot. I felt gaining a spot in the Irish outfield was still a realistic possibility if I could continue to improve at the rate I had as a junior. Larry Ike, the baseball pitching coach who helped me switch throwing hands the previous winter said in all his years of playing and coaching baseball, he had never seen a player successfully do what I was trying to do...except me. Now I needed to show Coach and Lizzy that I had regained the fifth tool in my softball skill set.

I was still careful about how I warmed up my left arm. Although I had been working on my southpaw action for months, I had built up the strength in my right throwing arm over the course of years. My left arm wasn't anywhere near as strong as my right arm had been in its prime. I didn't want to risk straining a muscle or tearing something. I couldn't afford an injury that would interrupt my training or put an end to my career altogether.

To get started, I would carefully stretch my shoulder. Then I was ready to pick up a ball and get to work. My dad and I followed the same throwing routine I had used during winter break. Wrist throws came first, then swim throws, the right angle drill, and finally some full throwing. After throwing from about 30 feet, we would gradually lengthen the distance until I was in deep center field and Dad was on the left field foul line. We'd long toss enough to get my arm stretched out good and then Dad would head to the plate to begin hitting balls to me in the outfield. I'd play left field and A.J. would position himself at second base and later at third base, ready to receive my throws.

Dad would hit me fly balls, line drives and ground balls and I'd react to each ball, getting into position to make the catch or field the ball cleanly. As I fielded each ball, I would come up throwing, using my legs, shoulder and arm to generate as strong and accurate a throw as I could deliver to A.J. We'd continue for 45 minutes to an hour or until my shoulder started to get tired. At that point I'd continue to field balls, but just roll them toward the infield. I wanted to do extra repetitions to work on my initial jump, refine the angles I took to track balls down, and practice my throwing footwork. I felt I could compensate for a throw that was not as strong as many outfielders' by getting to the ball as quickly as possible and coming up in position to release it quickly and accurately with strong footwork. Dad would hit deep balls to drive me to the fence and into the gaps, and if he was really on his game, he might even drive a few over my head to let me try to make a couple of "Say Hey" catches.

Before Dad's swing wore down completely, he would place a bucket on its side in front of home plate and I'd move up shallower in left field, about where I'd be positioned in a game if the Irish absolutely had to get an out at home. In those situations you had to gamble and play shallow because anything hit deeper to left would score the run regardless if the ball was caught.

Dad would hit balls out to me in the air and on the ground and I'd field them and immediately unleash a throw home, trying to hit the bucket on one bounce. I didn't hit it every time, but I tried to get it close. After about a dozen throws home, including at least a few really good ones, it was time to call it quits. We'd pick up the bats, gloves and balls, load up the car and head home. I had a date every night with an ice pack filled with Jolene's "secret" alcohol and water mixture before I'd be ready to get on with my off-the-field life. We followed our practice routine at least three nights a week and also during the day on weekends unless my shoulder and arm were stiff or hurting more than normal.

I had to listen to my shoulder and arm. If I was especially stiff or sore, I'd limit my workout to some hitting, stretching and maybe some light warm-up throwing. Kathy had cautioned me to train, not strain. There was no point in wearing my arm down so I couldn't throw properly or injured it. I was down to my last arm, after all.

In addition to hitting, fielding and throwing, I also had to keep up on my conditioning work. I still had an inch-thick summer workout plan for Irish softball. Some nights that meant running sprints from foul line to foul line on the softball field after we finished our drills. Other nights we'd go to the football field for extra sprinting and timed runs. I'd visit the high school weight room with A.J. as often as possible to work on strength training as well.

I was really lucky A.J. and Dad were willing to dedicate so much of their time throughout the summer to helping me train. A.J., in particular, had better things to do. In the spring, he had asked his coach at Limestone for a release from his commitment to play baseball at the South Carolina school so he could return home to play closer to his family. With release in hand, he discussed opportunities with two local college teams and accepted an offer to finish up his career at Grand Valley State University. He would be coming into his senior season trying to earn a spot in the lineup on a new team.

A.J. was as determined as I was to have a successful senior season, and he was spending a lot of time working on his game. Despite his own priorities, he was still willing to give up his own training time to help me work out. As much as I appreciated his willingness to help me out on the practice field, I was also glad A.J. would be coming back to West Michigan to play ball. Moving to South Carolina and playing ball with teammates from the Southeast was a great experience for him. Everyone should have the chance to follow their dreams. But now he had decided he wanted to finish his career closer to home. I would have supported A.J. no matter where he wanted to play, but I have to admit I was relieved he would be playing ball and going to school a lot closer to home than South Carolina.

The Writing on the Wall

With so much on my plate, summer almost flew by. In mid-August I completed my internship and spent the last couple of weeks of summer concentrating on softball training. Then it was time to head back to South Bend to begin my senior year. Moving day would be different this year. After spending my first three years in Welsh Family Hall on the Notre Dame campus, I had joined two teammates—Brittney and fellow pitcher and classmate Christine Ferrell—and rented an apartment just off campus. It was our first taste of being on our own and we had a lot of fun the first few weeks, decorating, planning meals and hosting teammates who still lived in the dorms.

I hit the books and the practice field hard. I was in the home stretch of completing my undergraduate degree and, as an athlete, wanted to build on the platform of hitting, throwing and fielding I had established over the summer. My internship had convinced me that I liked my work as an auditor and I was pleased to receive a post graduation job offer from PWC.

They wanted me to come to work right after graduation but they were also willing to allow me to work again as an intern in the summer after graduation so I could get a masters degree in accounting. Delaying my start date would also allow me to devote more time to studying for the demanding four-part CPA exam, an essential credential if I wanted to advance in my career. I quickly accepted the offer of a second internship in the summer after graduation with the understanding that a full-time job would be waiting for me after I finished graduate school.

Having an offer to work for a great firm removed some the pressure that's often part of the senior collegiate experience. I still wanted to finish strong academically and get accepted into graduate school, but my mind was sufficiently at ease to allow me to give my last season of softball my best shot.

The first order of business was to get ready for fall ball. Despite her earlier promise to use me only as a pinch hitter, I held out hope that Coach would test me in the field against live competition. This was really my last chance to convince her that I was ready to take control of an outfield spot. After three years, I knew she was well on her way to picking the starting lineup before the holidays began. Someone would have to be injured or really mess up for her to change her mind after we returned in January. With my suspect arm, looking good in practice wasn't going to be enough to sway her decision. I needed Coach to give me a chance to play in live competition.

As fall practices began, I tried to gauge if there was any chance I'd be part of the outfield rotation when fall ball began. It wasn't like Coach had led me to believe I was going to play. I was a pinch hitter, she'd said. That was supposed to be my role. I heard her, but I wasn't going to accept it as fact until I'd made every effort to change her mind. One factor was on my side. We had three fall ball weekends on the calendar this year. Maybe extra games would increase my chances of playing. That notion was quickly squashed when the first Sunday doubleheader—a twin bill against DePaul in Joliet, Illinois—was cancelled due to rain.

That left two more two-game sets: a three-way tournament at Melissa Cook Stadium with Loyola of Chicago and Western Michigan and a follow-up doubleheader in Ann Arbor with Michigan. Coach made her intentions pretty clear from the outset. I didn't see the field against Western and Loyola. She did put me in the field for a couple of innings at the end of the doubleheader against Michigan, but it was a token appearance....not a chance to compete for a starting position. I was probably the last one on the team to acknowledge it, but now even I could read the writing on the outfield wall. I really was just a pinch hitter now.

When reality sank in, I should have been devastated. Playing in the field had always been my favorite part of the game. I think I had always secretly dreaded the day when the last glimmer of hope to play in the Irish outfield would be extinguished. But now that that day had come, I wasn't overwhelmed with sadness or bitterness. Sure I was disappointed, but at the same time, I also felt oddly liberated. I was no longer burdened with the need to show Coach, Lizzy and Kris that I could throw. I was done pounding on the door with my injured shoulder to try to force my way in.

It wasn't that my desire was gone or even reduced. I was still driven to help the team win any way I could. And my loyalty to Coach and her staff hadn't changed. But after three years of giving my all to convince them that I deserved to play, I knew I had done all I could to change my situation. The time had come to reset my expectations. Although I had no control over my role on the team, I began to savor the things I could control:

I could control how hard I worked during this last year of my softball life, so I put maximum effort into every practice and workout.

I could control the pride I took in my progress as a lefty, so I kept working to make my throw better.

I could control the effort I made to get to a batted ball in the field, so I relished every chance to dive headlong to make catches in practice.

I could control my comeback as a hitter, so I took great joy in connecting solidly in batting practice and sending a line drive into the back of the cage.

And I could control the amount of fun I had being a teammate. So I got to know my teammates even better, enjoying their company, their interests, and the laughs we shared more days than not.

I was still the intense, ultra-competitive athlete who had chased her dream this far, but I knew my days as a softball player were slipping away. If the big accomplishments I had dreamed of were going to elude me for the rest of my career, then it was time to savor the things that were still mine...the things no injury could take away. Coach Greg had it right in the first place: softball isn't softball if you aren't having fun.

Senior Year

Perhaps one reason I was able to reset my expectations and put my own situation in perspective was the abrupt and unexpected end of A.J.'s baseball career. He had been given a scholarship to play for the Grand Valley State University Lakers in his senior year and was looking forward to playing his final year of college ball in front of his parents and grandparents as well as other family and friends in the Grand Rapids area. But after two weeks of fall practice, the coach took him aside and said he had changed his mind. He was going to focus on developing the underclassmen who had joined the team late in the summer. For the first time in his baseball career, A.J. found himself cut from the team.

It was another case of a coaching staff choosing players who had more future ahead of them over an upperclassman with most of his career behind him. A.J. felt betrayed. He had accepted the scholarship, enrolled in classes, and, most important, turned down offers from other colleges in the area to play for the Lakers. It was too late to change plans now. The scholarship was still his and so was the course schedule that would lead to his economics degree and a successful future career. But his dream was gone and it wasn't coming back.

I spent a lot of time talking to A.J. on the phone and helping him work through his disappointment. I had never seen him hurting so badly. He felt as though he had let down his family and maybe even me. I told him over and over that I would always be proud of him for never giving up on his dream, but also for being generous and kind in helping me battle to save my career. I also respected him for caring enough about his family that he changed the course of his career to come home and take a chance with a new team. Those actions said a lot more about A.J. as a person and meant a lot more to me and everyone else who loved him than whatever he might have accomplished on the diamond. It wasn't what we had planned on, but the sudden end to A.J.'s career as a college ballplayer meant we could see more of each other over the fall and winter. It was bittersweet consolation for what A.J. had lost.

Life as a senior marked the final cycle in my college career but it was also a new experience. Now I was one of the older sisters in our softball family with three classes of younger teammates behind me. I was moving forward without Katie, Smitty, Kathy and Amanda, my buddies from junior year. Also absent where the other teammates and friends who had graduated and moved away earlier in my career.

I still missed my buddies, but as the weeks of fall slipped past, I began to hang out with my classmates Linda Kohan and Stephanie Mola who were sharing a condo a few blocks from my apartment. Like me, Linda and Steph were charter members of 'The Cult'. We had been friends from the early days but hadn't spent as much time together as we were now. It turned out, we enjoyed hanging out, talking, and indulging in softball stories that inevitably turned any serious conversations into some serious laughter.

Steph's and Linda's place became a great place to go when the homework was done and it was time to relax. Our younger teammates would often migrate from their dorm rooms to join us at the condo, adding fresh voices to the mix. We enjoyed the company of girls in all three of the classes behind us, but the newest freshmen were a real breath of fresh air.

Dani, Alexa, Kasey and Kristina were about as diverse in personality as you could get, but they reminded us of ourselves as freshmen—brash and self-assured one moment, fun-loving cutups the next. They were serious about their softball, but not too serious about themselves, and that made them a refreshing injection of new blood. Although we sometimes had to gently nudge them into line, for the most part they fit right in, keeping the team loose in the dugout, on the field, and whenever we were together between practices and games.

Looking Ahead

All too quickly, fall gave way to Thanksgiving, which was soon followed by winter break. As my final year at Notre Dame moved quickly ahead, I found myself increasingly involved in post-graduate plans. I received word that I had been accepted into the master's degree program in accounting at Grand Valley State University and made plans to start classes the following fall after completing my second internship. I also started investigating financial aid options to help pay for my additional schooling. That was time consuming, and I would have loved to put it off, but scholarships, loans and other aid would be awarded in the early spring. I had to have everything lined up now so I would be eligible for the aid I needed to start classes in the fall.

While home for the holidays, I resumed the practice routine I had followed the previous winter, mixing throwing drills with hitting practice in the indoor practice facility we had used in the past or, if A.J. and I couldn't find an empty cage or floor space there, in my parent's garage and the snow-lined sidewalk in front of the house.

The second week of January, I headed back to South Bend for the start of our preseason preparations and my final academic semester at Notre Dame. I'd made the dean's list for the seventh time in the fall and was on track to graduate with honors in May, so I had decided to indulge myself a bit and take a slightly lower academic load for the first time since setting foot on campus. I wanted to have time to savor my last spring of Irish softball and a little less academic pressure would give me time to enjoy the company of my teammates, train and get any stretching and physical therapy I might need to keep my beat up body ready to play when Coach and the team needed me.

Helping me stay healthy and fit was our new athletic trainer, Nicole Alexander, a Florida graduate who had taken on Kathy's responsibilities in the fall. I'm sure when she reviewed my history and got a first glimpse of my shoulders and arms, Nicole must have thought she had inherited a physical wreck. But she dug right in and did a great job of getting me ready to play.

Although I was slated for pinch hitting duty, I continued to practice in the outfield and work on my right-handed glove work and left handed throw. I still had to concentrate intently on my work with the glove on my right hand. But by now I had replicated the range and catching ability I had always demonstrated wearing the glove on the left hand, a feat some viewed as almost as remarkable as my southpaw throw. The throw itself had continued to improve. On a typical play in straightaway left field, I could unleash a quick, accurate throw on a line to the cut off or to second or third base. My velocity on longer throws wasn't the equal of my healthy teammates' so trying to throw longer and harder was my daily personal quest.

I was also working hard in the batting cage to keep my timing intact and continue to generate maximum power from my modified swing. As hitters, we were lucky to have the chance to face a range of batting practice pitching styles in our workouts. There was Brittney and sophomore Jody Valdivia, who both threw hard, but brought their own unique movement patterns and changes of speed to the mix. My classmate Christine Farrell relied more on movement and deception than speed. When Coach threw, it gave us a chance to face a lefty who also had movement and deceptive speed. Finally Dawn Austin, our volunteer assistance coach and Penn State alum, took movement to another level, forcing us to raise our level of concentration, understand the strike zone, and learn to handle pitches that would dive out of the zone at the last minute.

I felt good in the cage and I was hitting the ball well, no matter who was tossing it. We had good pitching, so I was confident my success in practice would translate into great at-bats in games. If I had any worries, they were about how I would handle the pinch hitting role Coach had in mind for me. It would be hard to keep my intensity in check while sitting inning after inning. When the call finally came for me to head for the batter's box, would I be able to calm down, get a feel for the pitcher, then capitalize by driving the ball hard into a gap?

Southbound

True to her philosophy of seeking top competition to start the season, Coach had arranged for us to play several ranked teams in our annual swing through the South and West. We would start by playing in the Bama Bash hosted by the Alabama Crimson Tide, who were ranked number 1 in the preseason. Then we would head out to Palo Alto to play in the Nike Invitational hosted by Stanford, ranked number 5 early in the season.

For spring break we would travel to Las Vegas to take on UNLV and Texas Tech before traveling to the Los Angeles area to play UCLA, which would replace Stanford in the number 5 spot by the time we took the field at the Bruin's legendary Easton Stadium. On the heels of playing UCLA, we would head to Orange County where we would again play in the Judi Garman tournament hosted by Cal State Fullerton. There we'd face perennial powers including number 9 Oklahoma, number 12 Arizona, and number 6 Arizona State as well as rising Big Ten power Penn State.

It was a schedule that would ensure we would be battle-hardened before our conference season began. We hoped it was just the recipe needed to get us ready to challenge for top conference honors. Once again, a conference championship was our first goal, but if we somehow fell short, wins against ranked teams would improve our chances of gaining a berth in the NCAA Tournament, another one of our non-negotiable annual goals.

Our first stop of the spring was Valentine's Day weekend in Tuscaloosa, Alabama, for the Crimson Tide's Bama Bash. Considering the level of competition, we weren't planning on a love fest, but we also weren't expecting to get mercied 10-1 in five innings by our hosts. Our only threat to the Tide was built in the first on a hit batsman, a fielder's choice and two walks. A fielding error on a hard shot by Alexia Clay pushed a run across. Unfortunately, it was the only time an Irish base runner would cross the plate. Other than that it was all Tide the rest of the way. I didn't get called on to bat in game one, but was looking forward to Valentine's Saturday and a chance to contribute.

In the morning we faced East Carolina in the first of two games scheduled for the day. Two hits by Sadie and another two by Katie Fleury led the Irish attack as we beat the Pirates 2-1. Katie's solo home run in the sixth accounted for the winning margin. We were 1-1 on the season but had to face Alabama again in our second game of the day. The final score in the nightcap was just as lopsided as the one posted by the Tide the night before. They beat us 10-0, and the game ended in five innings again. Erin Marrone made a great catch for our side in the top of the first to quell a Tide rally, but the Alabama line-up was just too much for us to hold off forever. I saw my first game action of the season as a pinch runner in the fifth inning but was erased on a double play ball.

On Sunday morning, we took the field against Wisconsin in our last game before heading back to South Bend. It would have been nice to knock off the Badgers and even our record before getting on the plane, but it wasn't to be. Wisconsin won behind a 2-0 shutout pitching performance. Linda doubled and singled to lead our hitters but we couldn't string enough hits together to push across the runs we needed. I came to the plate as a pinch hitter with one on and two outs in the sixth, my first at-bat in the young season. The Badger pitcher drilled me with a pitch, giving us two runners aboard with a chance to tie things up, but our next batter fouled out to end the inning.

We had a lot to think about as we headed for home. Although Brittney and Jody had shown flashes of brilliance on the pitching rubber, our offense had been anemic. Our scoring output for the entire weekend was only three runs. We needed to pick it up if we were going to take advantage of the chance get some wins against top competition and set the stage for a successful Big East campaign. We had plenty of personal motivation, but we also knew that Coach was going to drive us even harder in practice. Our plane was still on the runway in Alabama and she already had her "game face" on. We had just a week to get ready for our next challenge, the Nike Invitational hosted by Stanford in Palo Alto, California. We had a feeling Coach was going to work us hard.

We started off the action in Palo Alto with a 4-1 win against Sacramento State, then lost twice to Stanford 2-0 and 5-2. We finally got our bats working with an 11-0 win in a rematch with Sacramento State before our final game of the weekend against Western Kentucky was rained out. I pinch hit three times in the tournament, with only a sacrifice bunt to show for the experience. I was still not comfortable coming off the bench to hit. I needed to calm down and just do what I had trained to do. Although my pinch hitting was a work in progress, we had performed better as a team. We hadn't defeated the Cardinal, but at least we had made it competitive compared to our performances against the Alabama the previous week. Meanwhile, we had defeated Sacramento State solidly in one game and very convincingly in the second. Now we needed to break through against a top team.

We headed to North Carolina the next weekend to play in the Wolfpack challenge at North Carolina State in Raleigh. Unfortunately heavy rains in the area prevented us from taking the field all weekend, depriving us of some badly needed game action. The weekend wasn't a total loss. With lots of time to kill, Coach arranged for a trip to the local mall and we also took in a movie, giving us a chance to become closer as teammates. We already spent a lot of time together, but normally that time was very structured for practices, training, travel or games. The cancellation of the weekend's games created a rare window of opportunity. Our schedules were clear so we might as well enjoy ourselves!

We headed home on Sunday to prepare for our annual Spring Break week on the West Coast. It was a good thing we would be playing a lot of softball in our stops in Las Vegas and California because—even though we'd had some fun in North Carolina—after a weekend away from game action, we were really ready to play ball.

On the Coast

Our first stop on our spring break jaunt was Las Vegas and the campus of UNLV. We were still a few hundred miles from the actual West Coast, but the palm trees, desert landscape, and glitter of neon on the famous strip made us feel we had arrived. Although I was seeing only limited playing time, I was excited to have Mom and Dad in town to share my last spring break as an Irish player. They had flown into Las Vegas and would be driving to our next stop—Brea, California—to enjoy more of the warmth and sun and watch us play ball.

In our Las Vegas opener we were matched against the Red Raiders of Texas Tech. We got off to a great start, taking a 7-0 win on the strength of Brittney's pitching and some timely hitting including two-run doubles by Heather and Linda and a triple by Bri Jorgensborg. I walked and scored a run in my only plate appearance. Next up that afternoon was UC Santa Barbara. We defeated the Gauchos 5-1, riding a four-run first inning to victory. Linda hit a three-run homer and Bri smashed another triple to contribute to the early rally. I came up with one on in the first and laid down a sacrifice bunt that moved Bri over to second. She eventually scored our fifth and final run to give us an extra cushion to lock up the win. Bri was on fire and stayed hot all weekend. She would be named Big East Player of the Week in recognition of her torrid hitting performance.

We headed back to our hotel in suburban Henderson for some down time with the parents who were in town to watch us. We were feeling good after getting two wins and knotting our season record at 5 wins and 5 losses. After enjoying an Italian meal hosted by the local Notre Dame Club, many of us sprawled out on the furniture in the hotel lobby and regaled our parents with stories of our wild lives as softball players. Not to be outdone, our parents countered with stories about their daughters' early years, drawing a lot of laughs from the other parents and quite a bit of razzing from our teammates. Coach's curfew cut the laughs short, but that was fine with us. We were tired and ready to get some rest so we'd be at our best to keep the winning streak alive in the morning.

We had a return engagement with the Red Raiders and Jody greeted Texas Tech with another seven innings of shutout frustration, adding a 5-0 shutout to the 7-0 gem Brittney had tossed the day before. Offensively we again rode a big inning, scoring four times in the fourth. A triple by my old roomie Alexia Clay drove in two runs to highlight the action. We had a rally going in the sixth when Coach called on me to pinch hit with three aboard and two down. I made good contact but lined the ball to second for the third out.

We faced off against the host UNLV Runnin' Rebels in our last game of the weekend. The home team came out strong, as the first three batters got hits, the third of which was a two-RBI double. We escaped the inning without further damage and Bri pulled us even with a two-run homer in the second, Unfortunately, we gave up three unearned runs in the bottom of the frame. The Rebels threatened again in the third but Steph Mola gunned down a Rebel runner at home with a perfect strike from right field to end the inning.

Steph then got it done at the plate, legging out an infield single that scored Christine Lux to cut the deficit to 5-3. That was as close as the score would get. We were really disgusted with ourselves, but not as upset as Coach was. Three Irish errors had resulted in an equal number of unearned runs and helped the Rebels take the win. My leadoff pinch hitting assignment in the fifth played a part in the frustration. I was hit by a pitch, which left an ugly bruise on my leg but didn't stop me from taking second on a wild pitch. Like our hopes of winning the tournament, I didn't get past second base. We were a subdued group as we boarded the bus and headed into the twilight for California.

Coming Through

Our week in the West continued Tuesday afternoon in Los Angeles as we took the field at UCLA's legendary Easton Field against the even more legendary Bruins, the team with more college softball national championships to its credit than any other. The Bruins jumped out to an early lead with a solo home run in the first inning, but we came right back in the second when doubles by Linda and Christine resulted in a run.

Both teams failed to score in the third, but in the bottom of the fourth, the Bruins manufactured a run with a single, a sacrifice bunt, a ground out and another single. The Bruins picked up an insurance run with a lead-off home run in their half of the sixth and three outs later they had the win. We'd competed hard and could have changed the outcome with a couple of key hits. But close didn't make us feel any better. We'd come to Los Angeles to win. Anything less was unacceptable. I would have liked to have had a chance to contribute, but with only three hits after our first inning rally, we didn't run through our lineup far enough for a lot of clear pinch hitting opportunities to present themselves. I'd made it as far as the on-deck circle late in the game, but that was as close as I would come to playing on the field I had seen so many times on television as a young travel ball player dreaming of playing college ball.

We had Wednesday off before play would begin at the Judi Garman Classic at Cal State Fullerton. I spent the day with Dad and Mom in Newport Beach, eating seafood and cruising the harbor on a tour boat. It was a relaxing break from the action and a chance to catch up with Mom and Dad. I'd be all business once we started play the next day, so it was nice to just enjoy the sun and my parents' company.

We started action Thursday against Penn State and the game was a real nail biter. Neither team recorded a hit until the fourth inning when freshman Alexa Maldonado led off with a double for the Irish. After Katie Fleury put down a sacrifice bunt to move Alexa over, the Nittany Lion pitcher retired the next two batters to strand her at third. Meanwhile, Brittney continued to hold the Lions hitless. We rallied again in the top of the sixth when Steph led off with a single and Sadie Pitzenberger was safe on an error. A fielder's choice erased our lead runner and a double play ended the threat altogether.

Penn State mounted a rally of their own with a one out walk and a single in the bottom of the sixth, but we got out of the jam with a force out at third and a strike out. We left one on in the seventh after Christine was hit by a pitch but the Lion pitcher managed to record the third out without damage. Brittney set down the Lions in order in the bottom of the frame to send the game into extra innings.

To keep the tournament reasonably on time, the rules called for an international tiebreaker format. The extra inning would begin with the runner who recorded the last out in the previous inning placed on second base. We had three outs to bring her home along with as many additional runs as we could score. Then the Lions, who were the home team in this game, would receive the same opportunity. If neither team scored—or we both tallied an equal number of runs—we'd do it over again until the tie was broken,

Starting with a runner on second base was such a huge advantage, it was critical for us to get the run across. If we didn't, there was a very good chance the Lions would win the game by doing so in the bottom of the inning. Since Bri had been our last batter, she would be placed on second base, but Coach decided to pinch run Christine Farrell in her place to give us some more speed on the base paths. Coach also decided to have me pinch hit to lead off the inning because of my ability to bunt. A leadoff sacrifice bunt in tiebreaker play was almost always the call so we could get the runner on second over to third where even a hard ground ball or a decent fly ball to the outfield would bring her home.

Coach's strategy was thwarted, though, when the pitcher hit me with a pitch, placing me on first but not advancing Christine from second base. Then the worst happened. Our next batter couldn't get the bunt down. She popped the ball up to first for an out, leaving Christine and me still occupying second and first base. The next two batters flew out to left field, preventing Christine from advancing to third. If we had been able to move Christine to third before we had two outs, either fly ball would have scored her. As it was, now we had to hold off Penn State in their half of the eighth inning to get another crack at it in the top of the ninth.

Unfortunately, the Lions did what we could not. Their first batter placed a successful sacrifice bunt on the ground to move the runner from second to third with one out. They had two chances to drive her home and the first one didn't even have to be a hit. A ground out somewhere deep or a reasonably deep fly ball to the outfield would probably be enough. The next batter made any thought of a close play at the plate a moot point. She singled sharply to left field for a walk-off win. We were 0-2 and had scored all of one run in 15 innings since arriving in the Golden State.

Our next opponent of the day wasn't going to be any easier to beat than our previous two. The Oklahoma Sooners were ranked fifth in the country coming into the game and it figured to be another tough game if we didn't get our bats going. Fortunately, Christine set the proper tone in the bottom of the second inning with a two-run homer after Linda had singled to get us started. Oklahoma scored once in the top of the third on a walk and a double with two down, but we escaped the inning still clinging to a one-run lead. The Sooners threatened again in the fourth with back to back singles before Jody retired the next batter for the third out.

We tacked on another run in the fourth when Heather led off with a single. Coach brought Christine Farrell in to pinch run for Heather and Linda followed with a sacrifice bunt to move her into scoring position. The move paid off as Christine Lux singled to drive the pinch runner home for our third run of the game. Brittney came into the game in relief of Jody and promptly retired the Sooners in order in the fifth and gave up a lone single in the sixth. Meanwhile it was three-up, three-down for the Irish in both the fifth and sixth. With one inning to play, it looked like we were going to get the upset win.

I was all but packing my gear, happy that we had the win in hand even if it meant I would remain on the bench. There was always next game. Then the Sooners decided they would have something to say about the outcome. Two singles, an intentional walk and two Irish errors later, they had come from behind to knot the score at three runs apiece. It wasn't pretty. We seemed to be self destructing right before the eyes of the large crowd on hand for the game. We had three outs to mount a rally if we wanted to avoid extra innings for the second time that day. I needed to refocus. The team might need my help to win it after all.

Christine got us started right with a lead-off walk, but the second Irish batter popped out on an attempted sacrifice bunt. Coach sent me to the plate to pinch hit with one down. This wasn't a bunting situation. We couldn't afford to sacrifice another out to move Christine into scoring position. I needed to get a hit. If I moved Christine to second or third without making an out, it would set the table for the rally we sorely needed to score the winning run.

I stepped into the batters' box and watched the first pitch go by. It was a nasty rise ball. I adjusted my batting position slightly, "shrugging my shoulders" to stand a little taller as Curtis had taught me. I wanted to be ready for a hittable pitch up in the zone. As the next pitch came in I could tell it was rising but I thought I could get on top of it and drive it. Swinging hard, I made an effort to keep my right shoulder above the ball, hammering through it with my right arm and hand. I hit it flush, sending a line drive up the middle for a single to the screams of my Irish teammates and coaches.

Christine was standing safely on second with me on first when freshman Dani Miller followed my hit with a clutch single of her own to load the bases with one out. The only thing we absolutely could not afford was a double play so Coach brought in Steph Mola to run for Dani to improve the chances the first base runner would make it safely to second on a ground ball. Sadie Pitzenberger came up next and bunted the ball back at the pitcher. With the game on the line, the pitcher hurried to make a play as Christine barreled toward home and Sadie, Steph and I charged just as quickly for the next base. The pitcher lost control of the bounding ball and, just like that, we had a walk-off win against the number 5-ranked team in the country. After three frustrating losses in a row, it was the breakthrough we had been waiting for.

As I ran from the field to join my teammates to celebrate in front of our dugout, Coach grabbed me, looked me in the eye and said, "Do you know how hard it is to do that?" I knew she was talking about getting on top of a good rise ball and driving it back up the middle, but she could also have been referring to coming off the bench cold to contribute a hit when we needed one badly. It was a great team win and a high point in the young season for me. If I was going to be a pinch hitter, I wanted to be great at it. Coming through in the clutch gave me a taste of how good that could feel.

Finding a Groove

The next evening we faced off against Pacific, a solid California team that we could not afford to take for granted. The Tiger's showed us they deserved our respect by jumping out to an early lead in the first on a two-run homer, then adding a third run in the fourth inning. We cut the lead to one in our half of the fourth but as we entered our half of the fifth inning, we still trailed. The way this season was going, any time we were behind we had good reason to be worried.

As we got ready to hit, Coach told me I'd be pinch hitting for my classmate and buddy, Steph Mola, who was scheduled to hit second. Steph was a slapping and bunting specialist but that wasn't what we needed in this situation. We were down by a run with only nine outs left to work with. Steph was the ultimate teammate. No one likes to miss a chance to hit, but she walked up to me in the dugout as I pulled on my batting gloves and offered some encouragement: "O.K. Beth," she said. "Do something I can't do!" It was her way of saying we need a big hit, something deep in a gap for extra bases.

After our leadoff hitter flew out to right field, I approached the batter's box and looked down to third for Coach's sign. Swing away. I dug into the box, holding my right hand up to signal the umpire that I wanted time to get comfortable. When I was ready, I took a practice swing and the umpire signaled, "Play ball". I watched the first pitch go by for a called strike. If I had learned anything from my last pinch hitting experience, it didn't hurt to watch the first pitch to see what you were dealing with. My last at bat hadn't instructed me to watch the second pitch go by, but I did this time for a second called strike.

I had dug a hole for myself. I'm sure Coach was thinking I better get the bat off my shoulder. Otherwise, I was wasting the opportunity to do some damage. Typically, a two strike count gives the pitcher a license to do just about anything. She can throw a ball outside the strike zone and hope I'll go fishing and miss. Or she can throw a strike and hope I'll be over anxious and hit a weak grounder or fly out. This pitcher decided to bust me inside with a fastball. I was ready. I blasted it high into the lights that illuminated the field under the night sky and took off for first at top speed, rounded the bag and roared toward second. At that moment the image of the left fielder turning away from the fence and back toward the infield told me all I needed to know. My first career home run had knotted the score at 3-3. My momentum carried me quickly around third and I rolled into home where I was greeted by the entire Irish team. After a lot of high fives, we moved as a pack back to the dugout chanting in celebration and I heard Steph beside me say, "That'll work!"

It turned out my homer was just what we needed to shake off the doldrums. With two outs, Alexa was hit by a pitch, Heather singled to move her over and Katie drove her home with a follow-up single of her own. Christine then padded our lead with a three-run homer to left center before Pacific finally recorded the third out. The 7-3 score held up as we retired the final six Tigers in a row. We had another win and had evened our season at 8-8. As a personal bonus, I was relived I would not go down in Irish softball history as a hitter who hadn't hit a home run!

My hot streak as a pinch hitter continued the next day against number 12 Arizona with a double in the fifth. Unfortunately our two-game winning streak screeched to a halt with a 10-1 loss to the Wildcats in five innings. Arizona scored three runs in the first, one run each in the second and third and then exploded for five runs in the fourth. The fifth inning was their only scoreless at bat all day. Meanwhile, we were held to one run on five hits with our only score coming in the first. It was an emphatic loss that dampened the high we had been riding the previous two days. We had one more game under the California sun before boarding our flight back to the Midwest to begin playing ball the way lumberjacks did...bundled against the damp and cold.

Our final West Coast matchup was against defending national champion Arizona State, ranked number 6 in the nation. The game was close into the third when Arizona State pushed a run across on two hits and an error. After that initial score, Brittney kept the Sun Devils at bay until the sixth when the first two hitters homered to extend the lead to three runs. We saved our best for the seventh and last inning, but it was a case of too little, too late. Linda led off with a single and Coach put Kasey in to pinch run and called on me to pinch hit. I found a pitch I could drive but this time I didn't find a hole. The third baseman barely lifted her glove to snag my line shot, then quickly threw to first to catch our runner off the base for the double play.

With two down, we still weren't out of it. Dani came in to pinch hit and doubled to left. Alexia Clay also entered as a pinch hitter and was safe at first on a fielding error, moving Dani to third. Our rally and the game ended there when a grounder to second base resulted in a force out. Unlike our loss to Arizona, we had played better against the Sun Devils. But we didn't hit well enough to take advantage of Brittney's strong pitching performance and capture the win.

We had tested ourselves against some of the nation's best teams in tournaments in the South and West but had only an 8-10 overall record to show for it. It didn't show up in the wins and losses, but we hoped playing strong competition had prepared us to battle for a Big East Championship and an extended run in the NCAA Tournament. After a week of proving I could come off the bench and contribute in clutch situations, I had reason to believe my bat could be a big factor in that success.

Back on the North Coast

After returning to South Bend from spring break, we dove right into our first games in the cooler air of the Great Lakes region with a double header against Toledo. We swept the Rockets, 15-0 and 9-1 to right the ship after the two losses that closed out our West Coast trip. Coach must have seen something she liked in my pinch hitting appearances because she decided to try me as the designated player batting second in the line-up. In the first game, Christine led a robust Irish offensive attack, driving in five runs, while Dani and Heather each had three RBIs. I hit a double in the third to drive in a run, contributing to a four run Irish rally in the inning. I also walked and scored a run.

In the second game I did my best to further reward Coach's confidence, smacking a drive off the top of the fence with the bases loaded and just missing a grand slam home run. As it was, the resulting triple brought in three runs in the nine-run Irish fourth. I then scored on Heather's follow-up single. After the all or nothing life of a pinch hitter, batting several times a game as the DP felt like a relaxing change of pace. Against the Rockets I was able to help the team with a sacrifice bunt and a walk in addition to my extra base hits.

We opened the Big East season four days later against St. Johns at Melissa Cook Stadium. True to form in a season marked by extreme highs and lows, the Red Storm shocked us in the first game by taking a 4-3 win. The game was scoreless until we pushed a run across in the fourth. But our lead was short-lived as St. Johns rallied for four runs in the sixth. Their outburst was powered by five hits including a couple of doubles, but was aided by a passed ball, a wild pitch and some aggressive base running. A two-run home run by Linda in the seventh made it close, but the Red Storm held on for the win. Coach had me serve as a pinch hitter instead of in the DP spot and my only chance to contribute came in the seventh. I led off but grounded out. It was probably too much to expect to come up big in every pinch hit appearance.

The nightcap started as a scoreless pitching duel until we scored two runs in the fourth. St. Johns came right back with four runs in the fifth to snatch the lead. We got a run back in our half of the fifth but it took a two-out rally in the seventh to gain the 5-4 win and save us from a Red Storm sweep. Katie and Bri jacked back-to-back home runs to save us.

I didn't get a chance to hit in game two and had only one at bat for the day but I decided not to read too much into it. So far this year, our offensive output had been a textbook case of feast or famine. Coach was still looking for a lineup that would consistently produce more runs and get us more wins. I was doing everything I could to earn a place in that conversation. I had learned in my junior season there was nothing to be gained by worrying about things I couldn't control.

Starting our Big East campaign with a split wasn't what we were hoping for. Fortunately, we had three non-conference games in the next three days before we'd hit the road for our first full Big East weekend. That would give us some game action to find our groove before facing our next conference opponent. First up was Ball State. The Cardinals made the drive over from Muncie, Indiana, for a single game on our turf. The game started with heartbreak for the Irish. Sophomore shortstop and lead-off hitter Sadie—who had come back from a season-ending knee injury in her freshman campaign to become one of our leading offensive threats—re-injured her ACL going into first base. For the second time in two years, season-ending knee surgery would be required.

Sadie's injury meant Katie would move over to shortstop from second base. Coach installed Dani at second and moved me into the DP spot, batting second in the lineup. We faced off against my old Finesse teammate, Elizabeth Milian, who brought her usual good stuff to the game. Unfortunately, her teammates were not up to the task defensively. We scored five runs, four of them unearned in a 5-1 win. I was the beneficiary of a Cardinal error in the third, reaching safely on a grounder to the right side, stealing second and eventually scoring on a three-run homer by Dani who continued to light it up in her freshman campaign.

A day later we faced off against Western Michigan University from nearby Kalamazoo and sent the Broncos home with two defeats. We won 6-1 in the first game, but only after allowing the Broncos to jump out to a one-run lead in the first. I walked with one down in our half of the first, and hustled all the way to third on a single by Heather. Christine sent a sacrifice fly to the outfield to bring me home with the tying run. After retiring the Broncos with no runs in the second, we rode home runs from Alexia Clay and Katie Fleury to score three runs and take a 4-1 lead. We pushed another run across in the fourth on three hits and got our final run in the sixth on a homer by Bri. I finished the game with two walks, a double and single.

In game two, Dani was clutch in the first inning, clearing the bases with a grand slam after three walks had loaded the bases. After Western scored one run in the top of the third, I lead off with a double in the bottom of frame. I got as far as third but the Bronco pitcher got the third out before I could score. The score remained unchanged until the sixth when we mounted a four-run rally. A couple of hits, two walks, and a wild pitch allowed us to stretch the lead to 8-1. I walked and scored our final run, capping my second straight game with two hits and two free passes. Sadie's injury had forced Coach to juggle the Irish hitting lineup and had given me a chance to expand my role. Getting on base eight times in our sweep of the Broncos was an important first step in my effort to show her that I could help the team win.

While I was excited to have the chance to play, I felt horrible for Sadie. My own struggles with injury and inability to get back on the field gave me a unique insight into the frustration and the physical and emotional toll she was experiencing. Like me, Sadie wasn't going to waste time feeling sorry for herself and she sure didn't want her teammates' sympathy. But I felt no one should have to go through what Sadie was experiencing. To play softball almost your entire life to get the chance to compete for a great university, only to have your dream snatched away over and over again...it really confirmed the notion that sometimes life really isn't very fair.

On the Road in the Big East

Friday night after our defeat of Western Michigan, we headed for the airport for our first weekend of conference play. Our destination was Washington, D.C., home of Georgetown University, where we would play a Saturday doubleheader. The Hoyas were newcomers to Big East softball in 2009 after starting their Division I softball program just four years earlier. After a split in our Big East doubleheader opener against St. Johns, we wanted to take care of business and get two wins against Georgetown. We came out strong.

I came up with one down in the first and put a charge into a ball that sailed over the fence in left center for a home run and the lead. The score remained 1-0 until the top of the fifth when Irish freshman catcher Kristina Wright was hit by a pitch with one out. My classmate Christine Farrell was called on to pinch run and made it to second as freshman centerfielder Alexa Maldonado legged out a bunt single. Our next batter flew out, but I worked the Hoya hurler for a walk to load the bases.

That brought Heather to the plate and she came through with a single up the middle to drive in two runs and move me around to third. Kasey O'Connor came in to pinch run for Heather just in time for Christine Lux to send a rocket down the right field line for a home run. Our lead was now 6-0. The score remained the same until the bottom of the seventh when the Hoyas mounted a four run rally on two walks, a pair of singles and a triple before Brittney recorded the final out to take the win.

The start of the second game was delayed for about an hour by rain showers passing through the Capitol area, which was a concern because we had to catch a flight to Tampa for a Sunday doubleheader with South Florida. Coach quickly calculated when we'd have to be off the field and on our way to the airport to catch the flight. It looked like we could still fit the second game in if we played at a fast pace or the game was shortened by the run rule. Whatever happened, we were going to make our flight; failing to do so was not an option.

We mounted an 8-1 lead in the first five innings of game two on the strength of a balanced hitting attack led by Heather, who had three hits. All that productivity on offense ate up valuable time, though. Coach's departure time limit arrived before we could complete the game or score the additional run necessary to mercy the Hoyas. With the game suspended before the outcome was officially in the books, none of our run scoring would count unless we needed the win badly enough to return to Georgetown at a later date to finish the game.

Our trip to the airport was mayhem. After dashing straight from Georgetown's field to the bus, we changed from our uniforms into travel clothes as the bus worked its way through the Washington, D.C. traffic. As soon as our feet hit the pavement outside the terminal, we grabbed our bat bags and duffels and sprinted for check-in, into the security lines, and finally to our gate where we just made it in time to board our flight.

We paid for our hurried boarding in D.C. when we landed in Tampa. Only a portion of our luggage arrived with us. That led to some anxiety Saturday night and Sunday morning but, fortunately, our equipment and uniforms arrived in time for the start of our first game against the Bulls on Sunday afternoon. South Florida had established itself as a force to be reckoned with since joining the Big East three years earlier. The outcome of the day's games would provide an early measure of how strongly we would compete for a conference championship.

The start of game one was delayed by rain but the showers finally passed through and it was time to play ball. Dani got us started in the second with a solo home run. I came up in the third and worked a 3-2 count before following Dani's lead with a homer of my own. South Florida scored one in the fourth but Brittney pitched her way out of a bases loaded jam to end the threat. We nursed our precarious 2-1 lead into the seventh when I doubled to drive in Alexia Clay for an insurance run. South Florida scored a run on a bases loaded walk in the bottom of the seventh before we recorded the third out on a line drive to Katie at shortstop.

Game two was equally suspenseful but for different reasons. We gave up two runs in the first on two throwing errors to fall behind the Bulls with the game barely underway. We mounted a rally in the fourth after I singled to lead off, Heather was safe on an infield hit and a walk by Christine but the Bulls pitcher got out of the inning without allowing a run. Fortunately, Alexia came up big with a pinch hit three-run home run in the sixth to give us our first lead of the game. We scored our fourth run of the day in the top of the seventh on consecutive one-out singles by me, Heather and Linda. After a Bulls pitching change, Dani doubled to right to score two more runs and stretch our lead to 6-2. South Florida got two runs back in the bottom of the frame, but Jody put the final touches on the victory to give the Irish our first-ever sweep of the Bulls.

To cap our rainy weekend, the delayed start of our Sunday doubleheader caused us to miss our flight home. We would have to wait to catch an early flight Monday morning. That meant another night in a hotel, but Coach was feeling pretty good about our performance against the Bulls. She rewarded us with a great dinner and even let us order an appetizer, a sure sign that she was happy with us.

It had been a demanding weekend with long flights, rain delays, sprints through airports to catch flights, lost luggage...just about every calamity a traveling college softball team can expect to encounter. But we were in high spirits as we flew home with three victories and very nearly a fourth to show for our efforts. I was feeling good about how I was settling into my role as the designated player. In the second game with the Bulls, I'd added two hits, a walk and a run to my 2 for 4 and two RBI performance in game one. Coupled with a two run, two RBI, performance in the first game against Georgetown, including a home run and a walk, it had been a good weekend at the plate.

Apparently the Big East coaches agreed. They named me Big East Player of the Week on the strength of a .562 batting average with a 1.125 slugging percentage in six Irish wins, including a pair of home runs and three doubles. The League noted that I had four multi-hit games, scored seven runs and collected seven walks. My four hits in seven at-bats at USF were highlighted for helping us gain an important sweep of a strong Big East rival.

It was nice to get the recognition but the season was young. I wasn't about to relax now. We had a lot of softball yet to play and we had set our sights on something more important than individual honors. Someone was going to take home a Big East Championship and an NCAA World Series Championship would also be won at the end of the season. Anything else we accomplished during the season, individually and as a team, was just a step on the way to those two goals.

Back to Work

Back in South Bend we were greeted by more rain...enough to rain out a planned Tuesday afternoon game with Indiana University Purdue University Indianapolis (IUPUI). Northern Illinois came to town the next day and brought our offense to life as we scored 11 runs to our opponent's 4. There were four Irish home runs in the game which, coupled with six Husky errors, led to the lopsided score. Significantly for me, Coach showed she had taken note of my offensive performance. She moved me from the second spot in the batting order to the leadoff position. The team needed a table setter who would find a way to get on base and then use her base running ability to advance and score. It was a great vote of confidence and I planned to do everything I could to not let Coach or my teammates down.

Coach also moved my classmate and buddy, Linda, up in the order. She would take over the number two spot, which gave rise to a new ritual every time we prepared to go to the plate. Although Linda was a great bunter, she really liked going to the plate in situations where she could swing away. Throughout her career, she had hit a lot of doubles and home runs. As the number two hitter, she would be called on to do a lot more bunting if I managed to get to first base ahead of her. If I managed an extra base hit, the bunt would be off and Linda could hit away.

Whenever I led off an inning, Linda would encourage me to hit a double into the gap. I'd respond by telling her I'd be waiting at second base when she came to the plate. Of course, it was all in fun. Short ball or long ball, we would both do whatever it took to win. With 13 doubles, a triple and five home runs on the season, I did my best to give Linda the chance to swing away, but I also singled 28 times, walked 25 times and was hit by a pitch 5 times. Some of those were in leadoff plate appearances with Linda waiting on deck. Sorry Linda...sometimes you just can't buy an extra base hit!

In the wake of our nonconference win we were focused on the upcoming weekend and scheduled Big East doubleheaders with Pittsburgh and Seton Hall at Melissa Cook Stadium. We were on a roll in the conference and were anxious to maintain our momentum. The best way to win a conference championship was to control our own destiny by winning every game the rest of the way.

Pittsburgh had other ideas. The Panthers held us to six hits while racking up a 5-2 win in game one. Pitt scored three in the second inning and, although we managed a run in the third, the Panthers got two unearned runs in the fourth to extend their lead. A final Irish run in the sixth was all we could manage the rest of the way. It was the first time in ten games we had been held without a home run. Maybe we should have saved some of those midweek knocks against Northern Illinois for the weekend.

Game two was a different story. We got our bats untracked and recorded a 7-1 victory behind a strong pitching performance by Jody. I tried to get us started with a leadoff single in the third. I stole second and moved to third on a single off the bat of Linda. Heather hit a ground ball to short and I was running as the ball came off the bat. A perfect throw by the shortstop gunned me down at the plate but left two runners aboard for Dani who doubled to drive them both home. We scored two more in both the fourth and fifth innings and tallied a final run in the sixth while Pitt scored its lone run in the fifth. Jody overpowered the Panther hitters, recording 14 strikeouts and allowing only three hits in seven innings of work.

After splitting our matchups with Pitt, we were determined not to let the same thing happen Sunday against the Pirates of Seton Hall. Brittney and Jody did their part by throwing consecutive shutouts. Meanwhile Irish batters slugged 20 hits on the day as we rolled to 9-0 and 13-0 wins. Both games lasted just five innings, and the early finish eliminated any excuse for not finishing up our homework that night for our Monday morning classes.

Brittney threw a four-hitter in the first game while our offense started early, scoring three earned runs in the first inning to chase the starting Pirate pitcher from the game. I led off with a single and Linda doubled to send me home. Then, after a sacrifice bunt by Heather, Christine hit a two-run shot over the fence. Erin padded our lead, coming to the plate with the bases loaded in the fourth and depositing a long ball over the fence for a grand slam. We scored two more before the fourth inning ended to provide the margin necessary to end the game in five innings under the run rule.

Game two began just as decisively as we scored five runs in the first, four runs in the second and four runs in the third. I started the bottom of the first with a leadoff double. Linda drove me in with a single. Dani had a three run home run later in the inning and Alexia Clay singled to drive in Katie to make it a 5-0 game. The Seton Hall bats seemed to come alive with several hard hit balls in the second, but we played good defense to prevent the Pirates from mounting a rally. In the second, we scored four unearned runs on two hits and three Pirate errors. We followed that with a four-hit, two-walk third inning to tack on our final four runs. Lost in all the scoring was Jody's second consecutive pitching gem. She was pitching a no hitter before giving up a single in the fifth, the only Pirate hit of the day. With hits in each of the weekend's four games, I had hit safely in nine of our first ten league games. Mine wasn't the only hot Irish bat. Not by a long shot. But considering where my season had begun, I had come out of nowhere to become a consistent contributor to the team's success.

Dueling with Blue Demons

Our next action pitted us against Big East arch rival DePaul. The Blue Demons made the short trip from the North Side of Chicago to South Bend for a Wednesday afternoon doubleheader that could be pivotal in deciding who would win the regular season conference championship. The Blue Demons were ranked number 22 in the nation and we expected a battle in both games.

DePaul jumped out to a three run lead in the first two innings of the opener, but it could have been worse if Brittney had not gotten the third out in the first with the bases jammed. We came back to tie things up in the fifth inning as Linda hit a two run homer after I drove Erin home on a shot at the Demon shortstop that was originally called a hit but later rescored as an error. Christine then followed with a two run blast of her own to give us a 5-3 lead.

Two, two-run home runs by the Blue Demons in the top of the seventh swung the score back in DePaul's favor, but an Alexia Clay single followed by doubles by Heather and Christine gave us the two runs we needed to knot the score. After a scoreless eighth, DePaul pushed across the go-ahead run in the second extra inning on a walk and a double. We had a chance to tie it again in our half of the ninth as Alexa doubled to lead off and I singled. A great throw from the Demon outfield gunned Alexa down at the plate. I advanced to second on the play but was left stranded there.

After using three pinch runners and two pinch hitters, Coach had exhausted her outfield options in the first seven innings. She had no choice but to move me from designated player to right field. I was finally an outfielder again. Lucky for the Blue Demons they didn't hit one my way in the course of six outs. After almost two years on the sidelines, I was ready to make a play!

In the nightcap we came out determined to prevent a DePaul sweep. We scored runs in four of the first five innings as Jody held the Blue Demon bats at bay, giving up only one earned run on four hits with eight strikeouts to her credit. Linda got us going with a solo home run in the first. A walk by Erin followed by a double by Alexa gave us a second run in the second. DePaul came back with a run in the third on a single, a sacrifice bunt, and a stolen base, which placed the leadoff batter on third base. An Irish error allowed the score.

Erin and Dani tallied RBI singles in the bottom of the third to increase our margin to 4-1, which turned out to be a good thing because DePaul got a solo home run in the top of the fourth to make it 4-2. We picked up another run in the fifth on a solo homer by Christine, which capped her dominating five hit, two home run, and four RBI performance for the day. That wrapped up the scoring, as we earned the split by a 5-2 final margin.

We weren't happy with a single victory in two tilts with the Demons. It felt like we had let DePaul steal a win from us in the first game. We hoped that loss wouldn't spell the difference between a regular season championship and second place.

Hanging On

Team practices and warm-ups before games throughout the season still found me throwing with the other outfielders, working on a quicker release, increased leg action, improved coordination, and a stronger delivery. I knew the odds were still stacked against me. We had too many great athletes capable of playing the outfield. But Coach's and Lizzy's decision that I was going to hit but not field didn't mean I was exempted from practicing at my position. They expected me to participate in every defensive drill. That was fine with me. I enjoyed practicing and pushing myself to get better. I couldn't imagine sitting on the sidelines during practice.

My throw was actually getting better every day. Even my teammates noticed and commented on it. I think it made them happy to see my effort pay off, even if the progress was gradual. I was convinced if I could have another year to work on it, I would be throwing like a natural born southpaw. For now, I could only give it my best effort. I might not ever see the outfield in live game action again, but I knew in my heart I was doing everything I could to keep that door open, even if just a crack. If nothing else, I would always have those two innings against DePaul as proof that I had overcome tall odds to give Coach another outfielder to draw on when game circumstances depleted our bench.

There came a time late in the season when I was forced to make a difficult choice. My left arm and shoulder were becoming increasingly sore and I was concerned that, if I continued to throw all out in practice, my ability to hit might be affected. I couldn't afford to jeopardize my role as the DP to continue to chase a goal that would likely remain out of my reach. With only a few weeks left in the season, Lizzy had already told me that I had earned my role as the DP and that wasn't going to change.

She said to focus on my hitting and stop working my left arm so hard. I knew she was right so I eased up a bit. I continued to make every throw in practice and warm-ups, but I didn't try to gun them all. I needed to finish strong at the plate to help the Irish win a regular season league title and a Big East Tournament Championship, and make a run in the NCAA tournament. It was time to give up my personal quest to become an outfielder so I would be in the best possible condition to help us reach our team goals.

Meanwhile, my right shoulder was also growing tired from the exertion of hitting. As the strength of my top hand waned, I applied everything I knew about my swing to keep the hits coming. In one practice session in the final weeks of the season, Lizzy said I was dropping my hands as I started my swing. Ordinarily I would have welcomed her coaching to fix the flaw as quickly as possible. But this was different. I didn't have the luxury of time to correct the problem and lock in the solution. The end of my career was just a few games and relatively few at bats away. As Lizzy began to instruct me on the proper correction I stopped her and said, "Lizzy, it's the end of the season and I'm still hitting the ball well. I don't think it's a good time to try to make adjustments." I was relieved when she considered for a minute, then said, "You're right. Keep doing what you are doing."

Actually, I wasn't just dropping my hands, I didn't realize it, but I was also dropping the bat head to a position almost parallel with the ground as I triggered before starting the swing. My Dad said later my swing looked a little like the flat cut that Rod Carew used in the Major Leagues. I'm not sure why the former Minnesota Twin chose that style, but in my case, it wasn't really intentional. With the strength waning in my right shoulder, I was just trying to make it possible to swing with a stronger left shoulder, arm and hand. I needed my left side to pull my weakened right shoulder through the swing to get the bat into the hitting zone on time to drive the ball hard.

Fortunately, I still had quick enough hands to help me maintain my timing as my trigger position changed and my swing became shorter and increasingly powered by my left side. Without a strong right side to hammer the ball, my power was somewhat depleted. Fortunately, my line drive hitting style was still producing a steady diet of hard singles and doubles and I continued to get on base at a high rate in keeping with my role as a leadoff hitter and table setter for the hitters behind me.

Rolling On

After our split with DePaul, Coach might have been concerned about a team letdown. But the next afternoon, we dispelled any such fears by clobbering Valparaiso in a doubleheader at Melissa Cook Stadium, 11-0 and 17-9. It was just the tune-up we needed for our weekend doubleheader at Connecticut in league action.

Saturday morning in Storrs, Connecticut, dawned cloudy with the threat of rain. Our Saturday doubleheader against the Huskies would be our only action of the weekend and we really wanted to get both games in. We started strong in game one as Linda and Heather combined with back-to-back doubles to give us the lead. Christine followed with a two run home run to up the score. After Alexa and Erin worked their way on base, Alexia Clay hit a three-run bomb to give us a six run lead.

I found a little extra top hand and smacked a homer to left in the fourth to make it 7-0 before Connecticut pushed two runs across in their half of the inning. We managed another run in the sixth and then exploded for four more in the seventh punctuated by Bri's opposite field two-run shot. The 12-4 final score gave Brittney the win on a five hitter.

A steady rain fell throughout the latter innings of the game and led to the cancellation of game two, a disappointing end to a promising day. As it was, in just one game, we had seven hits for extra bases including four home runs on the day. Alexia Clay had four RBIs to go with her two hits and Bri chimed in with a two-for-two day after entering the game in the fourth. If we continued to hit like that, I liked our chances in the league race.

The following Tuesday we made a midweek road trip to Madison to take on the Wisconsin Badgers in doubleheader action. It was a chance to avenge our early season loss to the Badgers in Alabama and we made the most of it, sweeping the home team,

5-0 and 4-2. I led off with a single in the first game to get us started. After advancing to second on a ground out, I came home on Christine's single.

The score remained at 1-0 until the top of the seventh when Alexia singled to right and Steph was safe at first on a sacrifice bunt. Alexia went all the way to third and Steph reached second base courtesy of some sloppy fielding by the Badgers. When things settled down, I was intentionally walked to load the bases, but the Badger pitcher then unintentionally walked Linda to force home a run. Steph came home on a passed ball, then Heather singled to center to drive me home. A walk to Christine reloaded the bases in time for an RBI single by Dani for our final score. Brittney's eight strikeout shutout set the table for the win, allowing us to nurse our narrow early lead until the final inning when we put the game away.

Game two was also close until the late innings. Neither team scored until the fifth when Erin lined a home run over the left field fence to give us the lead. We scored again in the sixth on Linda's single and Christine's triple. A walk, a triple and a single allowed the Badgers to tie the game in the bottom of the sixth, setting the stage for another late Irish rally. Erin singled to short to lead off the seventh, advanced to second on an error and stole third before Alexia Clay homered to right to give us the lead for good. Jody pitched a three-hitter to keep us in the game until our final rally.

I had three hits on the day and hit the ball hard right at Badger fielders for outs in other at bats, prolonging what was becoming a season-long streak of making solid contact at the plate. It was probably the longest hot streak of my entire softball career. More important for Irish fans and players alike, a couple of solid wins against a Big Ten opponent was a good platform to prepare us for the upcoming weekend of Big East action on the road at Villanova and Rutgers.

Moving Up
In the Big East

As we flew to Philadelphia for our Saturday doubleheader against Villanova we knew we were entering the pivotal point in our season. So far our Big East campaign had produced mixed results. Our first-ever sweep of South Florida was a high point, and we'd looked strong against Seton Hall, Georgetown and Connecticut. But we had split with St. Johns, Pittsburgh and DePaul, giving us a 9-3 record. If we were going to finish on top of the regular seasons standings, we needed to sweep more Big East doubleheaders. Splits just were not going to get the job done.

In the first game with the Wildcats, we were locked in a scoreless pitching duel until the fourth inning when our offense caught fire. I started the rally with a single to right center. Linda's sacrifice bunt was both successful in moving me over and misplayed by the Villanova infield to allow her to reach first. Heather followed with a bunt single and, running aggressively, I made it all the way around third and was safe at home for our first run. Linda turned on the jets as well, landing on third base. Christine Farrell came in to pinch run for Heather and quickly stole second, which set the table for Dani who responded by singling to drive in both runners. Three runs were all we would need as Brittney threw a four hitter. A rally in the fourth was the only threat Villanova could muster in the game, but they left runners on second and third when the third out was recorded by the Irish defense.

Despite getting two runners on in both the first and second innings of the second game, we were unable to score until the fourth inning. Dani Miller got us started with a solo home run, continuing a torrid hitting streak that would last 20 games. After

Erin and Alexia Clay were hit by pitches and advanced a base each on a wild pitch, both scored on Alexa's single. Then I singled to drive in Alexa, giving us a 4-0 lead. Villanova got one back in the bottom of the fourth on a solo home run, but we exploded for three more runs in the seventh. The rally started with a single by Christine, a walk to Katie Fleury, and an RBI double by Erin. Katie was caught in a run down between second and third, but we weren't done. A home run by Alexia Clay capped the scoring with two more runs. Jody gave up only three hits and had seven strike-outs in the 7-1 win. It looked like our hitters and pitchers were peaking together.

On Sunday we woke up in New Jersey to face off against Rutgers. The Scarlet Knights scored first in game one, with a single, a sacrifice bunt and a double accounting for a run in the second inning. After the home team threatened again but was held scoreless in the bottom of the third, we got things going in the top of the fourth. Linda doubled to lead off and scored on Heather's bunt single. Christine also laid down a bunt single and Kasey O'Connor, running for Heather, made it to third on a throwing error by the third baseman. A single by Dani brought Kasey home.

Dani made it to second on a throw to third that gunned down Christine. Erin followed with a single to drive Dani home for our third run in the inning. We picked up a final run in the sixth on singles by Heather and Christine, a Wildcat throwing error and a wild pitch. The 4-1 margin held up as Brittney survived back-to-back Wildcat singles in the sixth by getting consecutive ground outs and recorded the final three outs in the seventh to complete the win.

A two run rally by Rutgers in the first inning of the second game gave us a scare, but we scored four times in the third to take the lead and held on to win 4-3 to record our second sweep of the weekend. I got us started in the third with a leadoff walk but was erased on the base paths on a fielder's choice. That still gave us a runner at first with one out and set things up for a single by Heather, which moved pinch runner Christine Farrell to third. Heather made it to second on the throw to third. Coach sent Kasey in to run for Heather to give us a better chance of collecting two runs on a single to the outfield. That brought Christine Lux to the plate. Although we were accustomed to watching our slugging first baseman launch long flies over the fence, the outcome of this at bat was unexpected. Christine swung and missed on a third strike but the catcher dropped the ball. Christine took off for first base, drawing the throw needed to complete the strike out. The routine play became a debacle for the Scarlet Knights as their first baseman dropped the throw. Christine reached first safely and our other Christine scored from third on the play. Not content to cut the Rutgers lead in half, we stayed aggressive. Dani took one of her trademark mighty cuts and doubled to drive in two more runs. Katie then followed with a single to score Dani, giving us a two run lead.

A solo home run allowed Rutgers to narrow the margin to 4-3 but that was as close as it would get. Jody finished the game to give us the win and we flew home with a 13-3 Big East record. We were in position to control our own destiny in the race for the conference title.

The Place I Call Home

Even though I was living off campus, I still attended classes every day and found lots of reasons to stop by and visit teammates and friends who lived in the dorms. Whenever I got the chance, I planned my long training runs to wind through campus so I could enjoy the tree- and flower-lined pathways that traversed the quads and passed between the campus landmarks that had been the backdrop of my four years at Notre Dame.

The time I spent on campus seemed to become more special to me as spring progressed. I knew my career at Notre Dame was coming to an end and I paused to savor the beauty of the place whenever I could. Notre Dame felt like my home to me now, just as that Michigan player had said it would at a softball camp long before. I was going to miss everything about this place when graduation and my season were in the past.

I had collected a lot of memories in my four years in South Bend. As a freshman, I recalled scrambling to find my classes the first few days, barely noticing the sights and sounds of the bustling campus. As one of seven freshman softball players, I rarely found myself spending downtime alone without company. In our first autumn on campus, we would set out in a pack on our bikes heading across campus to visit teammates' off- campus apartments, run an errand at a nearby store, or just get out of the dorms and classrooms to see the sights.

On football Saturdays, I stood for hours at the bookstore and in the tailgate parking lots selling raffle tickets to help fund our trip to Italy. Always competitive, I really worked the friendly crowd in my zeal to outsell my teammates. I suspect many of the Irish fans who bought tickets from me did so because they found my tongue-in-cheek hard sell approach pretty amusing.

Watching freshman classmates from southern states try to control their bicycles when the first snow arrived provided just one of many hilarious memories of the times I shared with teammates from across the country. I didn't have a sister growing up, but now it seemed like I had gained nearly 30 of them in my four years as a member of the Irish softball team.

As grueling as the academic load had seemed as a freshman, as a senior there was something satisfying in the memories of rushing to classes, mandatory study periods at DeBartolo, or to LaFortune, Reckers or other meeting places to work on group projects. Not only had I been successful academically, I had learned a lot about collaboration, leadership, planning, and personal discipline along the way.

One thing I remember vividly was the almost nightly ritual of walking back to my room in the calm solitude of the familiar campus pathways, lit only by a few lights and, sometimes, the moon and the stars. Whether shuffling through autumn leaves, leaning into a winter wind, or sidestepping the puddles left by a spring shower, it was a peaceful interlude between the day's busy schedule and the bed and night of sleep that awaited me back at the dorm.

One particularly important part of each weekday evening while I was living on campus was the walk I would take to Notre Dame Circle beneath the famous Golden Dome. There, free of the thick concrete walls of Welsh Family Hall, I would find the cell phone reception I needed to call A.J. and learn about his day and share the details of mine. On many nights I would also call Mom and Dad to see how they were doing and wish them a good night.

I had discovered early on that the people of Notre Dame had a lot to do with making the campus feel like "my" place. From the first day, it had never seemed cold or impersonal. Academically, Notre Dame was clearly a place where excellence was expected. But it was also a place where everyone was valued and respected. Socially, the university had been open and welcoming from my first days on campus. As an athlete I had a built-in, formal support system both academically and socially. Yet, even on my own away from the team, I found the other students in my classes were friendly and easy to get to know. Although softball and my off-the-field effort to regain my health consumed the majority of my free waking hours, I enjoyed getting to know others in my classes and the dorm.

Outside of class I made friends with members of other men's and women's sports teams. My softball teammates and I attended their games and they attended ours. Off the field, we discovered we had a lot in common, whether we had come to Notre Dame to score touchdowns or goals; slam home dunks or knock the ball over the fence. It was relaxing to hang out with the other athletes and compare notes about sports or figure out what we were going to do when the weekend arrived. In the evening, sometimes a card game would break out. I found playing cards almost irresistible and, unless I had a serious conflict, I sat with athletes from other Irish teams intent on winning every hand but really just enjoying the good natured razzing and spirit of camaraderie that surrounded the card games.

I've heard friends who attended other schools say they never really knew a professor. Often they were rarely taught by one. It's different at Notre Dame. Among the academic staff, undergraduates are the main attraction. The university has highly respected graduate programs and important research is conducted on campus, but the primary mission of Notre Dame is undergraduate education. From my first day of classes, I could see that the professors who taught me cared about their students and were committed to helping them succeed.

Our professors went out of the way to make us feel comfortable as freshmen. One of my professors invited his entire class to his family's home for dinner one night. Most faculty members went out of their way to get to know each of us individually. As we settled in, they challenged us but were fair and encouraging. Most of all, they were committed to helping us develop our minds and really learn, not just memorize the material to pass a test. Their commitment to us as people was obvious during our games at Ivy Field and later, at Melissa Cook Stadium. We could look to the sidelines at almost any home game and see some of our professors cheering in the stands alongside family, friends and other fans.

Of course, the people who really made Notre Dame more than just a place to attend class and play ball were my Irish teammates. I knew I would miss spending so much time with my softball sisters once my career ended. We spent countless hours together on the field, during workouts, in the locker room, in study halls, on buses, in restaurants and hotels, and on flights across the country. We shared wins and losses, dreams and disappointments. We forged strong bonds of friendship and loyalty. We weren't always of one mind, but we were always united as one team. We would always be teammates and many of us would remain friends for life. But in a few weeks, I would take the field with them for the last time and four special years in my life would come to an end.

As the weather grew warmer and the campus flowers came into full bloom, these and other memories of my Notre Dame career seemed closer to the surface than ever. I had always known that, after graduation I would miss the big things—pep rallies, football Saturdays, basketball at the JACC, to name a few. But I now knew that the memories closest to my heart were the smaller things that formed the underlying texture of my life at Notre Dame. Those were the experiences that made this place feel so much like home.

Homestand

The Wednesday after our return from the East Coast, we hosted the North Dakota State Bison in a doubleheader at Melissa Cook Stadium. The Bison, who would go on to earn Summit League and NCAA Regional championships before falling in the Super Regionals to Arizona State, were making a first ever visit to South Bend. We were glad to have the competition, especially since a scheduled Tuesday game with Northwestern had been cancelled due to rain.

I led off in the bottom of the first with a double to deep left. After advancing to third on a fly out by Linda, I came home on a sacrifice fly by Heather to give us the early lead. In the third I hit a deep ball that barely missed leaving the park. I settled for a double instead of a home run and it looked like we were in business again, Unfortunately, I was the victim of a nice catch by the centerfielder on a fly ball hit by Linda followed by a great throw that beat me back to second base.

Brittney held the Bison scoreless until the seventh when an Irish fielding error led to two North Dakota State runs. We tried to mount a rally of our own in the bottom of the final frame as Erin walked and moved over on Steph's sacrifice bunt. The Bison intentionally walked me and then were able to get the third out before we could push a run across to tie it up. It was only the third time that season we had given up a lead after the sixth inning and it broke our season-long undefeated streak at home against non-conference opponents.

After letting the first matchup get away, we had our game faces on as we started play in the second contest. Linda and I singled in the bottom of the first and were both moved over on a ground out. Christine was walked intentionally to load the bases and I was forced out at home on a fielder's choice. Linda and

Christine then both came home on Katie Fleury's ground ball through the legs of the second baseman. We added a run in the fourth when Alexa slapped an infield single. I put down a sacrifice bunt which allowed Alexa to use her speed to get all the way to third base. She scored on a fly ball off the bat of Linda. We scored our final two runs in the sixth when I singled with one out and Linda smacked a home run to tally the final two runs in our 5-0 win. Jody continued her strong pitching, hurling a three-hit shutout. We weren't happy with the split, but the midweek competition kept us game-ready for our date with Big East rival Syracuse, which would be coming to Melissa Cook Stadium on Saturday.

The place was packed to capacity when we took the field to play the Orange and we aimed to please our loyal fans. After working the count to 2-2, I singled to left center to lead off. Linda sacrificed me to second and one batter later, Christine doubled to drive me home. Dani came up next and was safe on a throwing error by the third baseman, allowing Christine to score. Syracuse got a lead-off single in the top of the second but Brittney retired the next three batters to preserve our lead. Linda homered off the scoreboard in the third to extend our lead to 3-0. After a scoreless fourth and fifth, we struck again in the sixth as Katie walked and Erin singled. Both advanced on an errant throw and Katie scored on a ground ball out. Brittney got the final three outs in the seventh to gain a four-hit shutout.

We kept the big crowd on pins and needles in game two, allowing the Orange to take a one run lead in the fourth on a solo home run. But our fans let out a collective sigh of relief at the end of the fifth as we put up three runs in the inning. Alexa was hit by a pitch to lead off, Heather walked and Christine slapped a triple to right field to drive in the first two runs. Dani followed with a single to score Christine.

Syracuse was determined and leveraged a solo home run, a single and a double in the top of the sixth to tie it up. We responded in the bottom of the inning as Alexia Clay singled to lead off. Christine Farrell came in to run for Alexia and promptly stole second. After I walked, Linda singled to score Christine. Running hard, I took home on a throwing error on the play and Linda showed equal determination making it all the way to third base. A fly ball by Heather brought Linda home. Three outs later and we had a 6-3 win and another Big East sweep under our belts with only two conference doubleheaders left in the regular season.

Providence

We traveled to Providence for our last regular season road trip of the Big East season. It was an unusual Thursday conference doubleheader, but our travels came off without a hitch. The Friars might have wished our bats had been lost by the airline. We slugged five home runs in the doubleheader, taking the first game 9-1 in five innings before closing out a 7-1 victory in the second game.

In the top of the first I did my job as the leadoff hitter, earning a walk and moving to third on Linda's double. I scored on a ground ball and then Dani hit the first of our long balls to give us a 3-0 lead. In the third inning Christine and I again figured in the scoring although differently than in the first. I singled to lead off and, with two outs, Christine launched a pitch over the fence to increase our lead by two.

The Friars made a little noise of their own in the fourth when a leadoff walk was followed by two hit batsmen. An infield single brought one run home and left the bases loaded before Brittney put out the fire with a fly out and strikeout. We padded our lead in the fifth as Linda was hit by a pitch, Heather and Christine walked and then Dani knocked one over the fence for a grand slam. We retired the Friars in the bottom of the fifth, ending the game by run rule.

After three scoreless innings in the second game we were wondering if we'd used up all of our hits in game one. Fortunately, a double and two walks produced a run in the top of the fourth. Providence came back to score a run of their own in the bottom of the frame, putting us back where we started. After a hit batsman and a walk in the top of the sixth, Katie drove a long single off the fence to give us a one run lead. But we didn't really unleash our bats again until the seventh. I led off by sending a pitch over the fence for a home run. Not to be outdone, Linda immediately followed with a blast of her own. Now it was 4-1, but not for long. Heather walked, Dani doubled and Erin followed one batter later with an RBI single. Alexia then singled to drive Dani in and Bri drove Erin home with another single to close out the scoring.

My home run had my teammate, Steph, wide-eyed for a moment or two as the ball left my bat. There was a stiff breeze blowing in from the outfield and Steph had bet us before the game that no one could send the ball through a distant archway visible beyond the left center wall. My ball was hit a ton right at the arch and, as it drilled into the wind, Steph thought I had done the impossible. She was relieved to see the wind knock the ball down well past the wall but well short of the arch.

As nice as it was to get another Big East sweep, putting the finishing touches on a "bonus" win at Georgetown made the week even better. Coach arranged for us to fly from Providence to Washington, D.C. so we could finish the second game of our March 28 doubleheader with the Hoyas. The rain-delayed game had to be interrupted on the original date so we could catch our flight to South Florida. Sitting on an 8-1 lead with one out in the bottom of the fifth, we wanted to log the win to keep pace with DePaul in the race for the regular season championship.

At this point in the season, the team was feeling pretty loose. Coach, on the other hand, was just as intense as ever. As we boarded the vans in Washington, D.C. to head over to the Hoya's field, she was obviously concerned that we would not maintain the focus necessary to maintain our seven run lead for another five outs. We conspired to try to loosen her up. Caravanning through the streets of Washington in four vans, we ratcheted up our antics at every traffic light. First Dani jumped out of our van and started asking street vendors about their hats and purses as Coach stared at her in shock from one of the other vans. At the next light, I got out and pretended to window shop at a nearby toy store before getting back in the van as the light changed. Finally Linda ran to Coach's van where she pretended to wash the windshield. We could see Coach gesturing emphatically at us the entire time. She clearly wanted us back in the van and focused on the five outs we had left against the Hoyas. Our teammates, on the other hand, were cracking up. Messing with Coach wasn't something we did often, but a seven run lead with only five outs remaining had us feeling pretty confident she would forgive us later. We decided to enjoy the moment to the fullest.

Then reality intruded on our fun. The van driven by volunteer Assistant Coach Dawn Austin got caught in traffic and became lost. After our antics, Coach was already on edge. Now she was really beside herself. We were at the field for 40 anxious moments before Dawn's van arrived. I'm sure when Coach writes a book about her career as a softball coach she'll recall our return trip to Georgetown as one of the days that she had reason to question why she decided to pursue this profession. Fortunately, we backed up our earlier confidence by taking care of business on the field. Aside from a run in the seventh by Georgetown, we managed to complete an 8-2 win and a sweep of the Hoyas to make us perfect against Big East opponents on the road.

We had time on our hands until our flight back and, as we expected, Coach quickly forgave us for our pregame antics. She decided we should take a tour of our nation's capitol. It was one of the few times in our hectic collegiate softball travels that we could take time during a business trip to see the sights. We savored the chance to relax and take a van tour of the monuments, stopping for a couple of photo opportunities along the way before heading to the airport to fly home for our next challenge: Louisville was coming to town.

My Senior Day

The doubleheader with Louisville was the designated 2009 Senior Day for my class of Irish Softball. It was the final Big East regular season matchup on our home field and friends, family, alumni and a lot of loyal fans would show up to commemorate the careers of the five remaining members of the class that had arrived on campus four years earlier. We weren't the seven player "cult" that showed up filled with confidence, secure in the knowledge that our softball futures were in front of us. Now there were five of us, with four years of softball and academics behind us and the rest of our lives ahead of us

We were older and hopefully a bit wiser than when we arrived in the fall of 2005. Four years and a college education will broaden anyone's view of the world. But some life lessons happen less obviously. Welcoming three additional classes of freshman into the Irish softball fold during our careers inevitably led to us to take younger teammates under wing and serve as big sisters as well as friends. As we became juniors and seniors, it was clear that we needed to provide leadership and vision for the team in order to build team unity and a shared mission to help us pursue our championship goals.

Caught up in travel, practice, extra throwing and hitting, and the intense competition of every game—not to mention completing my accounting degree and setting my career plans—I had occasionally been distracted from the season's bittersweet march toward the end of my career. But the realization that "this was it", the end of a special chapter in my life, was never entirely out of mind. Senior Day simply brought that reality to the forefront.

I had been on the field for three previous Senior Days and I thought I was ready for my own. Those earlier celebrations had been emotional as senior teammates and friends marked the end of their softball careers. While saying goodbye to friends hadn't been easy, I had always known I could still lean on my teammates and coaches for friendship and support the next year. Now that my own Senior Day had arrived, I knew that I was the one who would be leaving while my teammates and coaches would be moving forward to play without me.

Senior Day isn't a day of mourning, though. It's a celebration and that's how it felt as I welcomed family and friends to South Bend. My Grandma and my uncle came from Southeast Michigan and two aunts and two cousins came from Pennsylvania. A.J. brought his Grandpa, parents and brother. And De came with other friends from back home. Of course Mom and Dad were there, too.

My brother Andy also came to watch me play and participate in the ceremonies, and having him join me made a special day even more meaningful to me. After serving as an inspiration in my earliest days of softball, Andy hadn't shared much of my high school, travel ball and college softball playing experience. Our lives just seemed to go in different directions. But in recent years we had become closer and I was really glad that he drove down from Grand Rapids to be there for me. After all, if he hadn't picked up a ball and started playing catch with my Dad in the backyard so many years before, I might never have decided I wanted to play ball, too. Andy had completed his degree at Ferris State University and was just starting his career. In a sense, my Senior Day marked a new beginning for both of us.

With all the off-the-field distractions, we had to be careful to maintain our focus on the most important event of the day, our doubleheader with Louisville. The Cardinals were always a tough opponent and we'd been eliminated at their hands early in the previous year's Big East Tournament. Louisville was also running neck and neck with DePaul and Notre Dame for the conference championship, which meant they arrived in South Bend with plenty of motivation to take us down.

As seniors, we felt this two-game set was too important to let the festivities of Senior Day get in the way of our best effort on the field. We talked to Coach about not holding the traditional on-the-field ceremony between games. Although that had been the custom in previous years, we felt it allowed the emotions of the day to come to the surface prematurely and interfere with the business we needed to take care of on the field. We agreed that a ceremony after the games would allow the team to maintain focus until our business on the field was complete.

With the official ceremony rescheduled, we were ready to play ball. The stands were packed and you could feel the excitement in the air as we took the field against the Cardinals. Brittney responded by retiring the first three Louisville hitters on consecutive ground outs. Now it was time for Irish hitters to produce some runs. Batting leadoff in the bottom of the first, I watched a ball and a strike go by. Then I squared up the next pitch, driving a single into centerfield. Standing on first I looked around and it seemed like the huge crowd of Irish fans was going crazy. A leadoff hit never felt better! I made it to second base on a wild pitch but Louisville's pitcher put an end to our early fireworks by retiring the next three Irish hitters to end the inning.

Both teams managed an unearned base runner in the second but neither of us scored as the opposing pitchers recovered to keep things under control. Louisville converted two singles and triple into two runs in the top of the third inning, but we responded in our half of the inning. I singled to left with one out and, a batter later, Heather sent a single of her own to the same field. Christine was up next and also singled, bringing me home. A fielding error by the right fielder allowed Heather to leg it home as well while Christine ended up on third. The next batter was retired to end the inning, but we were tied at 2-2 going into the fourth.

Louisville hit the ball hard in the fourth. The first two batters produced a fly out and a single, respectively, while the third drove a line drive right into Brittney's glove. She tossed to first to double off the base runner to end the inning. We left two runners on in the bottom of the fourth and Louisville did the same thing in the top of the fifth before the Irish finally cashed-in in the bottom of the inning when Christine homered with the bases empty.

The Cardinals moved the tying run all the way to third base in the sixth but were again unable to score. Meanwhile Katie singled to lead off for us in the bottom of the frame and Erin drove her home with a double. Alexia sacrificed Erin to third and Bri was hit by a pitch to gain first base. She stole second to eliminate the possibility of a routine double play and I hit a ground ball to shortstop that brought Erin home for our second run of the inning and a 5-2 lead going into the last inning.

We were feeling confident with Brittney on the mound, despite the steady contact Louisville's hitters were making each inning. Three more outs and we'd be half way to a sweep. After the first Cardinal batter struck out, we were on our way. An infield single to second base looked harmless enough. But then Louisville's catcher and soon-to-be Big East Player of the Year, Melissa Roth, smacked a home run to right center. Our lead was now just one run. We still only needed two outs, though, so we weren't panicking.

When the next two hitters landed on base courtesy of a single and a hit batsman, Coach decided it was time to worry. She brought in Jody to see if she could put out the fire and preserve the win. A dribbler right back at Jody became an infield single and the Cardinals had the bases loaded with one out. Jody showed she was up to the challenge, striking out the next batter to get us to within one out of the win.

She finished the job by enticing the next hitter into a pop up behind second base. We watched as the right side of our infield converged on the ball to make the routine catch. With two outs, the Louisville base runners were in high gear sprinting without much hope toward home. They were as surprised as we were when the catch was muffed and the ball ended up on the ground. Two runs crossed the plate before the ball was recovered. Jody retired the next batter on three straight strikes but the damage was done. We went down in order in the bottom of the seventh to give the Cardinals the win. We had allowed them to snatch victory from the jaws of defeat.

Our decision to eliminate the traditional Senior Day celebrating between games was looking better all the time. During the intermission, no one was feeling like celebrating anything, least of all Coach. Just as in our doubleheader against DePaul, we had allowed game one to slip away. We were devastated but knew we had to rebound from the loss quickly to avoid a sweep. There was some serious work to do to salvage a split on the day and preserve our chances of finishing on top in the Big East regular season standings.

In game two, Louisville jumped out to a one run lead in the top of the first, but Linda got that one back for us with a home run in the bottom of the inning. Unfortunately we squandered an opportunity to score more by leaving two runners on base. After Jody retired the side in the second, we wasted no time mounting another rally. Erin doubled to lead off. Two outs later, I doubled to drive her across and give us a 2-1 advantage.

Louisville went down harmlessly in the top of the third and we wasted Heather's double in the bottom of the inning. Fortunately, Louisville was also leaving runners on base. The Cardinals got two singles in the top of the fourth without a run to show for it. Finally, in the bottom of the fourth we showed what we were capable of. Alexia led off with a single and was moved over on a sacrifice bunt by Alexa. That brought me to the plate. I extended the count to 2 balls, 2 strikes and then slashed a double down the left field line bringing Alexia home. Linda then jumped on a 3-1 hitter's count and singled to right, driving me in. Heather accelerated our run generation with a home run that scored pinch runner Kasey ahead of her. Christine added a double of her own before the Cardinals retired the last two Irish batters without allowing another run.

After our experience in game one, we weren't taking a 6-1 lead for granted. True to form, Louisville came back in the top of the fifth, scoring two runs on a lead-off double, a hit batsman, a wild pitch, then a single that brought two runs home. Erin did her part to re-extend our lead with a leadoff home run in the bottom of the fifth to make it 7-3. We were six outs away from a win, but we had to finish the job. This seemed awfully familiar.

I'd be lying if I said it didn't worry me when the Cardinals' leadoff hitter smacked a home run in the sixth inning. The next two hitters singled to increase the tension. It seemed impossible that we would squander another lead. We were better than that. Jody got the next hitter to fly out and a line out double play put an end to the threat. There was poetic justice in that line drive to end the inning. I'd been victimized the same way against Louisville in the previous year's Big East tournament on a line drive to short. A couple of feet one way or the other and the outcome of that contest and this game might have been altered entirely.

After Heather's leadoff walk in the bottom of the sixth, we were retired in order, setting the stage for whatever last inning heroics Louisville could muster. They kept it interesting until the end, with a leadoff double and a single that put two aboard. But this time we corralled the game ending infield pop up to earn the split. The 7-3 win wasn't a thing of beauty, with 13 hits on our side and 11 for Louisville, but a win's a win!

After the game we sat down to a steak dinner on the plaza outside the stadium and the coaches called the five of us up one at a time to say a few words about our Notre Dame careers and the marks we'd made in our years with the softball program. I kept my sunglasses on so no one could see if my eyes leaked a few tears. Coach said my perseverance in the face of adversity was an inspiration. Kris commented on my positive attitude and credited my parents for doing a good job raising me. Dawn became emotional as she recalled the good times we enjoyed together. Lizzy, who worked closest with me as my position and hitting coach, emphasized my refusal to give up, But she concluded that, in my case, sometimes trying harder wasn't the best recipe for success. "You seemed to do your best when you 'tried easier'," she commented. I couldn't disagree, but if I had not tried as hard as I could for as long as I had, I don't think I would have had the chance to learn that lesson.

Big East Tournament

As it turned out, our inability to hang on to late leads against DePaul and Louisville cost us the chance to win or share the top spot in the final regular season standings. We finished a game behind DePaul and a half game ahead of Louisville. It was disappointing to come so close to a regular season championship only to let it slip away. But finishing on top of the regular season standings wasn't the only conference prize in our sights. We could still win the Big East Conference Tournament, which was the only league honor that would earn us a championship ring. While we were already confident of getting into the NCAA Tournament based on our 38-15 record and the strength of our schedule, winning the conference tournament would cement that opportunity with an automatic berth.

Once again, the tournament would be held in Louisville on the home field of the Cardinals and the scene of last year's disappointing early tournament exit. We boarded the bus for Louisville Wednesday morning and checked into the tournament hotel that afternoon. We would begin play Thursday afternoon but first we had a date with the annual Big East Softball Awards dinner Wednesday evening. We were in town for one reason and one reason alone: to win the tournament championship as a team. Attending a ceremony focused on individual awards seemed a bit at odds with our goal, but it was an annual event and a team obligation. We were used to it by now.

As it turned out, seven members of the 2009 Irish squad took home all conference honors, a great showing and really an indication of how well the entire team performed. I was thrilled to receive first team honors along with sluggers Christine and Dani. Linda, Brittney and Jody took second team honors and Erin earned a spot on the third team. It was the second straight year that seven Irish players earned all Big East honors. Considering that the season began with me sitting on the bench, earning a spot on the all conference squad had to be one of the biggest individual turnarounds in Irish sports history. But as I said, we weren't in Louisville to bask in individual awards. Gratifying as it they may be, we wanted that championship ring.

While Coach attends the annual Big East coaches' meeting the night before the tournament begins, Irish players traditionally gather with the assistant coaches for spirited team games in the hotel lobby. This year it was charades. Although there was plenty of laughter and we razzed each other mercilessly, there were no complaints of excessive noise from hotel staff and other guests. We headed to our rooms relaxed and ready for the action on the field to begin.

Our first game in the tournament would be against the number seven seed, St. Johns. Although we were seeded second, we wouldn't be taking the Red Storm lightly. We had split our double-header with them early in the season and it had taken back-to-back home runs in the seventh inning of game two for us to avoid being swept. Jody made an early statement by retiring the Red Storm in order in the top of the first inning. Leading off in our half of the first, I drove a single into right field. After Linda sacrificed me to second, Heather came through with one of her patented doubles into left field to get the RBI. A fielding error by the third baseman allowed Heather to take third base and Christine's fly out to right field was enough to bring her home. When the inning ended, we had a two run lead to build on.

Both teams went down in order in the second and the parade of outs continued in the third, punctuated only by Linda's infield single. A leadoff double and a sacrifice bunt that was misplayed into an error resulted in St. John's first run of the game in the fourth. Things didn't get interesting again until the bottom of the fifth when Alexia and Alexa singled with one out. Up next, I hit the ball into center field where it dropped in, but the alert center-fielder quickly scooped up the ball and threw to second to force Alexa as Alexia motored into third. I stole second to join Alexia in scoring position but the Red Storm got the third out before either of us could cross the plate.

St. Johns threatened again in the top of the sixth after the leadoff hitter walked, was sacrificed to second base and advanced to third on a ground out. She was stranded there as the next hitter lined out to Dani in right field. In the bottom of the inning our hitters finally gave Jody some breathing room, tacking three more runs onto our 2-1 lead on doubles by Christine and Katie, a walk to Erin and a triple by Alexia. Jody retired the Red Storm in order in the seventh and we had advanced to the second round of the tournament with a 5-1 victory.

Friday afternoon we were scheduled to face off against our second opponent, host Louisville, which had beaten Connecticut to advance. We had to weather a six-hour rain delay before we finally took the field to face the Cardinals. We stayed loose by touring nearby Churchill Downs, the shrine of horse racing just south of the Louisville campus. Our warm-up suits were a violation of the track's dress code, but we pulled some strings with a local contact and were able to tour the luxury boxes above the grandstands.

As the skies cleared, we finally took the field against the Cardinals. They would be the visiting team and bat first in the contest. Although the leadoff Louisville batter was hit by a pitch and advanced all the way to third, Brittney recorded the third out without damage. Linda doubled for our team in the bottom of the first, but we couldn't bring her home either. After the Cardinals went down in order in the second, we wasted a single by Erin in another scoreless at bat. Louisville's frustration continued in the third as three Cardinal hitters went down in order. but Irish hitters stirred things up in the bottom of the inning. I doubled with one out and Linda singled to move me to third. Two straight outs ended the inning with runners at second and third and no runs across.

The Cardinals tried a rally of their own in the top of the fourth. The leadoff hitter was safe on a bunt single and, with one out, stole second. The next batter walked and an infield single to first base loaded the bases. The next batter sent a grounder to Heather at third and she gunned the ball home to force the lead runner at the plate. There were two down but the bases were still loaded. Brittney struck out the next Louisville hitter to escape the jam.

Dani singled to lead off in our half of the fourth, and she moved to second on Katie's sacrifice bunt, but that's as far as she got as the next two Irish batters were retired. Brittney set down three Cardinal batters in order in the fifth and we came to the plate in the bottom of the inning knowing that letting our opponent hang around deeper into the game could cost us our run at a championship.

It appeared the Cardinals' were also feeling the tension. Alexa led off and was safe at first on an error by the Louisville third baseman. Linda then singled to the pitcher and Alexa came all the way around and scored on a throwing error while Linda took second. Heather smacked a double to drive Linda home and, with two down, Dani smacked a follow-up double to drive in our third run. That was all we needed to put the game away. Except for a Louisville double in the seventh, Brittney retired the rest of the Cardinal batters without incident.

I am sure the Cardinals felt like they had given the game away as we capitalized on two fielding errors to score two and arguably all three of our runs. But we had given them a win with an error a week earlier in South Bend, the only blemish on our Senior Day. Turnabout was fair play. Now we were just one win away from a tournament championship. Our bitter loss to the Cardinals in the prior year's tournament had been avenged. It was time to take down our arch rival DePaul in the championship game.

Championship Game

The championship was a pitchers' duel from the start. Both pitchers brought their "A" games with them, using a mix of great velocity, movement and location to keep the opposing hitters off-balance and guessing. Brittney retired the first five DePaul hitters in a row and Becca Heteniak, the Blue Demon ace, retired the first nine Irish hitters she faced. With two outs in the second, DePaul hit consecutive singles but Brittney got the next batter on a ground out back to the pitching rubber. Then after Heteniak's three-up, three-down third, Brittney proceeded to retire the next three DePaul hitters in the bottom of the inning.

Heteniak's streak of consecutive outs was marred in the fourth by an error on Linda's one out ground ball. Christine Ferrell came in to pinch run and took second base on a wild pitch after two were out. Christine Lux walked and Christine Ferrell took third on another wild pitch. A pop out to the catcher ended the inning before we could cash in on DePaul's mistakes.

DePaul did its best to capitalize on our failure by building a rally around a two-out double and a walk before Brittney fanned the next batter. Erin recorded the first Irish hit, singling with one out in the top of the fifth. But the half inning ended on a fielder's choice and a ground out. Three DePaul hitters went down in order in the bottom of the fifth. By now, the pattern was well established. Both pitchers were going to have the upper hand, allowing only the occasional hit or unearned base runner, but dousing any threat of a rally before it could really get started. This game would probably be lost by the first team to lose focus, or won by the first to take the competition up a notch.

That brought me to the plate to lead off in the top of sixth. I had a pop out and a swinging strike out on my resume for the game so far. I'd been victimized by rise balls both times. It was time for a different approach; time to make her throw me something I could hit. With Heteniak that would mean recognizing each pitch, laying off balls I couldn't touch, and fouling off anything I couldn't drive into the outfield. Of course, luck would play into it. Foul balls on high strikes can turn into outs if they are popped in the air or tipped to the catcher for strike three. The umpire can call strikes where I see balls. Heteniak can just burn me with great pitches that move more than I can adjust to them.

I didn't have time to think about all of that. In fact, I really wasn't thinking about very much at all. I was all eyes, hands and instinct—the sum of everything I'd learned from KBL to that moment. I don't recall how many foul balls it took to construct the 3-2 count…enough to cause the Blue Demon ace to put a little something extra on a final rise ball in an effort to blow it past me. That something extra was enough to make the pitch sail far enough high and outside to give me a free pass to first base. Coach Greenman used to call long at bats against a great pitcher the "battle". Is a walk still a "free pass" if you have to win a battle to earn it? I was willing to let someone else worry about the answer to that one. I just wanted to make sure this was one free pass DePaul would end up paying for.

With me standing on first with no outs, Coach knew it was time to pull out all the stops. It was only the sixth but it already felt like we were in extra innings and living on borrowed time. This game had all the makings of a 1-0 shutout win for somebody. If we were going to be the team with the run, we needed to make the most of this opportunity. That meant asking our next batter to lay down a sacrifice bunt to move me to second so I could score on a single.

There's nothing tougher to bunt than a hard rise ball, a lesson Heteniak reinforced on the next pitch. The bunt attempt was popped up, sailing foul and landing softly in the DePaul first baseman's glove. I was still on first base and we had two more outs to work with, but now the window of opportunity had closed part way. It might take a hit bigger than a single to drive me home. The good news was, we still had the heart of our order coming up. At least Heteniak would have to deal with our thumpers, the big RBI producers who batted in the middle of our lineup. Heather was at the plate.

The Blue Demon pitcher knew who she was dealing with. She worked cautiously around the edges of the strike zone and fell behind Heather by a 2-1 count. It's one thing to be careful, but walking Heather would do what our failed bunt attempt had not accomplished...move me into position to score on a single. She couldn't afford to miss the strike zone again because giving Heather a 3-1 count would tip the balance hugely in the Irish batter's favor. Heather knew the situation and probably saw the next pitch coming almost before it left Heteniak's hand.

The Irish third baseman coiled, triggered, and lashed out powerfully at the ball. She didn't miss. With a good jump off first base, I had to decide if there was a chance it would be caught. I saw immediately that the ball was out of the infield, sailing hard, long and into the right center gap. Once I knew the ball would hit the grass, I was already thinking past second base toward third. Only a miracle throw from right center field could beat me there. As I rounded second there was a higher stake decision to make. Should I try for home? Coach and I had to decide quickly, was it time to take it up a notch?

If I'm not running like I want to score when I round second, there's no way it's going to be possible. My job is to cover ground as quickly as I can and not worry about what Coach will decide. Her role is to keep an eye on how quickly the Blue Demon outfielders are retrieving the ball and making the throw into the cutoff. If she doesn't like what she sees, she'll put up her arms and get me to hit the brakes. As I cut the angle to round third, stopping was the last thing on my mind. I could see Coach outside the base line, wind-milling furiously. We were on the same page. There'd be no playing it safe. The Irish were turning it up a notch and going for home.

Now it was all on me. I had to sprint hard for the plate and beat the throw. I wasn't watching anything but the position of the catcher. She was parked just up the line from the plate waiting for the throw and the chance to tag me out. My path to the plate was outside the line. Without slowing, I hit the dirt feet first on my left side and aimed wide of home. Still sliding, I rolled onto my stomach, extended my right arm and hand, and felt my fingertips drag across the smooth surface of the plate as my momentum carried me past. It was a perfect slide-by, just as Coach Greenman had taught me...as far out of the range of the catcher and a possible tag as I could get and still touch home. I heard the umpire call me safe, but I already knew it. I leaped to my feet and, fists clenched, roared to salute Heather over on second base. "Yeah!"

Back in the dugout I calmed down in time to watch Heteniak regain control and retire the next two Irish hitters, leaving our potential insurance run on second base. We had the narrow lead, but were six outs away from the win and the championship. Getting six outs can seem like an eternity in softball. It's hard to shortcut the process. Unlike games played to a timer, our game can't end until you record all the outs. We'd been reminded of that fact several times this season. In the bottom of the sixth, a fielding error with one out gave the Blue Demons life. But an Irish double play quickly erased the threat. That was one shortcut, but there was still another inning to play.

We had three outs of our own to try to extend our lead but we were retired in order in the top of the seventh. That set the stage for DePaul's last stand. After a leadoff ground out, the second DePaul batter suddenly dispelled any notion that the Blue Demons were going down easy. She doubled to deep center field to put the tying run in scoring position. Now a big hit like Heather's, or even a solid single, would bring the run home and make it anyone's ball game again. The next hitter barely made contact and couldn't get the ball out of the infield, but it turned into a squib single and moved the lead runner over to third while putting the winning run on first. There was still only one out, and now just about any kind of a hit—or even a fly ball to the outfield—could score the run. The runner on first stole second before we could get another out. Now the tying and winning runs would both score on a solid single to the outfield. We needed two infield outs like we needed air to breath.

I watched as Brittney toed the rubber and delivered the pitch to the next DePaul hitter. Like Heather, the batter took a mighty hack and connected about as hard as you can hit a softball. Luckily the ball had eyes for Christine's big glove at first base. She caught it without changing position and, thinking fast, unleashed a snap throw to Heather at third, catching the lunging lead runner off of the base for the third out. We'd managed shortcut number two... an almost miraculous first to third game-ending, double play. Eighteen Irish softball players, our coaches, and support staff all converged on the infield yelling and screaming at the top of our lungs, slapping hands, hugging and trading high fives.

Watching on TV in Pennsylvania, my cousins laughed as I clutched the championship trophy like I would never let it go. I have to admit, I wanted to hold onto that moment forever! I was so proud to be part of all we had accomplished as a team. We had done it...the Fighting Irish were Big East Champions!

Last Run at Regionals

Winning the Big East Tournament for the first time since our freshman year was exhilarating. For five seniors, it represented the fulfillment of the promise Coach had seen in us when she recruited us as juniors in high school more than five years earlier. Yes, we still had other goals, but the experience of the past two years had shown us how difficult it was to earn that championship ring in the Big East. We felt great. Now we wanted to earn that elusive trip to Oklahoma City and the College Softball World Series.

After arriving back in South Bend, we learned we would be traveling to Ann Arbor once again to a Regional hosted by the number 7 Michigan Wolverines. This was our chance to give the Wolverines a fight for the regional title and redeem ourselves for our early exit in the previous year's Regional tournament. After a couple of days of practice, we boarded the bus for Ann Arbor with our sights set on winning the first Regional title in Irish Softball history.

We started play against Cleveland State, the number three seed, on the first evening of Regionals and beat the Vikings 3-1 in a game that was delayed by rain for an hour after five innings had been played. The win set up a matchup with Michigan. Unlike a year earlier, this time we played the Wolverines tough, allowing only a solo home run in the first six innings. Heather matched the Wolverine's output with a one-run homer of her own, but Michigan eked out a narrow 2-1 victory by pushing a final run across in the seventh. So close but so far away. That's how we felt as we found ourselves sent to the losers' bracket by the slimmest of margins. With our backs against the wall, we beat Miami of Ohio 5-3 to gain a rematch with the Wolverines.

The rematch with Michigan was every bit as close as our first meeting. Pitching and defense kept us even for most of the game, but in the end the Wolverine batters did what we were unable to do: score runs. Coach Hutchin's team got the game's first run in the sixth and added three more in the seventh to take a 4-0 win and end our season.

As luck would have it, I came up with two outs and two on in the seventh and hit a shot on a 1-2 count. A ball with eyes would have found a hole, but this one was drilled right at the ankles of Teddy Ewing, Jessie Merchant's successor as Michigan's shortstop. The ball reached her hard on the short hop and deflected off her glove. She kept it in front of her as Greg Youtzy had taught me to do so many years before, scooped it up and threw me out by a step. As I ran through the base I slowed to a trot and raised my hands and forearms over my helmet, trying to swallow past the lump in my throat and hold back my tears.

I turned back toward home plate taking in the scene from the field one last time. My softball dream was over. There was nothing left to do but shake hands with Coach Hutchins and her Wolverines; hug Mom, Dad, and A.J.; and join Coach and my teammates on the bus for one final trip together, back home to Notre Dame.

Afterword

I never wanted to be known as the injured player, or the one who made the "crazy" decision to throw left handed because her right shoulder couldn't perform any longer. I just wanted to be recognized by my teammates, my coaches and my opponents as a good softball player, an athlete they respected for her skills, aggressiveness, intelligence, and sportsmanship. But if others find in these pages the inspiration to overcome setbacks of their own and the encouragement to blunt the discouraging words of others, then telling my story has been worth the risk of being known from here forward as the player with the bum shoulder.

Or perhaps I should say, _one_ of the players with the bum shoulder, knee, wrist, ankle, or other injury. The truth is, in just about any college softball program, there is probably at least one girl with a story something like mine. During my Notre Dame career, I watched many other athletes struggle against physical adversity. It's hard to find a softball player who hasn't had to deal with injuries, as well as just plain physical wear and tear.

The medical histories of a few of my Irish teammates stand out in my memory. There was Kenya who pitched courageously her entire senior season with a torn ACL. Heather, who fought back from serious ACL repair to become an all-time Irish great at third base. Erin, who had all the makings of greatness and achieved it despite a heartbreaking string of injuries to her ankle, shoulder and ACL. Linda, who separated her shoulder and kept on playing after enduring the pain of replacing it in the socket when it would pop out during games. And there was Sadie, who overcame two knee surgeries, a hip injury, a concussion, and broken bones in her face, but fought tenaciously to get back on the field and terrorize opposing pitchers and batters with her bat and her glove.

The great thing about these and other Irish women is that they did not allow their careers to be defined by their wounds, or even by what happened between the foul lines when they were healthy. They worked hard in the classroom and contributed their time in the South Bend community. Each left Notre Dame ready to lead a full, rewarding and generous life.

I feel an obligation to remind young athletes who read my story that chasing your dreams should never mean abusing your body or neglecting your physical health. Hindsight is always 20/20, but if I had known then what I know now about the condition of my shoulder, I would never have played in pain for three years when surgery could have corrected the problem and allowed me to chase my dream with a healthy shoulder, less pain, and without doing further harm to my body.

I can't emphasize enough to athletes of any age, DO NOT TRY TO PLAY THROUGH PAIN. Pain is your body's warning system, telling you something is wrong. See a doctor and find the cause of your pain. While it is true that my attempts to learn what was wrong with my shoulder failed to result in an accurate diagnosis or the proper treatment, I am an exception. Most of the time, the problem can be diagnosed and the right surgery or treatment prescribed to fix it or at least manage it. Pursue your dreams with all the passion and intensity you can muster, but listen to your body and treat it with the respect it deserves. It's the only one you have.

At the end of senior year, I finally received an MRI scan of my shoulder. The surgeon who reviewed the results—a different doctor than the one who had treated me previously—discovered that my labrum, rotator cuff and bicep were badly torn. He said the damage had clearly occurred much earlier and likely stemmed from the summer after my freshman year at Notre Dame. In hindsight, playing summer travel ball that last year might have been too much, too soon for my surgically repaired shoulder to bear. The doctor said if the shoulder had been repaired right away after the injury, my recovery and rehabilitation would have been relatively quick, about the same amount of time as after my initial surgery as a freshman.

But three years of abuse as I pursued my softball dream meant a more significant surgery and a longer recovery. I delayed having my second surgery until the fall after graduation so I could complete my follow-up internship with PWC and get my first few weeks of graduate school under my belt. This time, my rehabilitation lasted almost a year before I regained most of my normal range of motion. The build-up of scar tissue in the shoulder led to a mid rehab trip to the surgeon so I could be anesthetized and the arm could be manipulated to break up adhesions and scarring in the joint while I was under the anesthetic. Despite my recovery, my doctor has advised me not to resume throwing right handed if I want to avoid injuring myself again. Fortunately, I'm a pretty good left hander now so I'll still be able to play catch with my kids someday. I have also become an ardent golfer, and find I can swing a club pretty well from the right side. As they say, golf is the game of a lifetime. For me, softball—at least from the right hand side—is not.

Some of my former teammates have said they were ready to move on when their careers at Notre Dame ended. It was a little harder for me. Despite my injury, my first spring without softball was difficult. I missed the game and the team camaraderie that was such a big part of my life for so many years. Still, I felt like I had given everything I had to achieve my dream of playing college softball. I had no regrets and left no unfinished business on the diamond. The dream I ended up living wasn't the one I had envisioned when I set my sights on a college softball career. But it was a pretty great dream nonetheless.

One lesson I can take from my college softball experience is the importance of letting go of the past and always looking ahead to the next challenge with positive anticipation. Today, as the NCAA commercials say, I am joining most college athletes in "going pro in something else". After graduating from Notre Dame's Mendoza College of Business, I received my Masters in Accountancy at Grand Valley State University in my hometown of Grand Rapids. I squeezed in my shoulder rehabilitation and a job as an academic graduate assistant while finishing my degree. I also took advantage of the interlude before starting work to sit for the four CPA exams, passing all four in my first try.

A.J. and I made it through four years of our long distance relationship and are still together today. And in the fall of 2010, I started my career at PWC. I plan to chase my career and life dreams with the same intensity I applied to softball. Dreams may not always come true easily, but in life as in softball, I still believe, impossible is nothing!